UNDERSTANDING ATTACHMENT

PARENTING, CHILD CARE, AND EMOTIONAL DEVELOPMENT

JEAN MERCER

Westport, Connecticut
London

Library of Congress Cataloging-in-Publication Data

Mercer, Jean.
    Understanding attachment: parenting, child care, and emotional development /
Jean Mercer.
      p. cm.
    Includes bibliographical references and index.
    ISBN 0–275–98217–3 (alk. paper)
1.   Attachment behavior.   I. Title.
BF575.A86M47   2006
155.4'18—dc22   2005019272

British Library Cataloguing in Publication Data is available.

Library of Congress Catalog Card Number: 2005019272
ISBN: 0–275–98217–3

First published in 2006

Praeger Publishers, 88 Post Road West, Westport, CT 06881
An imprint of Greenwood Publishing Group, Inc.
www.praeger.com

Printed in the United States of America

The paper used in this book complies with the
Permanent Paper Standard issued by the National
Information Standards Organization (Z39.48–1984).

10 9 8 7 6 5 4 3 2

For Andrew—

one securely attached little guy—

and his secure base people.

Contents

Preface

I first thought about writing this book while I was sitting in a court-room. I was observing the trial of two unlicensed therapists who had managed to kill a child they were treating and who had done so partly because they did not understand the facts about attachment (part of this story is told in Chapter 7 of this book). Expert witness after expert witness testified, and the word "attachment" was used many times—but no one said what it meant. I looked at the jury to see if they looked confused. They didn't seem to be having any problem. I waited for the judge to ask them if they understood the term, for the prosecutor—for anybody at all—to inquire whether the jury understood this important issue. No one did. No member of the jury asked for a definition, either.

During a break, I sidled up to one of the prosecutors and asked her whether anyone was going to tell the jury what attachment was. She smiled pleasantly and murmured something, but her thoughts were obviously on other issues, such as conviction. I minded my own business, then, because I thought what the therapists had done was seriously wrong, and I wanted them to be convicted, too. If the prosecutor could manage without having the jury understand what attachment was, that was fine with me. (They were convicted and are serving sixteen-year sentences, by the way.)

Nevertheless, I was puzzled. "Attachment" is referred to and discussed daily in the twenty-first-century United States. As you will see in this book, legal decisions about children are made on the basis of this concept. We seem to be living in the "Age of Attachment" rather than the Age of

Aquarius. Twelve members of that jury apparently thought they knew what the word meant. Yet my experience as a professor and a lecturer is that attachment is far more difficult to understand than most other psychological concepts. And my experience as a daughter, a mother, and a grandmother is that, once understood, the idea of attachment is of enormous help in understanding family love and family relationships. I wanted to make the attempt to pass on what is known about this fascinating topic.

I had seen at the trial and elsewhere the possible consequences of mistaken beliefs about attachment. I had also fielded some questions over the years that showed how confused even child care providers are about attachment ("Isn't there a disease about that? Something called separation anxiety?"). But how to help people understand? The scientific and clinical literatures about early emotional development and attachment are highly complex. The number of published pages alone is a daunting challenge, even though modern work in this area began only about seventy years ago. No sensible layperson, and few professionals other than those working directly on the topic, would care to sit down and try to make his or her way through all that has been said about attachment.

What I have tried to do in this book is to select the most important work on attachment and to summarize it, stressing the concrete reality and applications of the ideas rather than research design, statistics, or even abstract clinical concepts. In the course of this, I have included some material that is important because it is probably wrong; readers need to know that not every statement made about attachment is thoroughly validated. I have also tried to show how our understanding of attachment has changed through recent history—and how it continues to change. We have by no means come to a complete understanding of this aspect of human life, and we need to recognize this fact by leaving the end of this story open for speculation, but not for wild fantasy.

I have tried to write about attachment in a way that will be accessible to educated readers who have no background in child development or mental health issues. Most of the language is nontechnical, and where I have had to use technical terms, I have defined them. For those readers who are interested, there is some material about research design and research conclusions, but those who want to get on with reading about attachment will probably not be much troubled if they skip those parts. There is a minimum of biology included, and a small amount of discussion of animal behavior, because human beings are not alone in the animal kingdom in their emotional connections to family. Most of the story of attachment comes from the disciplines of psychology, psychiatry, and anthropology, however.

New parents sometimes inadvertently use the word "human" when they mean "adult." Although they embarrass themselves by doing this, they are really quite right. Although an infant is a member of the human species, he or she is not human in the full, mature, complete sense—the sense that involves being a member of a group and caring about others. It is the development of attachment that makes the baby a real human being and prepares him or her to take his or her rightful place among other humans. How this happens to almost every individual is the real subject of this book.

Our own family experiences cannot be the only source for understanding emotional ties, but they can help us flesh out the sometimes dry bones of systematic research. I have tried to include here some examples from my own family life. In addition to personal experience, we can benefit from the fact that attachment, separation, and loss have been the subjects of songs and stories for generations. Literary treatments range from Biblical descriptions of the prodigal son and the judgment of Solomon to modern forms— the orphan status of Donald Duck's and Mickey Mouse's nephews, the adoption of Superman, the lost father of Luke Skywalker. Orphanhood and the lost or estranged parent have traditionally received the most emphasis; as the blues song tells us: "Motherless children / Have a hard time / When they mother is dead." More recently, the focus has been on family relationships that are present but only partially satisfactory, as *The Simpsons* shows us. The modern concern seems to be conveyed by Philip Larkin's poem, "They —— you up, your mum and dad. / They do not mean to, but they do." Artistic and literary descriptions of attachment can be vivid and compelling, but they are not in themselves sources of information because they are restatements of our own beliefs, and that is why we like them. It may be valuable while reading to think from time to time of great writers' depictions of "disorder and early sorrow," or even of the mother of James James Morrison Morrison Wetherby George Dupree, who went downtown without consulting her three-year-old and, A. A. Milne tells us, was never heard of since.

The hardest part about studying attachment may be abandoning old assumptions and starting from scratch in our understanding of family emotional connections. I hope this book will help readers accomplish this important task and come to a new comprehension of a basic part of being human, the source of some of our deepest pleasure as well as of our greatest emotional agonies, without which we would not belong to the family of man.

chapter 1

What Is Attachment?
The *Study* of
Emotional Ties

"I don't want to breastfeed my baby, because he's going to have to go to day care, and I don't want him to cry because he's attached to me," announces the mother of a newborn boy.

"How's Susie? Oh, she's doing fine, especially when you consider that we never had a chance to bond with her," says the father of a lively toddler.

A nurse remarks, "A lot of my time at that job went into helping mothers bond with their babies."

A mother tells her husband, "I like this day care center because they keep changing Tommy's caregivers. I don't want him to get attached to them."

A character in a detective novel comments, "He was ready to murder— he never had any deep attachment after his mother."

Consoling a jilted friend, a woman explains, "You can't really blame him for being commitment-shy after his mother deserted the family like that."

A grandmother advises, "He just has that blanket because he's insecure. You should take it away from him."

Another grandmother says, "We had never seen our grandson, but we read him a story and we bonded right away."

A newspaper article describes a military interrogator as moving closer to a prisoner "in order to bond with him."

A book by a high-ranking intelligence advisor claims that terrorist leaders can be detected on the basis of their childhood experiences.[1]

A judge orders a bonding assessment before making a child-custody decision.

THE IDEA OF ATTACHMENT

What are all these people talking about? The specific situations are different, but there is a common theme: the emotional ties that exist between human beings and guide their feelings and behavior. A term often used to describe such ties is *attachment*. Attachment, in one form or another, is a fact of every human life.

Every normal human being over a year of age likes some people better than others. We choose to spend more time with the people we prefer, if we can, and we seek them out when we are unhappy. When we are young children, we feel safe with our special people; when we are adults, we try to protect such people if they are young or vulnerable. If we are both adults, we may choose them as sex partners, helpers, or companions. We generally prefer people who are most familiar to us. If we are separated from them for a long time, we are distressed, and if they die or desert us, we grieve. We do not react in the same way to the loss of unfamiliar people. This pattern of emotional relationships is present in one form or another in all cultures and people. A person who feels and acts the same about everyone is regarded as strange, and *is* strange.

A person's special preferences for others can be called *liking* or *love*. In newspapers, television programs, and ordinary conversations, the words attachment or bonding are often used instead of the meaningful but less exciting everyday words. No matter which term is chosen, however, the intention is to describe the fact that humans prefer to be with certain people and are indifferent to—or even avoid or hate—others.

What Are We Talking about, When We Talk about Attachment?

How can a word or two refer to all the different comments quoted on the previous page? Can attachment be defined so broadly as to include all those situations? In fact, attachment is not very easy to define. One highly skilled and educated clinical psychologist, when asked to define this term, replied, "I don't know, but I know it when I see it!"

Attachment has a multitude of meanings and implications, but its first and most important aspect involves *emotion*. Human feelings about attachment are among our most poignant and powerful, disturbing and gratifying emotional experiences. Love, devotion, grief, mourning, jealousy, and anxiety are all connected to attachment. From the two-year-old who watches out the window for Daddy to come home to the lover who torments himself by imagining that his partner is with someone else, we human beings have intense experiences of attachment-related emotion.

Attachment is not just a matter of our personal emotional experiences, though. In addition to *attachment emotions*, we have *attachment thoughts*. These are our beliefs and ways of thinking about relationships with other people. They can include not only our own individual love relationships but also what we expect others to think and experience, even about relationships in which we play no role ourselves. Attachment emotions and thoughts combine to form an *internal working model* of emotional and social relationships, a set of feelings, memories, ideas, and expectations about people's interpersonal attitudes and actions.

Adults may or may not want to talk about their attachment thoughts and emotions, and young children may not have the ability to do so. Much of what we know about attachment comes from the study of attachment behavior. The fascinated, engrossed gaze of the new father on his tiny baby, the anxious pacing of the mother whose teenager is late coming home, the wail of the toddler who sees his mother leaving the house—these are all actions that tell us something about each person's attachment-related thoughts and feelings.

Is Attachment the Same throughout Life?

The comments about attachment quoted at the beginning of this chapter dealt with individuals of a variety of ages, from infancy to grandparenthood. All of those people were said to show attachment in some form, and so they most probably do. But infants, parents, and grandparents do not have exactly the same attachment behaviors, emotions, or thoughts. Like many other aspects of human life, attachment develops; it changes as a result of age and experience.

The natural development of attachment is one of the reasons that there seem to be so many events being described by a single word. During different stages of life, attachment behaviors, emotions, and thoughts have different age-appropriate characteristics.

Attachment is probably most easily observed in infants and toddlers from about eight months to two years, and most readers will have seen at least a little of these young children's characteristic behavior. Young children's attachment seems to involve powerful feelings, the desire to be near the preferred person, and the fear of separation or of the approach of an unfamiliar adult. (Unfamiliar children are not such a problem.) During this period of development, the child may be generally fearful and distressed by loud noises, strange places, big dogs, and even loving but unfamiliar grand-parents. Large groups of people may also seem threatening—as one two-year-old complained tearfully, "Too many PEE-PUL!" Young children's attachment emotions can be seen in behaviors like crying, showing fear, or laughing and snuggling with a look of pleasure. Infants and toddlers are likely to show *stranger anxiety* and *separation anxiety* as very obvious attach-ment emotions.

Infants and toddlers show characteristic attachment behaviors, including moving toward familiar people and away from strangers and making or avoiding eye contact. Young children also use social signals like calling out or raising their arms to ask a caregiver to pick them up. They may show characteristic *reunion behavior* when a familiar person has been away, and they may display *mourning* if the loss is permanent, with intense crying, withdrawal, depression, and problems playing and sleeping.

As toddlers get better at crawling and then walking, they display a new kind of attachment behavior, using a familiar person as a *secure base.* In se-cure base behavior, the toddler explores a new environment or person by briefly leaving the familiar person, then checking back by returning, getting in the adult's lap, talking, or perhaps just making eye contact across a dis-tance. In the absence of a familiar person who can serve as a secure base, exploration does not occur so easily. Children of this age may use a *transi-tional object* to help them explore or take comfort in a strange place. This may be a familiar "blankie," a pacifier, or a stuffed toy; and, just as only a familiar person brings comfort, only the right object serves the purpose. The transitional object is not a substitute for the familiar person, and by this age, the child probably will want both for maximum comfort.

During the later toddler and preschool periods, children respond to threat-ened separation with aggressive actions, such as *temper tantrums.* Tantrums are often a response to the child's perception of a loss of contact with an adult attachment figure. (Our relatives, the baboons, throw tantrums when their mothers refuse to carry them as they grow too heavy.) Anger continues to be part of our response to loss throughout life, as does mourning behavior that resembles the young child's. Although we tend to emphasize the posi-tive feelings we have toward attachment figures and the longing we feel when separated from them, attachment relationships also involve negative emotions. This is very evident when an attachment figure has been lost and the resulting mourning includes anger, frustration, resentment, and profound sadness. Ongoing attachment relationships can also involve negative feelings mingled with the positive ones. Ambivalence is evident in toddlers' responses to their mothers, such as the *rapprochement crisis*[2] in which the toddler simultaneously demands help and pushes it away, the eye-rolling teenager's sarcastic frustration with parental protectiveness, or the struggles of many married couples to be "close enough but not too close." It may well be the case that the importance of attachment relationships comes from the melding of strong but contradictory feelings and behaviors.

Most of our basic attachment behaviors are in place by the end of the late toddler period. By that age, we are already inclined to try to stay close to those we care for, to look at and talk to them when we are distressed, and to cry or act sad when we are separated for a long time. Angry tantrums can also be part of our attachment behavior. As we get older, more mature, and more in control of our emotions, we learn to inhibit or to dissemble some of our attachment-related impulses. The wife seeing her soldier husband off on a deployment may want to cry or even rage at him, but she tries to keep a brave face so he will think of her with pleasure in the weeks to come. The child of divorced parents learns to keep the peace by acting as if he does not mind when a parental visit is arbitrarily cancelled. The widow or widower may not weep at the funeral service, but waits for a private time and place before expressing attachment feelings.

With maturation, of course, we also learn about the world, and we understand, as a young child does not, the implications of some events for attachment concerns. A diagnosis of serious illness triggers adult fears of loss even before the sick person changes much in appearance or behavior. A newspaper photograph or television news report can bring up vivid emotions of anxiety in adults, but would be dismissed by a young child as just a picture. A wife may recognize that her husband is talking a little too often to the attractive neighbor and may begin to respond with anticipatory grief and anger, although *really* nothing has happened yet.

What Is Bonding?

So far, we have talked about attachment, love, and liking, and about the connections between these feelings and thoughts about other people. What happened to *bonding*? Why is it not mentioned? This term is frequently used in people's descriptions of preferences for friends and relatives. "The mother and the baby bonded." "We went fishing and did a little male bonding." "My sister says her cat is unfriendly, but it bonded with me." Television programs, newspapers, even courtroom discussions speak of bonding as if the term is clearly understood.

The word bonding was originally used to refer to a father or mother's sudden development of positive, protective feelings toward a baby born to them or a very young adopted infant.[3] When people spoke of bonding in that sense, they usually meant to imply certain ideas: (1) that bonding involved the feelings and behavior of adults toward babies, not of babies toward adults;

(2) that bonding involved a dramatic, irreversible shift in the adult's emotional life; and (3) that bonding was needed for the child's sake because it enabled the adult to do the hard work involved in early parenthood.

As time went on, however, there were some questions asked about these assumptions, and the term bonding became popularized and used more frequently with less and specific meaning. Today, you will often hear people talk of bonding and attachment as if they were a single process. Nursing professionals sometimes use bonding as a name for the things they do to foster a good relationship between a new baby and mother—things like encouraging skin-to-skin contact or showing the mother things the baby can do.

Whatever meaning bonding once had seems to have been lost, as the term has been used more and more loosely and carelessly. This book will not use the word "bonding" without the accompaniment of a clear definition, and then only with respect to a very narrow range of human relationships. It might be good for readers to think twice before using a word that communicates so many different things to different people. Although attachment has its own confusions, it still maintains a common enough meaning to be useful—and we really have no substitute that carries all the meanings of attachment emotions, attachment behaviors, and internal working models that grow out of early relationships.

APPLICATIONS: ATTACHMENT AND REAL LIFE

Don't people just naturally understand attachment? Don't we all have intuitions that help us manage our relationships with other people? Why do we need to think about these natural parts of life?

Certainly most of us have learned a lot about emotional connections through observation, but modern life often places demands on us that are more than we can deal with on the basis of our casual experience. We would like to be sure that we are doing the right things when we make decisions about difficult matters like child care or adoption. Although human beings are resilient, we would like to feel confident that our decisions will have the best possible outcomes.

There are a great many practical situations in which people need to apply an understanding of attachment. Whether that understanding is correct or not can have a real impact on the success and happiness of human lives, especially those of children and families.

Daily Problems of Childrearing

Especially in the infant and toddler period, problems related to sleep are often connected with what appear to be attachment issues. Fearfulness and tantrum behavior have similar connections. Such behaviors are usually worsened if a caregiver is sick or depressed, or in cases where there has been some change, like moving into a new house or the birth of a new baby. Applying attachment concepts to these practical problems can be helpful for parents or other caregivers.

Child Care

When children are cared for in groups outside their family homes, their experiences can play an important role in their development. Regulations governing day care centers should include applications of what we know about attachment. For example, the numbers of children cared for by individual day care staff members, staff turnover, and the ways that caregivers interact with children are all related to attachment issues and can help or hinder early emotional development.

Parents choosing day care arrangements need help in understanding the role these experiences have in determining their children's development. Motivated and educated parents are a critical force in bringing about regulations that produce higher quality child care. A survey done by the organization Zero to Three[4] showed that many U.S. parents believe it is a good thing for young children to have several different caregivers. Parents with this misunderstanding may opt for child care arrangements that are potentially harmful.

Foster Care

Foster care programs are an essential factor in the lives of thousands of children whose parents are not able to care for them effectively. These children may be placed in foster care because they have been neglected or abused, or because the parents are unable to provide adequate housing or other necessities. The parents may be young, poorly educated, or mentally or physically handicapped, and drugs or alcohol may have played a part in the family situation.

Although it might seem logical to expect that children in foster care would welcome and appreciate a home without neglect or abuse, in fact, these children suffer from being separated from their parents, and they need sympathetic responses to their reactions to loss. The age at which foster placement occurs is an important factor here. Foster parents need to be able to work with children reacting to separation, and as we will see later, they may need to be chosen for personality characteristics that enable them to provide a good emotional environment for children.

Foster care programs need to take into account attachment issues, such as the need for familiarity, consistency, and continuity of care. Frequent changes of foster care placement do not give necessary support to early emotional development. Along the same lines, foster care placement needs to involve permanency planning: the attempt to guarantee a secure long-term placement for the child as soon as possible rather than an open-ended arrangement without a sense of a secure home.

Kinship Care

For some children, a substitute for placement in the foster care system is kinship care. When the parents are not successful in providing an appropriate home, a child may be placed with a family member, not informally, but with the approval and supervision of the state's child protective services agency. Attachment is an issue in kinship care just as it is in other foster care placements, unless the child has had a longstanding familiarity with the family member. As we will see, the genetic relationship is no substitute for the experience of a familiar relationship, and movement in and out of kinship care needs to be planned as carefully as any other form of care.

Adoption

Of all practical situations, adoption is the one that seems to have the greatest relevance to attachment. When adoption occurs, children are asked to undergo and adjust to separation from familiar people, then to develop a new attachment for the adoptive family. Adoptive parents do not just want to care for and rear an adopted child; they want to create a new family relationship and new emotional ties between themselves and the child.

How well the new connections work, and what the adoptive parents need to do, depends strongly on the age of the child at the time of adoption. As we will see, applying the abstract concept of attachment to real-world situations requires attention to age differences. Adoptive parents need to understand how a child's emotional ties change with development and how the family needs to handle children in different circumstances. Even if they have raised other children successfully, adoptive parents may need help and training in order to do well with adoptees.

A highly demanding situation for adoptive families involves foreign adoptions. Children adopted from other countries can be difficult to communicate with because of different language backgrounds and what may have been serious experiences of neglect and abuse. They may have had little opportunity to form attachments in the past, and they may also have physical and mental problems that interfere with emotional connections. Adoptive families who are trying to cope with all these problems can benefit from a clear understanding of attachment and the role it plays in children's lives.

Handicapping Conditions

Whether they are adopted or not, children with certain handicapping conditions may offer a challenge in terms of emotional development, as well as mental or physical growth. As we will see later, young children cement their emotional ties with their parents by communicating their interest in familiar people. They do so with the sounds they make, through eye contact, by following, and by expressions of pleasure or displeasure. Children with handicaps may not be able to communicate in the emotional ways their parents expect. For example, a visually impaired child may not look at the parents' eyes or facial expression and respond to it as a normally sighted child would, and the parents may interpret this as a lack of emotional connection. Parents of children with handicaps may also need to make a practical application of information about attachment.

Children with handicapping conditions or serious illnesses may spend significant periods of time in hospitals, receiving treatment or recovering from it. Information about attachment can help clarify their emotional needs during these periods, as well as the ways in which medical staff and parents can be most supportive.

Domestic Violence and Terrorism

When children are exposed to domestic violence, their emotional lives and ties to others may be distorted as a result. Mothers who live in fear of violence may be unable to create normal emotional connections with their children. For parents, foster and adoptive parents, or child care providers, an understanding of attachment processes may help in the care and guidance of children who have been traumatized by violence. The same is true for those who work with or adopt children who have been orphaned by civil wars and acts of terrorism.

Divorce and Custody

The frequency of divorce and remarriage in modern life means that large numbers of children are subjected to separations and the possibility of having to make new emotional ties. Application of information about attachment can make these situations somewhat smoother for children. It is important for parents to be aware of the emotional impact of these experiences on their children and to take this impact into account as they plan further life changes. It is also important for attorneys and judges to be aware of the effects of custody decisions on children's emotional lives.

School Issues

Although most readers will think of child care as a definite factor in early emotional development, many will assume that by school age, children are no longer vulnerable to separation or affected by other attachment issues. However, separation and loss can have an effect on children's schoolwork, play, and friendships, and schools can apply information about attachment in ways that might reduce the impact of divorce or changes in living situations. Such applications could be especially helpful for children in foster care.

Psychotherapy

Forms of psychotherapy that stress attachment are used in treatment of both children and adults. It is possible, although not certain, that some emotional problems are a direct result of difficulties in early attachment. It is evident that diagnosis and treatment of emotional disturbance must incorporate the appropriate application of well-established principles of attachment, or they risk doing harm rather than good.

UNDERSTANDING ATTACHMENT: USING THIS BOOK

Attachment and emotional development are not yet completely understood, but much is known and will be discussed in this book. This first chapter has presented some ideas about attachment and has offered definitions of some important terms used in the discussion of emotional development. Chapter 2 will provide some historical background and identify important events in the growth of the attachment concept as we know it today. In Chapter 3, we will examine one of the critical steps toward effective research on internal working models of social relationships: the invention and implementation of ways to measure attachment behaviors, emotions, and thoughts. Chapter 4 will describe the natural history of attachment and discuss some of the attachment changes characteristic of different stages of human life. In Chapter 5, we will look at work on the outcome of attachment experiences, examining the evidence that different personality outcomes result from different attachment histories. Chapter 6 will look at the possibility that mental illness can result from disturbed attachment experiences. It will discuss the possibility that attachment problems can be treated through psychotherapy and the use of the general concept of attachment in the therapeutic setting. Chapter 7 will describe some ways in which the attachment concept has been used and misused in popular discussions and in practical legal applications. Finally, Chapter 8 will address the changes in social life that may lead to differences in attachment experiences and the new directions in theory and research that may lead to a somewhat different view of attachment than was known in the past.

Outside the Scope

There are some basic matters connected with the study of attachment that are simply beyond the confines of a book like this one. Good research design and statistical analysis are critical to the understanding of any developmental process, but there is space here only for the most essential points about research evidence. Readers who want to know more can pick from an excellent array of books on the subject, such as Keith Stanovich's *How to Think Straight About Psychology*.

Infant determinism is another related issue outside the scope of this book. This much-debated notion posits that experiences during infancy have extraordinary influence over personality development and override most later life events. Rather than arguing about the details of this complex issue, this book will be based on the assumption that individuals are shaped by both early and later experiences.

Readers may be surprised to find little discussion of brain development in the chapters to come. It has become fashionable to link all aspects of child development to changes in the brain's structure and functioning. Both cognitive and emotional developments are often discussed with respect to brain growth, and facts about the effects of the environment on the brain are used to advocate for childrearing and educational practices. This book will not follow that popular pathway. In spite of the frequency with which these connections are made in the mass media and elsewhere, the fact is we do not have much real information about connections between the brain and emotional development. To assume that we do is to make an unwarranted assertion. In fact, most of the information we have is from animal studies that may or may not be relevant to human development.

In one discussion of this matter, child development and policy expert Jack Shonkoff[5] notes:

> Translations of science that go far beyond what is known, or that distort existing data, represent significant threats to its credibility in the arenas of both public education and social policy. One egregious example is the conclusion that young children who are abused or who witness violence to others sustain irreversible changes to their developing brains that result in permanent emotional damage and inevitable violent behavior ... later in life.... [T]here is absolutely no evidence to support [this].

In a comment particularly relevant to the study of attachment and the role of separation and loss, Shonkoff also states, "There are absolutely no data that even begin to address questions regarding differential brain effects related to the timing of an adverse experience, nor is there any neuroscientific evidence regarding the reversibility of such hypothetical insults." It is an attractive idea that everything about attachment might be explained by looking at brain development, but it is one that will be avoided in this book.

chapter 2

Babies, History, War, and Politics: Early Work on the Attachment Concept

Human beings have observed emotional development as long as history has been recorded, and have paid a great deal of attention to mothers' love for their children. The story of the judgment of Solomon, like other tales, stresses the love of a mother for her child—in this case so strong that the mother would rather lose the child and know it to be well than keep it and have it harmed. Traditional stories of this type gave less consideration to a child's preference for a familiar caregiver, but our forebears did have some concerns about children's feelings.

MOTHER LOVE

The mother's powerful preference and concern for her child were sometimes considered to be an instinctive response, a biological characteristic that humans shared with animals. (The difficulty of getting a ewe to accept an orphan lamb when her own has died was well known, for example.) At the same time it was recognized that an adoptive mother could develop a strong emotional connection to a baby, who would return her love. It was hard to argue that maternal love was based on some biological response, built in and already present at the time a baby was born. It was often assumed that the experience of breastfeeding caused maternal affection to develop, and, although our culture has largely forgotten the practice, adoptive nursing is possible for humans.

BABY LOVE

The idea that breastfeeding played a role in emotional preference was associated with the practice of wet nursing. Through the eighteenth and nineteenth centuries, and even the early 1900s, it was not uncommon for a family to hire a wet nurse—a lactating woman who was paid to breastfeed an infant. Some wet nurses lived with the family, and some took the child for long periods of time to their own homes, possibly at a considerable distance. This arrangement might have been made because the biological mother was sick or had died; it might have allowed the mother to carry on earning money with skilled work; it could have been based on the wish to allow the mother to start another pregnancy quickly; or it might have resulted simply from the wish for a fashionable figure and free social life.[1] Discussion of wet nursing usually stressed the possible dangers of a nurse with unwholesome milk, or the possibility that undesirable traits could be taken in with the milk. There was little concern about effects on the mother-child relationship.

Babies and Their Nurses

That the wet nurse could become very fond of the nursling was taken for granted, and some wet nurses remained in the household for many years after the child was weaned. That a child could come to prefer a nurse to the mother was an observed fact, but usually not a source of concern, even when the nurse and the child were abruptly separated upon weaning. Eighteenth-century paintings showed toddlers shrinking from visiting mothers and turning toward the familiar nurses they had come to prefer.[2]

Historical evidence of the impact of separation from a wet nurse who had become an attachment figure was occasionally recorded. An account written in 1841 of a two-year-old boy brought to his parents' home by his wet nurse described him as enjoying "the best of health" during the two weeks the nurse stayed, but when she left:

> [He] grew pale, sad, and morose. He showed himself unresponsive to his parents' love and refused the dishes that had been his favorites only a few days before.... The little boy whose failing became increasingly apparent, spent whole hours in sad immobility, eyes fastened to the door through which he had seen pass the woman who served him as mother.... The doctor decided that the only way to save the child was to call the nurse back immediately.[3]

This strategy was effective; the child was allowed to spend another year with the nurse, and a gradual separation at that time left him in good health.

The obvious cause of the children's preference for their wet nurses was the experience of breastfeeding, the wet nurse's primary responsibility. It was generally ignored that wet nurses also bathed, dressed, played with, comforted, and even slept with their charges, all possible sources of emotional connection. This view has not changed greatly, and in fact the average person in the United States is convinced that breastfeeding is desirable because it creates mutual love, although, as we will see, there is little evidence to support this idea.

Baby Love and Religion

For many eighteenth and nineteenth-century parents, a child's attachment to mother or nurse was interesting, but usually inessential; it was cute, basically harmless, and important only when the grieving child seemed in danger of dying after separation from the loved adult. But some parents during this period had a particular concern that their children have special emotions connected with their parents—emotions that were thought to play a part in their religious lives. For different religious groups in the United States and European countries, the relevant feelings might involve fear, respect, awe, love, or pleasure. These differing emotions were all desired because they were expected to help achieve one goal: cheerful obedience to parents at an early age.[4] No doubt these parents, like modern mothers and fathers, found an obedient child more pleasing than an unruly one, but the parent's convenience was not actually the major concern. Children were to obey the authority of parents as training for the obedience to God that would eventually save their souls—and the absence of which would damn them for all eternity. Parents had the fearful responsibility of shaping the child's attitude toward the goal of salvation, and they were warned against yielding to their own affection for the child, an emotion that might interfere with the work of child training. It was the child's emotional response to the parents that was of critical importance; the parents' love might be better suppressed than expressed.

FORMAL THEORIES OF ATTACHMENT

So far, our discussion on the history of the attachment concept has dealt with informal, unsophisticated ideas shared by average parents and their medical advisers. By the end of the nineteenth century, however, some writers began to develop formal concepts of human emotional development that included attachment processes.

Sigmund Freud

Freud based his thinking about attachment on the belief that feeding creates the child's emotional preference. Though development of the concept eventually surpassed this early idea, the foundation of attachment for Freud was what our grandmothers called "cupboard love."

To discuss what Freud thought on a given matter is not as simple as it may appear. Freud's ideas developed and changed in the context of a long and eventful professional life. His conceptualization of the events of the first years of life did not change greatly, however, even when some of his ideas about human motivation altered.

To understand Freud's view of what we now call attachment, we need to examine his ideas about the nature of infant personality as stated in about 1916. The newborn was seen as being driven by a combined need for food and desire for the pleasure of sucking. Initially, in this view, the young child's interests are narcissistic and focused on the self. Even when at the breast, the baby concentrates on its own bodily sensations and gratifications. Nursing mothers take advantage of this by cleaning the baby's ears or cutting nails while there is no resistance because the child is absorbed in sucking. Gradually, though, that outside object, the breast, comes to be of interest and is gratifying in and of itself. The mother becomes a love object, not just a useful contraption for presenting the breast. Staying near the mother then means security and happiness, and the threat of separation becomes a cause for anxiety.

In order to disconnect the pleasure of feeding from the experience of play and comfort, we would have to look for cases where one adult fed the baby and another played and comforted it. In Freud's day, as in our own, this would have been an uncommon situation. A baby may have more than one caregiver, but each one generally provides a full spectrum of care when on duty. Freud's view of feeding as a necessary cause of the child's emotional preference emerged from the confusion of social and biological factors (just as had earlier been the case when people thought about wet nurses). The related fact that caregivers and feeders were almost exclusively female led to the assumption that the mother was the focus of the child's early emotional life. In addition, Freud stressed biological drives like hunger because of their obvious connection with medicine and the natural sciences—fields with respectable foundations of evidence that reached far beyond what existed at the time for social and behavioral studies.

Ian Suttie

Freud's many followers, and some of his opponents, maintained that the emotional preference of the child for the familiar caregiver arose from the gratification of being fed. However, this belief plays little or no role in the modern concept of attachment.

In fact, late in Freud's life at least one thinker was already abandoning the assumption that childhood emotional preference was founded on feeding experiences. Dr. Ian Suttie argued that the child's need for the mother's love was a primary necessity in itself and did not have to be connected with the satisfaction of hunger.[5] Suttie was far more inclined than Freud to examine social and cultural factors and to note that not all groups of people have the same childhood experiences, but, like Freud, he was not greatly concerned with the smaller details of the child's development of emotional preferences for people. Suttie's early death prevented him from elaborating on these ideas.

The Ethologists

While Freud and Suttie were considering early emotional development in humans, a quite different group of thinkers was approaching some related problems by studying the behavior and development of animals. The German researcher Konrad Lorenz was a leader among them.

Lorenz worked in a discipline that attempted to explain behavior primarily in terms of hereditary factors, with little emphasis on the role of learning. Focusing primarily on animal behavior, ethologists had little interest in the effect of cultural differences on the individual. Their mission was to describe behavioral characteristics of animal species, but there eventually were some attempts to apply ethological concepts to human beings.[6]

Ethological theory had at least as strong an influence on modern ideas about attachment as Freudian theory did and, thus, needs to be examined. Before the twentieth century began, there had been many studies of animals using a natural history approach, but ethologists brought to their tasks a clear theoretical system that went beyond simple observation. Certain assumptions guided their work:

1. Ethologists emphasized the role of instinct in determining behavior. Their definition of this term was rather precise and quite different from the loose, everyday use today, when many English speakers say "instinctively" to mean "automatically" or "involuntarily." For example, someone might say, "When the dog ran across the road, I instinctively slammed on the brakes." Although, from the ethologists' viewpoint, instinctive behaviors were indeed both automatic and involuntary, they were also inborn and unlearned, as opposed to the learned behavior that is involved in driving a car. The concept of instinct included a number of other assumptions as well.
2. Animals were assumed to inherit particular patterns of complex behavior. Ethology was not concerned with a brief, simple reflex response

like an eye blink, but with complicated actions, such as a mother mouse caring for her offspring by following them and returning them to the nest if they crawled out. Behaviors like this have many steps and must be flexible and elaborate, guiding the mouse to follow her pups in different directions or to sniff them out behind an obstacle.

3. Ethologists assumed that inherited behaviors were species-specific. Members of the species who are capable carry out these species-specific behaviors (for example, a male opossum does not carry young in a pouch, of course). There might be instinctive behaviors found only among males or only among females of the species, and similarly there might be instinctive behaviors that occurred only at a certain point in development, not in older or in younger individuals.

4. Ethologists assumed that instinctive behaviors had some real connection to survival of the species. The types of behavior most likely to involve instinct would be eating, drinking, defense, courtship, mating, and care of the young; behaviors like intelligent learning and problem-solving were much less likely to be instinctive. Of course, the most important aspects of instinct from the perspective of this book are those related to attachment issues: possible instinctive reactions of the young to their caregivers, reactions that could mesh with the adults' instinctive care behaviors in ways that facilitate survival of the young and of the species.

5. Ethologists assumed that instinctive behaviors were usually directed toward something in the environment and contributed to survival. Generally, the objects that receive the animal's instinctive behavior also release the behavior by providing the kinds of stimuli that cause the behavior to begin. If the stimuli are the wrong ones, a normal instinctive behavior may not occur. A baby animal that is sick or malformed may not release its mother's instinctive caregiving behavior, and a mother who behaves inappropriately may not release the baby's instinctive responses to her.

   To say that a behavior is instinctive does not mean that it will occur in its perfect form under all circumstances. Nor does it mean that the outcome of instinctive behavior is always appropriate. A suspended, stuffed head of a female will release the male mating behavior in some bird species. The males approach, position themselves, and copulate with her nonexistent body just as they would with an intact live female.

6. The idea that instinctive behaviors are connected to their objects opens the door to an important ethological idea about learning. By definition, instinctive behaviors are unlearned, but an animal might need to learn something about the objects toward which instinctive acts can be

directed. Hunting and eating prey may be instinctive, but a wolf that encounters a porcupine learns rapidly that a tender rabbit is a better target than a painfully prickly beast. The ability to learn about the potential objects of instinctive behavior is especially important for adults' care of the young and for the young animal's appropriate response.

A female sheep, for example, quickly learns the smell of her own lamb and will care only for that one, butting away any wandering orphan that tries to nurse. This devotion to her own lamb helps ensure its survival, which would be endangered had the mother not learned to recognize her own. Similarly, lambs, calves, and the young of other species quickly learn to follow their own mothers, not just any female of their species (most of whom would not care for the little one). These animals' instinctive behaviors have to be combined with individual learning for the best survival results, so the parallel with human attachment is obvious.

IMPRINTING

Ethologists were especially intrigued by a rapid type of learning they called *imprinting*. This type of learning was most obvious in young birds, such as ducklings, whose early and later life experiences alter the object of their instinctive behavior.

Young ducklings have the innate, unlearned behavior, in the first few days after hatching, of following a moving object. In their natural life in the wild, that object is most likely to be the mother duck, who has made her nest and laid her eggs in a relatively solitary place. In other settings, however, the ducklings will follow other moving objects that happen to be present: other kinds of birds, cats, dogs, people, or even toy trains. The instinctive following seems to be released by the movement the duckling sees, not by the kind of object that is moving.

Within a few days after this hatching and following, however, the young duckling stops following just any moving object. It now restricts its following to the kind of object that it initially saw and followed soon after it hatched, whether this object is its own mother, a human caretaker, or even something dangerous like a fox. The duckling is now considered to be imprinted on the object it followed earlier and only that or similar objects can release the instinctive following reaction.

Imprinting is, by definition, a form of learning because it involves a change in behavior that depends on experience. It is an unusual type of learning, though, because it only happens quickly and effectively during a specific time period. (Ordinary learning happens in roughly the same way at most times during an individual's life.) Imprinting has a different speed and pattern than other kinds of learning. To think of it another way, imprinting is based not just on experience but also on an interaction between the two basic mechanisms of development: experience and maturation. Human attachment also involves both experience and maturation.

CRITICAL PERIODS

The time during which imprinting works best is called a *critical* or *sensitive* period. Time is essential to the idea of imprinting, because an experience at a particular time has an effect on development that it would not have had earlier and will not have later. It is in this window of time that critical and special processes appear to occur. Many critical periods happen early in development, a point that we will need to keep in mind when we examine modern thinking about attachment.

If you have been around farm animals, it probably does not surprise you at all that ducks follow moving things, even things that are not at all duck-like. What may be more surprising is that the duck's imprinting experiences during an early critical period have a long-term effect on the duck, even after it has passed the early following stage. As the imprinted duck becomes mature and gets ready to mate, its preference for a partner is determined not just by ordinary duck beauty and charm, but by the effects of the imprinting experience. The duck remains extremely resistant to change and now courts another duck, or a human being, or a toy train, the choice depending on the early following experience. Zookeepers must be very cautious when hand-rearing birds that imprint, or they will find it impossible to breed them as adults. Bird caretakers have been known to use a hand puppet to attract the young bird's interest, as unrequited love for the zookeeper may later cause the bird to reject mates of its own species.

THE FOUNDATIONS OF
ATTACHMENT THEORY AND WORLD EVENTS

By the 1930s, much of Freudian theory and ethological theory were already in place. It would have been possible to blend these two views and to produce the theoretical approach to attachment that emerged in the 1950s and later, but this blending did not occur.

World events in the 1930s and 1940s simultaneously postponed theoretical advances and piqued interest in early emotional life. The commitment to "total war" during World War II delayed advances in theory. However, due to circumstances resulting from the war, large groups of young children were separated from familiar caregivers. This had occurred for individuals in the past, but reactions could not readily be recorded.

Given the numbers of children involved during World War II, the possibility of observations on early emotional development increased, and research interest grew.

Even before the war began, social and medical changes had already begun to call attention to the effects of separation. Until well into the twentieth century, young children who needed intensive medical treatment fell into two categories: if poor, they were likely to die untreated; if affluent, they received surgical or medical treatment in their own homes. By the 1930s, advances in medical techniques and an increased awareness of infection made it more likely that children would be hospitalized, but until the advent of antibiotics, fear of infection set severe limits on visits by parents. During this period, large numbers of children experienced not only fear and pain but also abrupt separation from their parents. One man who was a child during this time recalls his tonsillectomy at age three. His mother brought him to the hospital, handed him to a nurse, and then left, returning for him as instructed ten days later. He did not speak again for a year after this event.

Separation and Evacuation

As fathers joined the military during World War II, countless children in the United States and European countries, as well as those in Asia, experienced separation from their fathers. Their mothers' anxiety, depression, and involvement in war work nearly amounted to a second separation. The death of a father in combat made a child's loss permanent, and often exacerbated the mother's preoccupation. Although wars throughout history have had similar effects on children, the total involvement of combatant nations in World War II made for an extraordinarily large number of affected children.

In the United States, though fears of invasion caused families to prepare for evacuation of their homes, no serious evacuation program was ever initiated. In Britain, however, constant German bombing of London and of shipping and industrial areas caused immense damage to residences, and consequently, many deaths of women and children. The British government began programs to evacuate infants and children, with or without their mothers, to safer rural areas, where they stayed for months or years, often billeted in private homes. Evacuation of British children was abrupt and hurried. One author wrote a few years later, "In a few days almost three-quarters of a million children were separated from their parents.... History has here made a cruel psychological experiment on a large scale."[7]

Observation of the evacuated children yielded confusing results about the effects of separation, with frequent bedwetting as the most common problem. In fact, it was quite difficult to understand the results of this cruel natural experiment to some extent because of the large numbers of children and the chaotic conditions. Simply keeping track of trainloads of children with their gas masks and identification papers had to take precedence over data collection. And, of course, the primitive theories about emotional development meant that most observers would have no idea what to look for in the children's moods or behavior.

Some famous observations have survived from this time period, however. Anna Freud, who went to Britain with her father just before war broke out, worked with Dorothy Burlingham on observational material they eventually published as *War and Children*.[8] Much of their work stressed defense mechanisms—ways in which children protected themselves emotionally against the profound anxiety of separation from familiar people and places. A well-known report from Freud and Burlingham described the case of Billie, a three-year-old separated from his mother. He initially managed his anxiety by repeating to himself that his mother would come to get him, that she would put on his coat and pixie hat, and so on. When told by a well-meaning or impatient staff member not to keep saying these things, Billie ended up nodding his head repeatedly in a tic-like way that made sense only to those who had witnessed his earlier distress.

From this period, we also have Anna Freud's sympathetic descriptions of the emotional concerns of young children in wartime—their terror of sirens and of people wearing gas masks, and especially of separation from the familiar. One case states, for example:

> Jim was separated from a very nice and affectionate mother at 17 months.... He formed two strong attachments to two young nurses who successively took care of him. Although he was otherwise a well-adjusted, active, and companionable child, his behavior became impossible where these attachments were concerned. He was clinging, over possessive, unwilling to be left for a minute and continually demanded something without being able to define in any way what it was he wanted. It was no unusual sight to see Jim lie on the floor sobbing and despairing. These reactions ended when his favorite nurse was absent even for short periods. He was then quiet and impersonal.[9]

Separation: The Kindertransport Arrangement

While the evacuation of British children was providing a glimpse into the effects of separation on early emotional development, European children were also showing the effects of war. One well-defined group was comprised of German Jewish children brought to Britain just before war began in earnest. Immigration of these children—without their parents— was a result of the efforts of British refugee organizations after the homes of

German Jews were attacked in November 1938. Two thousand children under the age of seventeen were brought to Britain by Kindertransport trains, and then boats across the English Channel, before war broke out in September 1939.

Observations by Anna Freud and Dorothy Burlingham showed how the younger children coped with this abrupt, terrifying, often permanent separation from familiar caregivers. One group of small children was described as turning to each other for help and comfort, rather than accepting nurturing from strange adults.

John Bowlby

During and following World War II, a new and important formulation of ideas about emotional development was offered by the theorist whose name is invariably linked with this topic: John Bowlby.[10] "Attachment theory" and "Bowlby's attachment theory" are almost synonymous terms today, although, as we will see in Chapter 8, another form of attachment theory, not identical with Bowlby's work, is beginning to emerge.

Bowlby's theory of attachment involved ideas about human development that were somewhat unusual for their time, although not completely unique. He believed that the emotional attachments of infants and toddlers to their caregivers were based on social interactions, not on physical gratifications, and that they were built into human beings as a result of adaptation during early evolution. He saw a developmental timetable for attachment emotions and behaviors that was determined by an inherited human nature, not by learning. Most importantly—and, from the modern viewpoint, most questionably—Bowlby considered early attachment experiences to have a powerful effect on personality development. He was particularly interested in the impact of attachment history on mental health and on criminal behavior. As a leader in the international discussion of child development, Bowlby was in a position to stress this view, and a world that had so recently seen thousands of children separated from their parents was ready to listen carefully. It was within the context of Bowlby's thoughts that most of the events about to be described occurred.

Planned Separation: The Kibbutz Movement

A movement for social change that began in the nineteenth century was doubly connected to the study of emotional attachment in the twentieth. The kibbutz movement began with concern about the negative impact of close family ties on individual autonomy. The childrearing arrangements that grew out of this concern did, and still do, provide new information about social and emotional development.

The kibbutz (a word simply meaning group) is a form of community organization created (long before the founding of the modern state of Israel) by some of the early European immigrants to Palestine. A form of communal living with Utopian goals, the kibbutz is based on a philosophy of social and economic equality in which tasks and rewards are shared. Equality of the sexes was and is one of the goals of kibbutz life.[11] Though, in the past, most kibbutzim strongly emphasized agricultural work as a source of income, the manual work involved could be difficult for men and women to share equally.

Like other social groups, kibbutzim were not and are not identical, and no single description can give an accurate picture of the two-hundred-odd groups now in existence. However, these modern groups developed out of a much smaller number, all of which shared similar social philosophies, especially with respect to the functioning of families and of childrearing— a complex question in a society trying to achieve gender equality.

A major part of the early kibbutz members' social values was a reaction against the close family relationships of the shtetl, the small, beleaguered Jewish community, historically typical of rural Europe. Shtetl life had been narrow and sometimes dangerous, as its members were often forbidden to own land and at times were threatened with attack from their non-Jewish neighbors. (European Jews living in urban ghettoes battled these problems too, but had more contacts with the wider world.) Intense family relationships, combining love and hate with the ambivalence characteristic of important emotional ties, arose as families clung together in defense against a hostile outer world. Poverty, danger, and some traditional Jewish beliefs combined to reduce the opportunities open to women, and to make connections with children a parent's critical emotional focus.

The early kibbutz philosophy rejected this whole system in favor of an organization that would foster the development of the individual. Family relations were seen as stifling rather than supportive. Intense emotional ties between parents and children were considered a source of dependence and weakness, rather than the autonomy valued by the immigrants.

In their desire to avoid the suffocating emotional connections they recalled from shtetl family life, the founders of the kibbutz system did not plan for marriages or children. They planned instead for an egalitarian, communal life in which one's relationship to the whole group was more important than intimate, interpersonal ties. Like most human beings, however, they did develop some interpersonal relationships and some babies were born.

According to one original kibbutz member, Joseph Baratz,[12] "[Our] women didn't know how to look after babies." Baratz's group eventually chose one woman to care for all the babies in a house. She was assigned to this purpose, while the other mothers continued to participate in farm work.

Other kibbutzim adopted similar solutions, with one or more separate "children's houses," where the children eventually came to sleep as they got older, as well as spending their days there. Mothers who were breastfeeding in the babies' first months came in to nurse their infants, but they had their own jobs to do and did not visit freely; the caregivers had their child care work and did not encourage mothers to participate. Except for the period of breastfeeding, the children became the children of the kibbutz, rather than of their individual parents.

In the infants and toddlers' houses, the children's lives were rather different than what previous generations had experienced. Although parents felt a special interest in their own children, social pressure worked against its expression, as this would have implied that these individual parent-child ties were more important than those to the whole community. Parents' energies were consumed by the demands of the adult group.

The children's house caregivers did their jobs, but they did not want or try to create intimate relationships with the children. Caregivers changed according to their shifts, and when children reached given ages, they were transferred to a new house with new caregivers. Nighttime care of the younger children was a special issue because the regular caregivers were off-duty at night. Some kibbutzim tried to have every adult take a turn sleeping in the infants' house, but most adult members were unwilling and unskilled at dealing with a crying baby. Some slept through the cries and others pretended to; as a result the chances that a child would be comforted at night were low and unpredictable.

The outcome of the kibbutz pattern of child care was that babies had only one consistent source of social experience: other babies. Adults were constantly coming and going, changing shifts, or altering their visits once the babies were weaned from the breast. Only the babies in nearby cribs stayed the same, and almost all of them would stay together for many years, as the age group transferred together from one house to the next.

For the infants of the kibbutz, as for few other children, food and comfort were thus separated from predictable and familiar social and emotional interactions. Other babies could not comfort a distressed infant, but they could provide the security of familiarity. Toddlers and older children could actually offer comfort. As Bruno Bettelheim described this:

> At night, small children have only their mutual comforting to rely on, since it may take quite a while for the single night worker to hear a child who wakes up crying.... Even when the night watch is finally summoned by the child's anxious cry, the person who comes when

the child thus awakens from a nightmare, deeply shaken, is more or less a stranger and can therefore give only small comfort. But as likely as not, when the night watch gets there, he finds that some other child has already soothed the anxious one.[13]

RECENT EVENTS AND THEIR CONTRIBUTION TO THE UNDERSTANDING OF ATTACHMENT

Evacuation of children during World War II was not the last cruel psychological experiment that has given us information about children's responses to separation and loss. More recently, events gave rise to thousands of adoptions from foreign countries, providing an unhappy opportunity for further research on early emotional development.

Reasons for Adoption from Abroad

Social changes in the United States, Canada, and Western Europe in the 1980s and 1990s made adoption of young infants more difficult. Concurrent with this, couples were experiencing an increased level of fertility problems. Unmarried parenthood had become more socially acceptable, and more girls wanted to care for their unplanned babies rather than relinquish them for adoption. Large numbers of older children needed homes, but couples seeking adoption most often wanted newborn infants they could care for from the beginning—not an unrealistic wish, considering the many problems an older child might bring to the family. Racial prejudices also played a role, as many families of European backgrounds preferred, for a variety of reasons, not to adopt children of color, and indeed many social workers preferred to place minority children with the few available minority adoptive families.

Adoption of children born within an industrialized country could also be fraught with difficulties relating to the legal rights of the birthparents, issues about termination of parental rights, and the possibility that a birthparent could change the decision about relinquishment or bargain for continued contact with the child.

Foreign adoptions had considerable appeal in these circumstances. There were young infants available; racial backgrounds were in many cases more acceptable to parents of ethnic majority status; and there would be no contact with the birthparents, thus, no question of changed decisions about relinquishment. In many cases, adoptive parents could feel gratified that they were rescuing children from what were indeed vile, barbaric conditions.

In the 1980s, some questionable practices were associated with foreign adoptions. Stories circulated about children who had been kidnapped or whose poverty-stricken parents had been tricked or bribed into giving them up. However, a foreign adoption industry rapidly developed to guide Western parents in their adoptive process and to guarantee it was legal and ethical.

Romanian Adoptees

Under the rule of the dictator Nicolae Ceausescu, the small, poor country of Romania developed a frighteningly large population of children who existed in institutions. (Existed is the correct word; to say they were cared for is stretching the meaning of that term.) From 1965 until 1989, Ceausescu and his party enforced social regulations intended to double the population and provide plenty of cheap labor. Women were not allowed access to birth control or abortion until they had had four or five children.

Because of the country's extreme poverty, Romanian families were, in many cases, unable to care for the children they bore. Orphanages were established to "warehouse" children from poor families, and it became socially acceptable to place children in these institutions. A large proportion of the orphanage children came from Romany or Gypsy families, an ethnic group considered inferior and undesirable. Children with birth defects and problems, such as fetal alcohol syndrome, were especially likely candidates for orphanages.

Conditions in the orphanages were almost unimaginable. Children received little care, often being tied into cribs and given food in bottles until a late age. There were few toys, little opportunity for free movement, and almost no social stimulation or responsiveness from adults. Medical care was minimal, and special needs children received no treatment for their problems. Malnutrition was common, as were skull deformities caused by lying in the same position for long periods. Many had hearing problems as a result of untreated infections. There is little doubt that physical abuse, as well as neglect, occurred at the hands of attendants and older children. Considerable numbers of the children were HIV-positive. Because of the institutional conditions and their pre-existing problems, many of the orphans showed severe developmental delays, failing to walk or talk until well after the expected age.

In 1989, at the end of the Ceausescu regime, there were over 150,000 children in these Romanian institutions. Sadly, the changes in Romania's social practices under that regime persisted after the fall of the dictator, and abandonment of children by poor families has continued.

Beginning shortly after Ceausescu's fall, Western families began to adopt children from Romanian orphanages, and they have continued to do so until very recently. In 2004 Romania formulated a policy prohibiting many foreign adoptions.

Russian and Other Eastern European Orphans

Although the Romanian orphans accounted for a great number of ne-glected children needing adoption or foster care and although the Romanian situation gained the most attention due to its abrupt change in national policy about foreign adoption, other Eastern European countries have been major sources of adoptable children. In those countries, parents of babies with physical handicaps are encouraged to institutionalize their children and make them available for adoption, as are those whose poor living con-ditions inevitably lead to developmental problems in the children. Though adoption of these children has been encouraged, recent news stories about the number of deaths of Russian adoptees in the United States have caused concern in Eastern Europe, which may bring about new policies on foreign adoption.

Adoption from China

In 1979, China instituted a "one-child" policy, limiting most families to one completed pregnancy. The goal was to balance food production and population size, thereby reducing poverty. This policy, of course, was strongly at odds with the traditional Chinese desire for large families, as well as the previous Communist policy of encouraging childbearing, and it took some time for the rule to be enforced. There is still considerable resis-tance to family limitation, but rewards for small families and penalties for larger ones have been effective.

The one-child-per-family policy stresses delayed marriage and childbear-ing, the trade-off being fewer and healthier births. When more than one child is born to a couple, the parents may try to avoid consequences (such as being restricted to a small apartment) by failing to register the birth, though this ploy makes it difficult for the child to obtain an education. There are exceptions to the one-child rule, and it seems to be the case that the policy was intended for one generation only and may be altered in the foreseeable future.

Because of the Chinese preference for a son to carry on the family line, the one-child rule has a particular significance: the birth of a girl makes a second attempt for a boy unlikely. As a result, abandonment of baby girls began not long after the policy was initiated. This practice is in line with the old Chinese tradition in which midwives had a box of ashes available for the suffocation of a newborn girl, hastening the possibility of a new pregnancy and the birth of the much wished for boy.

In one study of abandoned Chinese babies, almost all were healthy girls and only a few were boys, all of whom were sick or handicapped.[14] Most abandonments occurred in the first six months of life, the children often being left in places where they were likely to be found, or if they were sick, at hospitals.

Adoption of Chinese orphans by Westerners began in about 1994 and increased in frequency at a rapid rate. Girls are generally seen as manageable, quiet, and affectionate, and Westerners stereotypically think of Asians as cooperative and intelligent. In addition, these children are babies, making them even more desirable.

The Hague Convention

The increasing occurrence of foreign adoption in the early 1990s brought about an agreement called the Hague Adoption Convention (also called the Convention on Protection of Children and Co-operation in Respect of Intercountry Adoption), which was signed in May 1993. The Hague Convention is intended to prevent commercial trafficking in children and other possible abuses, as well as protecting the adults and children involved in international adoptions.

The Hague Convention is implemented in the United States by the Intercountry Adoption Act of 2000, which sets standards and accreditation criteria for adoption services and procedures for safeguarding children. In the United States, the State Department serves as a central authority for international adoptions. In addition to accrediting intercountry adoption agencies, the central authority has the essential task of preserving records on international adoptions.

Research on Development after Adoption from Abroad

The Hague Convention set rules for record keeping, a crucial part of research on the developmental impact of adoption from abroad. Adoption agencies and adoptive parents have also kept records, but information about early foreign adoptions is not necessarily very reliable.

The results of the cruel psychological experiment inherent in large numbers of foreign adoptions are, of course, of enormous interest to present and future adoptive families, and also to theorists and researchers studying attachment, separation, and loss. As adoptions from Romania increased, a group called the English and Romanian Adoptees (ERA) Study Team began a major research project.[15] One goal was to examine the outcome of this type of separation experience, something Bowlby's work predicted would be disastrous.

The research done by the ERA Study Team was extremely difficult. The serious developmental problems caused by the experiences of the Romanian orphans could never be studied through experimental (randomized controlled trials) techniques for ethical and practical reasons. The alternative, the quasi-experimental type of study done by the ERA Study Team, yielded such a mass of puzzling variables that it is difficult to determine cause and effect or to know whether a child's condition was a result of the orphanage experience, abandonment, a combination of the two, or the orphan's treatment following adoption. This work involves multiple questions and looks at the immediate result of the children's orphanage experiences and the children's ability to recover when placed with adoptive families, making the resulting data exceedingly complex.

One built-in problem with this type of study is the factor of spontaneous developmental change. However dreadful the conditions, a child who survives continues to develop, although not necessarily at a normal rate or along a normal trajectory. Changes in adopted children are to some extent simply the result of continuing maturation, though the nurturing provided by the adoptive family also plays a role. Recovery from a harmful experience may largely be a matter of resilience—one's natural ability to get back on a normal developmental pathway. All studies of child development have to deal with this factor, as did the Romanian orphan research.

The research on the Romanian orphans had other problems. It was difficult to know what the conditions had been before the children were institutionalized. Family poverty, maternal malnutrition, maternal depression, prenatal exposure to alcohol or drugs, problems at the time of birth, genetic issues—these could all increase a child's vulnerability to deprivation and lessen the child's response to better care following adoption. Although orphanage conditions were uniformly abominable, another difficulty had to do with knowing an individual child's experiences. Something that clearly made a difference was the length of time the child spent in the institution. Children who were very appealing might have received a bit more attention, and even the experience of being with slightly older children could have been beneficial (depending on the other children's characteristics).

The results of the ERA Study Team's work are far from simple. Some of the children, in fact, recovered very well from their experiences after several years of adoptive life. Others did well medically, but showed problems in their emotional and cognitive development. Importantly, there was support for the idea that separation is only one of many important factors in development and may have a critical impact if followed up by poor parenting.[16]

Do the statements in the last paragraph apply to children in U.S. foster homes as well as to Eastern European orphans? It would be fair to say that attachment theory has not yet integrated the ERA findings. It may be that the conclusion above applies when a child has been exposed to many risk factors, but not otherwise. However, most children in the United States today do not experience separation except in the context of serious family problems and troubled lives, and the ERA Team's conclusion may well apply to ordinary foster care children, as well as to children dramatically rescued from appalling institutional conditions.

CONCLUSION

The understanding of attachment has grown gradually over the centuries, but theory development and research have progressed most rapidly in the twentieth and twenty-first centuries. Early psychoanalytic thought focused on the relationship between mother and child, theorizing the connection to be based largely on the child's physical needs. Later theories considered the possibility that social needs and behaviors are innate human tendencies rather than responses based on hunger and discomfort. Evidence from studies of children separated from their parents during World War II suggests that attachment and separation played essential roles in emotional development, and John Bowlby based an entire theory of attachment on this and later information. In the 1990s, new research was conducted when large groups of children were adopted from foreign countries where they had been institutionalized. This study suggests that separation alone does not play as important a role in emotional development as Bowlby thought, but theories of attachment have yet to respond to this work.

chapter 3

The Growth of Attachment Theory: Connecting Ideas through Research

The end of World War II allowed thinkers, who had for years been busy with national wartime concerns, the leisure and time to consider attachment. As we saw in the previous chapter, Britain had become the center of psychoanalytic thought as the Nazis destroyed German intellectual life. Ethological theory also found a British home with the immigration of the Dutch ethologist Nikolaas Tinbergen, winner of the Nobel Prize for Medicine, and his colleague Konrad Lorenz. In postwar Britain, psychoanalytic and ethological ideas came together, as did the material to which they could be applied: observations of children separated from familiar people.

FACTORS IN THE DEVELOPMENT OF A THEORY OF ATTACHMENT

With dreams of a better world, many postwar thinkers sought to improve conditions for young children's development. In order to accomplish this, however, more knowledge was needed about the foundations of social and emotional growth. Conditions and motivation were right for an intense, systematic exploration of early emotional life, and researchers began to focus on the details of development. For example, a paper published by Dr. René Spitz in 1945 discussed the occurrence of *hospitalism*, the slow development and fragile health of abandoned infants who received little individual attention in group care. Spitz noticed particularly that these babies developed odd reactions to strangers. Compared to the behavior of family children, for these children the "usual behavior was replaced by something that could vary from extreme friendliness to any human partner combined with anxious avoidance of inanimate objects, to a generalized anxiety expressed in blood-curdling screams which could go on indefinitely."[1] The implications for these children's emotional development were worrisome, but the research itself provided one of many steps in the formulation of a valid theory of attachment.

The new studies were also shaped by an idea shared by scientists in a variety of fields. For some years before the war, a sophisticated view of scientific work had been emerging, and in the form of *operationism*, this approach to knowledge influenced the investigation of attachment. Operationism takes the stance that communication about scientific knowledge is primarily communication about measurement. If I want to tell someone about an observation I have made, I must recount what operations—that is, measurements—I used in order to keep track of what I saw. Only if two observers share the same operations do they know whether they have seen the same thing, and only then can one check his or her observations against the other's. If observers of little boys and little girls' attachment behavior use different operations and different definitions, they are very likely to report that they find sex differences—even though the children may actually be very similar, if measured with the same ruler. The social sciences are particularly in need of operational definitions, and this was a real issue for the early developers of attachment concepts as they struggled to decide whether a child demonstrated attachment or not.

As theories about attachment were formulated, they were also guided by another concept connected with operationism: the idea of *falsifiability*. This term sounds like it means "fudging the data," but it actually is a way for researchers to keep themselves honest. Falsifiability is the possibility that expected research results will not come out the way a researcher thought they would, and research must be designed in ways that allow this to happen. A researcher abandons falsifiability if he or she throws out all the data that do not support the hypothesis—as sometimes happens in the study of parapsychology, for example.

When researchers stress falsifiability, they are allowing their developing theory to be guided by systematic empirical evidence. A theory whose predictions are not always supported by evidence must be modified, and modification is what modern theorists of early emotional development have attempted to do as they study attachment.

TWO THINKERS

Out of the foundations of time and place described above came two people whose work forms the essential basis of modern theories of attachment: John Bowlby and Mary Salter Ainsworth. Both Bowlby and Ainsworth had unusual qualifications in research as well as in clinical training. Both stressed excellent observation as the foundation of knowledge about child development, prefiguring the mantra of developmentalist Sally Provence: "Don't just do something; stand there and watch." Bowlby's and Ainsworth's lives and thought have been beautifully described by Jeremy Holmes and Inge Bretherton,[2] and much of the material below has been drawn from that work.

John Bowlby: Clinician and Theorist

The British clinician John Bowlby (1907–1990) brought to the study of attachment a variety of experiences and training. Bowlby combined an ivory tower approach with a persistent involvement with real-world problems. His interest in child development began with volunteer work at a school for children with problems of adjustment. He became familiar with one distant, disengaged, aloof boy, and with another who clung anxiously and stayed close to Bowlby. These children were Bowlby's first examples of what would later be seen as the two faces of attachment problems.

Studying to become a child psychiatrist, Bowlby also became involved with the British Psychoanalytic Institute at a period of rapid change in psychoanalytic thought about early development. In spite of Sigmund Freud's relatively small initial interest in the emotional events of the early months, psychoanalytic theory remained the only approach that had even a minor focus on early development, and this focus was sharpening. The British Psychoanalytic Institute was moving toward a formulation of object-relations theory, a set of ideas about the development of early relationships with people and the ill effects of separation and loss.

A leader in the British psychoanalytic group was Melanie Klein,[3] who proposed the possibility of direct psychoanalytic treatment of the very young. (Sigmund Freud had attempted treatment of children's problems only through the intervention of parents.) Klein eventually supervised Bowlby's early analytic work, but the two disagreed profoundly on certain issues—perhaps motivating Bowlby to demonstrate through research that he was right on some important questions.

Melanie Klein stressed children's internal conflicts between love and hate as the source of emotional problems. She considered the fantasy life of infants to be more important than actual family events in determining mental health. Bowlby disagreed, basing his opinion on real-world experiences, such as training with social workers at the London Child Guidance Clinic.[4]

In the little time available during the war years, Bowlby had begun his efforts to investigate the effect of children's real experiences on their emotional development. He studied the cases of forty-four delinquent boys at the London Child Guidance Clinic,[5] an investigation that his colleagues dubbed "Ali Bowlby and the Forty Thieves." Bowlby showed these boys to have experienced separation from their mothers and to have been deprived of maternal care.

Linking his research with clinical practice, Bowlby proceeded after the war to head the children's department at London's Tavistock Clinic. He changed the name to the Department for Children and Parents and used the parents' own childhood experiences as material in his work with their children. As Bowlby continued his clinical and research work, with its emphasis on family relationships, a number of ideas and investigations contributed to his thinking about emotional development. What began as a general viewpoint slowly became a theory of attachment.

Films of children suffering from the effects of separation provided Bowlby with evidence for the role of familiar caregivers in the emotional lives of the very young. James Robertson provided filmed material, such as *A Two-Year-Old Goes to Hospital* and *Nine Days in a Residential Nursery*,[6] which documented the child's confusion and grief upon separation, and his inability to respond positively to a reunion with the mother.

Experimental work on animals also provided evidence that influenced Bowlby's theoretical approach. Harry Harlow of the University of Wisconsin was studying rhesus monkeys in an attempt to determine how monkey mothers became capable of effective care of their young—and why they, like humans, were sometimes neglectful or abusive. Harlow's work focused on the animals' early experiences with caregivers. For example, he provided surrogate mothers in the form of monkey-sized wire figures; some held a bottle of milk and others had soft padding to which the babies could cling. Harlow's showed that although baby monkeys could survive these conditions, their later behavior was much affected by their experiences.[7] The ability to court and mate was impaired, and when the females did become pregnant, their treatment of their infants was inappropriate and harmful. Harlow's work substantiated Bowlby's belief that early experiences with caregivers could set a direction for good, or poor, social and emotional development.

As Bowlby became familiar with the ethological view, mentioned in the previous chapter, another type of animal research provided him with some essential ideas about attachment. The most important ethological concept, from the perspective of Bowlby's work, was the young animal's rapid connection with an adult. Imprinting was an intriguing phenomenon for several reasons. It involved a social bond that might be comparable to the emotional tie between human parents and children. It was not linked to feeding, demonstrating that social relationships could have their own primary motivations. It occurred very readily during a period of de-velopment comparable to the one that most interested Bowlby. Imprinting was also an event with a long-term effect on the individual's social and emotional life, as Bowlby thought might be the case for children.

Most theories develop gradually, but there comes a moment when they coalesce and are presented to the world in a nearly complete form. Bowlby's attachment theory reached this stage in the late 1950s, and it was published in several important papers.[8] These papers drew together Bowlby's ideas about the reasons for children's emotional attachments to their mothers and caregivers, about the observable behaviors that indicate attachment, and about the consequences of separation from a familiar attachment figure. Although Bowlby's ideas became further elaborated over the years, these papers are the true foundation of modern attachment theory.

Bowlby's Basic Theory

Any theory is a framework of ideas that connects observable events and helps to explain the ways in which events are caused. We derive hypotheses or predictions about the world from theories. If testing of these predictions does not give supportive evidence, the theory needs to be reshaped. As was mentioned earlier, a good theory must be falsifiable. It must be possible to know when the observations do not confirm the prediction.

Bowlby's attachment theory does meet these criteria. It connects observable events, such as social experience, separation, and later behavior; it allows us to make predictions; and it makes it possible to know when a prediction is wrong. (This does not mean, of course, that testing the theory is necessarily a simple matter. Research with infants and families has many pitfalls, and there are serious challenges to investigations where experimental manipulation is impossible, as is true about many aspects of attachment work.)

What Are Human Beings Like? Bowlby's attachment theory may be easier to understand if we first state some of its underlying assumptions about the nature of human beings. One important assumption is that humans share many motivations and behaviors with nonhumans. Although the ethological view says that some characteristics are species-specific, other characteristics are shared across species. More closely related groups, such as humans and monkeys, might be expected to share more motivations and behaviors than, say, humans and fish. Information about animals' lives may thus tell us important things about human beings.

A second assumption is that human motivations and behaviors can be genetically controlled, as well as learned, and that when this is the case their presence has been influenced by evolutionary factors. Such behaviors and motivations presumably contributed to survival long ago, in our environment of early adaptation. Because young human beings are relatively helpless (compared to many other species), factors that helped them survive their early years would be prone to natural selection. These factors would still be present in modern humans, even though technology and social organization may have made them irrelevant to survival. For example, babies in prehistoric times might have been more likely to survive if they stayed close to adults; modern infants still show this tendency, even though living in houses and other such changes have removed much of the value of this behavior.

The Theory of Attachment. Bowlby's theory of attachment included a number of clear statements about children's emotional ties to familiar caregivers:

1. Children's attachment to their mothers, or to other familiar caregivers, results from a basic human motivation. It is not based on gratification of physical needs, such as hunger. The desire to be near familiar people, a need in itself, is independent of other experiences and is a healthy and desirable part of human relationships. Even in adults, attachment should be seen as an important continuing factor in social life, not as regression to a baby-like dependency.

2. The infant behaviors connected with social interactions, *engagement behaviors* such as sucking, clinging, following, and signaling another person by smiling or crying, are all related to the development of attachment. They are also all *inherited*, instinctual behaviors characteristic of human beings. These tendencies were selected in the course of evolution because they made it more likely that babies would be attended to, cared for, and helped to survive.

3. Some of the actions that will form part of attachment behavior are already present between birth and six months of age, but they are not particularly focused on a specific one or two adults. After six months, the baby begins to crawl and to follow adults, and soon attachment behaviors begin to be directed toward a few familiar caregivers. From the standpoint of evolutionary advantage, this delay in attachment is an excellent arrangement, protecting babies from the traumatic experience that early separations might otherwise entail. If attachment already existed at birth or in the early months, the high maternal death rates that used to occur soon after birth would potentially have caused many emotional problems. It was a good bet that a caregiver who was still alive when the baby was six months old would probably live for another year or two, giving the baby time for secure emotional development. With modern medicine, maternal death rates are quite low, and separations do not necessarily take place in the very early months,

but this recent change does not erase the characteristics that evolved long ago.

4. *Separation anxiety* is an indication that attachment has occurred and therefore a normal and desirable event in emotional development. Ordinarily, the child's distress is soon relieved by reunion with the caregiver. When separation from familiar people is abrupt and long lasting, however, the child who has achieved attachment is not only anxious, but can be expected to go through predictable stages of grieving and emotional reorganization. Although the steps of infant grief are intense, worrisome, and demanding of adult support, they are nevertheless a normal and necessary response to serious separations. Neither separation anxiety, nor grief following serious loss, would be expected until after there had been a focus on a familiar caregiver, and as we saw above, this does not happen until six months at the earliest.

5. Although Bowlby did not emphasize this point, it is important to realize that attachment emotions and attachment behavior are age-related, with *upper* as well as lower limits. Just as the characteristics we have discussed are not displayed before six months, at the earliest, they do not occur in the same form after, perhaps, three years of age. The attachment behaviors Bowlby initially described are typical of the late infant period, the toddler stage, and the early preschool years. Emotional ties alter and modulate with age, and so do related feelings and actions, as we will see in a later chapter.

6. In later work, Bowlby suggested that attachment behaviors and emotions are connected with the individual's internal working model of the social world. This suggestion offered a way for attachment to change developmentally as the individual passed the age period in which instinctual factors played the strongest role. An internal working model is a set of memories, emotions, and thoughts that determines a person's expectations and attitudes, and that consequently shapes behavior. Attachment-related behaviors like preferring certain people, maintaining near or far physical distance from those attachment figures, seeking help from people, and displaying distress upon separation or loss are determined by this internal working model.

Of course, attachment-related behaviors are not necessarily directed toward a consistent set of people throughout a lifetime, nor are the behaviors themselves always the same. These facts show us that the internal working model changes with age and *experience*. For example, a baby girl may crawl rapidly to her mother and signal to be picked up when frightened by a loud noise. Thirty years later, she may look around to locate her husband when jostled in a crowd of people, or may move to protect her own baby, ignoring potential threats to herself. Her internal working model of social relationships has gone through thirty years of experience and maturation and now shapes a different set of feelings, attitudes, and behaviors than it did in the woman's own infancy.

Mary Dinsmore Salter Ainsworth: Attachment Ideas, Attachment Measurement

U.S.-born, Canadian-reared psychologist Mary D. Salter Ainsworth (1913–1999) made her own theoretical contributions to the understanding of attachment, but her work on measurement of emotional development gave attachment theory the *self-correcting* power that we demand of modern theoretical formulations. Without the ability to measure attachment, it would be impossible to create and test hypotheses, and, therefore, impossible to know whether attachment theory was a good description of early emotional life. It is for her measurement techniques and her organization of research programs that Ainsworth's name is joined with Bowlby's in the history of attachment theory.

Measurement in the Early Days of Attachment Theory. From the beginning of serious work on attachment, accurate measurement and empirical evidence were emphasized. Bowlby used case studies and narrative descriptions to find evidence to test his developing theory. One of the appeals of ethology for Bowlby was its meticulous description of animal behavior. Bowlby regarded all relevant empirical material as useful to the understanding of emotional life. Melanie Klein had forbidden him to interview the mother of a three-year-old he was treating, a factor in Bowlby's opposition to her thinking.

Following the war years, the films made by Robertson and by Spitz provided a new way of collecting and displaying information about child development. Many of us feel suspicious of evidence presented on film, knowing, as we do today, the ease with which editing can distort reality. Bowlby, too, was aware of this possibility, and he guided the making of some of Robertson's films in ways that made them reliable. For example, a child who was to be followed in one film was chosen at random from a group, and the hospital clock was included in frames as an indication of time-sampling.[9]

Ainsworth's Measurement Work. From the time of her doctoral dissertation, completed in 1940, Mary Ainsworth was fascinated with ways of recording memories, emotions, and behaviors. She was particularly interested in the problem of checking one type of measurement against another in order to achieve the highest level of accuracy. In her dissertation research, for example, she asked students to fill out surveys about their family experiences, but she also examined their autobiographical reports to make sure that the simple paper-and-pencil tests gave accurate measures of their complex life stories.

With her new husband, Leonard Ainsworth, Dr. Mary Ainsworth went to London in 1950 and by chance answered an advertisement that led to work with John Bowlby's research group. She became involved in data analysis of the material filmed by Robertson under Bowlby's guidance.

Although she admired Robertson's observational and descriptive methods, Ainsworth was still not convinced that Bowlby's ethological approach made sense. Her own interest in attachment issues led her to a study of school-age children who had been separated from their mothers for lengthy medical treatment. Her assessment classified these children into three groups: those who were happy and positive about reunions with their mothers, those who were ambivalent in their feelings, and those who were indifferent or actually hostile toward their mothers. As we shall see shortly, this three-way classification was later to form a crucial part of Ainsworth's measurement of early attachment behavior.

Cross-Cultural Work. During the 1950s, Mary Ainsworth spent time in Uganda with her husband, where she had the opportunity to observe mothers and children in a different culture. If attachment behavior was really species-specific and instinctual, as Bowlby was supposing, the observations made in Uganda should closely resemble the findings in England.

Ainsworth arranged to visit twenty-six families with babies. She went every other week to sit in the family living room and observe how the growing babies began to stay closer and be more attentive to their mothers. She gave special attention to the mothers' sensitivity to the infants' signals, the babies' tendencies to cry or to explore, and (through an interpreter) the mothers' reports of whether they enjoyed breastfeeding. As we will see in a later chapter, the results of this study were much as Ainsworth and Bowlby would have predicted; the infants of Uganda showed attachment much as the British babies did.[10]

Observations in Context: The Baltimore Project. In the early 1960s—when Bowlby had already published his three papers outlining attachment theory—Mary Ainsworth moved to Baltimore. It was here that she set up a complex research project for observation of mothers and infants.

Ainsworth's naturalistic observations were not only meticulous and detailed; they had an additional characteristic that made them particularly critical to the study of attachment. Like the Uganda work, Ainsworth's Baltimore observations explored the mother's contributions to the attachment relationship, not just the child's. The babies of mothers who were sensitive and responsive had babies who showed one pattern of attachment behavior, and those with mothers who were unresponsive and uninterested showed another. (Then, as now, it was not completely clear whether babies influenced mothers, mothers influenced babies, or each affected the other.)

Ainsworth's Baltimore research, a model demonstration of a new approach, involved the study of connected patterns of behavior, rather than old-fashioned frequency counts of events like crying.[11] More complicated and difficult to do than the older style of research, Ainsworth's work was also far more capable of displaying the complexities of developmental change. By demonstrating these complexities, Ainsworth made a critical contribution to attachment theory as Bowlby was elaborating it.

Showing how mothers' actions guided their children's attachment was valuable in itself, but it also demonstrated the importance of the internal working model of social relationships. Repeated acts by the mothers triggered responses in the babies, but these involved more than the primitive, instinctual level of action suggested by the ethologists. These repeated events let babies learn what they might expect from other human beings. They established a pattern of expectations and attitudes that started with the earliest relationships and would be generalized and applied to new people. For example, the expectations learned from a mother would also be extended to a child care provider and later to a kindergarten teacher, and so on. Importantly, the internal working model could change and develop as the child grew and had new experiences. Early instinctual behaviors did not change with experiences, but the internal working model of attachment could continue to alter, eventually giving rise to the individual's attitude toward his or her own child. Lest this description of the internal working model sound too cool and intellectual to have anything to do with attachment, let us recall that the model includes emotion and motivation based on the powerful early feelings of the toddler seeking his or her mother's comfort and fleeing the stranger's approach.

The Strange Situation: A Behavior Sample. Ainsworth was now interested in two new measurement problems. Visiting families in Uganda and in Baltimore had been enormously useful, but the collected information was very difficult to analyze. Families can be quite different. How can we compare them to each other? And, if the mother's behavior is so important, how can we possibly tease it out of the complications of real-life situations where mother, father, children, culture, home, and accident determine how people act?

Ainsworth wanted to establish some way of describing infant behavior which would allow her to compare babies, or families, or cultural groups without being confused by background details. She was especially interested in how infants behaved in high or low stress situations, but how could she create or reduce stress in a family, even temporarily? She needed a standardized test, one in which the situation could be controlled, all mothers and children had the same experiences, and trained observers could collect the same information each time. Only then would it be possible to make comparisons or even to find norms and understand what were frequent and what were unusual behavior patterns.

The result of Ainsworth's efforts was a test known as the Strange Situation. This measurement device has been the basis of thousands of research studies. Indeed, we may wonder whether the topic of attachment would ever have achieved its present eminence without the Strange Situation as a means of exploration, and as an answer to the question: how in the world can we compare these babies?

The Strange Situation. Like many other psychological tests, the Strange Situation involves a narrow sample of information drawn from a wide range of measurable factors. First, it is intended to test babies at about twelve months of age (although some researchers have not paid much attention to this). All the evidence shows that the great majority of babies of this age show attachment behaviors, readily and intensely. This is the best time to catch behavioral evidence of the child's emotional connection to a caregiver.

Second, the Strange Situation chooses a simple, common, mildly threatening situation, and keeps it very brief. Though an effort is made to limit unhappiness, the intention, of course, is to cause enough distress to the child to elicit attachment behavior. This approach produces stress at the level a child might feel when the mother steps away briefly when shopping, but not nearly at the level of attachment behavior that would occur when, for example, a parent and child are both terrified by a ferocious dog, a parent runs to help another child who is hurt and screaming, or there is domestic violence.

The Strange Situation: What Happens, What Is Measured. The Strange Situation is intended to assess the toddler's responses to a brief separation from the mother, followed by a reunion. It takes about twenty-two minutes altogether and requires a room with certain features and an adult who is a stranger to the child. There are eight steps or episodes in the Strange Situation procedure.

Episode 1: The mother and baby enter the room with an observer who shows the mother where she can put the baby down and then where she can sit.

Episode 2: The mother puts the baby down near some toys. The mother does not start playing with the toys, but she may respond if the baby starts, for example, to bring a toy, put it in her lap, or hand it to her. If the baby has not started playing after two minutes, the mother may take the baby to the toys. (For completeness, we should note that by this age normal babies can crawl or even walk alone; they can pick up toys, put them down, or throw them; they understand some words and may speak a little. Although they do not play in very complex, planned ways, they are interested in toys; they like to pick them up, mouth them, throw them, or bang them against things. If they are walking, they often like to carry things, especially big things.)

Episode 3: A stranger comes into the room, greets the mother and baby, and sits quietly near the mother for one minute. During the next minute, the stranger talks with the mother. Then for a third minute, the stranger gets down on the floor and tries to play with the baby. The mother then leaves the room quietly. The baby generally notices that she is leaving. (This introduces, in a mild form, the stress factor that interested Ainsworth.)

Episode 4: The mother is still absent. The stranger sits on her chair, but responds to the baby, if the baby tries to start play. The stranger offers comfort, if the baby shows distress. The mother stays out for three minutes, if the baby is not upset, but if there is distress, the mother returns and the stranger leaves.

Episode 5: The mother calls the baby's name from outside the door and then comes in. If the baby needs comfort, the mother offers it and tries to get play started; if not, she sits on her chair and responds, but does not start play. After three minutes, she leaves, saying, "Bye-bye, I'll be back soon."

Episode 6: The baby stays alone for three minutes. If there is distress, the stranger comes back.

Episode 7: The stranger offers comfort, if the baby is distressed, or else stays seated on the chair for three minutes. If the baby is too upset, the mother returns before the three minutes have elapsed.

Episode 8: The mother returns, the stranger leaves, and the mother spends three minutes, as she did in the first episode.

During the eight episodes of the Strange Situation, trained observers look at certain behaviors as they occur in each episode: The amounts of play and exploration that occur when the baby is with the mother or with the stranger and the amount of crying and the ease with which the mother can comfort the distressed child. And, above all, the observers look at reunion behaviors—the response of the child when the mother returns to the room.

Classification of Infants' Attachment. A test like the Strange Situation is not very useful, if every child is described separately and no comparisons or connections are made between children. One of the points of having a standardized test is that we can classify or group children who are similar to each other. We can then search for factors that might explain what causes individuals in one category to be different from those in another. Researchers who use the Strange Situation put children into categories on the basis of their behavior, and the categories they use are much like the ones Ainsworth used in the studies she first did while working with Bowlby.

In one careful study, the largest group of twelve-month-olds tested in the Strange Situation—about 65 percent—was classified as *securely attached*. These toddlers played and explored when with their mothers, but played a little less when the stranger came, in Episode 3. They began to cry shortly after the mother left. The reunion when the mother returned was a happy one. These babies actively sought contact with their returning mothers, and they were easily comforted and ready to play again. (This group was called Group B by the researchers.)[12]

The second group, Group A, was smaller and included about 20 percent of the tested babies. These *insecure-avoidant* children were less concerned with the stranger and did not necessarily cry when the mother left. The reunions were not happy for the mother or the baby. These children actively avoided the returning mothers, rather than seeking them, and actually snubbed the mothers who tried to approach them.

About 15 percent of the toddlers were classified in Group C, with *insecure-ambivalent* attachment. They were anxious and explored little, even in Episode 2 when the mother was present. During reunion with the mother, these children simultaneously went to her and pushed her away or resisted being picked up. The mothers did not seem able to comfort the distressed children.

A fourth classification, Group D, was applied to a small proportion of tested children by another research team.[13] The Group D children were designated as being *insecure-disorganized/disoriented*, and their behavior was quite unusual. In fact, although most of us have seen children who showed the A, B, or C patterns, the D pattern is not often observed.

Group D babies are most different from Groups A, B, and C in their reunion behavior. When the mothers returned to the room, these Group D children did not behave in uniform, predictable ways. Their feelings seemed contradictory, and they might vigorously avoid and then vigorously approach the mother. They might get into physical contact with her and then turn their heads to gaze away. They sometimes had facial expressions of fear, seemed confused and apprehensive, rocked themselves back and forth in a stereotypical way, or suddenly fell to the floor looking dazed. Babies who behave like those in Group D obviously need further investigation and possibly treatment. These issues will be discussed in a later chapter.

OTHER MEASURES OF ATTACHMENT

Fascinating and productive as the Strange Situation is, it is not the final step in measuring attachment patterns. As human beings get older, they continue to have emotional attachments to others, but the ways they show these attachments change with age. Even preschoolers placed in a situation like the Strange Situation do not behave in exactly the same ways as twelve-month-olds. By adulthood, people still have emotional bonds and important internal working models of social relationships; these are expressed in mature ways, not like those of an infant. (We would be very worried about an adult who cried when a loved one had been away for three minutes.) Individuals who are past the toddler stage follow different rules, and they cannot be tested in the same manner.

There has been work in assessment of attachment in preschool children, using techniques such as asking children to finish incomplete stories. Assessment of school-age children has proved more difficult, and the eminent child psychiatrist Charles Zeanah has expressed doubt that anyone is presently capable of managing this. One approach for preschool and school-age children has been the use of a Q-sort technique in which observers decide which type of attachment is characteristic of a given child.[14]

More recently, the attention of researchers has turned toward the assessment of adult attachment relationships, including connections with parents, marriage and friendships, and attitudes toward children. Again, this kind of measurement is not going to resemble the Strange Situation. Adults do not show the same responses to separation as toddlers do, though there are some similarities, such as behaving differently when around strangers or feeling ambivalent when reunited with a person who has made us feel deserted.

The study of attachment relationships in adults focuses on the internal working model of social relations, which has presumably changed, developed, and become far more elaborate as the years have passed. We may be able to get at that model more effectively by talking about relationships, rather than by looking at overt behavior. The Adult Attachment Interview is a way to do this.[15]

The Adult Attachment Interview uses open-ended questions about childhood experiences to get at the adult's internal working model. The specific experiences reported are meaningful. Stories of a family cooperating happily suggest a very different working model than do tales of bleak years in an orphanage or an abusive foster home. But analysis of the Adult Attachment Interview goes beyond the stories that are told to the way the interviewee tells them. Do the stories give an organized, coherent picture of the individual's thoughts about family history? Are there separate stories that do not form a consistent pattern? Does the individual speak in clear, descriptive sentences, or hesitate, trail off, begin again? Does the interviewee claim that he or she does not remember much about childhood family relations and dismiss them as a matter of little interest?

As was the case for the Strange Situation, responses to the Adult Attachment Interview can be placed into a few categories. Adults are considered to be in the *autonomous-secure* group, if they recount an organized story of childhood memories—whether or not they find the memories pleasing or satisfying. The term *preoccupied* is used to categorize adults who have many, contradictory childhood memories, but no way of organizing them into a meaningful whole. Finally, those who state that they have few or no memories of early family relations are classified as showing a *dismissing* pattern. Adults' responses to the AAI are quite reliable, that is, researchers usually find similar results each time, and these results do not seem to be related to other memory or intelligence factors.[16]

ATTACHMENT THEORY AND MEASUREMENT: LINGERING QUESTIONS

Our historical account has shown how attachment theory has grown over the last fifty years or more, but there are some broad issues and implications that still need consideration. The very idea of emotional attachment, as Bowlby described it, is attractive to some and almost repulsive to others. Some responses seem almost parallel to the early rejection of Freud's view of infantile sexuality. College students are often negative about the idea of attachment, perhaps fearing that the autonomy desirable at their present age would be impossible if attachment had already occurred. Others who are newly introduced to the attachment concept become thoroughly confused. They try to puzzle through Bowlby's theory and find it disturbing that they cannot reduce this complex system to one or two simple foundations. To close, we need to deal with some general questions about attachment theory, as it exists today.

Is There a Precise Definition of Attachment?

The simple answer to the question: what is attachment? is that it refers to a long-lasting emotional tie between a child and a familiar adult—one that lasts even after the child is an adult. Like most simple answers, of course, this one leaves much to be desired. Several points need to be considered in order to achieve a more exact definition and to go beyond knowing it when we see it.

A *tie* may be best understood as an internal emotional state that causes a predictable pattern of positive, attentive, interested behavior of one person toward another. In the case of attachment, however, there is a complication. Although we can assume that a tie lasts for a long time, the behavior pattern is stable and predictable only for short periods of time. The toddler's preference to stay close to a caregiver and his or her tears upon separation are predictable for just a few months; after that, the child will show this marked preference only when under stress. The preschooler who turns to a parent for help and care is showing a positive behavior pattern, but it is not the same pattern we see when an adult cares for a much-loved, elderly parent. A long-lasting emotional tie gives rise to different behavior patterns, as both the child and the caregiver change and grow over time.

Of course, much of the emotion connected with attachment is positive in nature. Our desire and preference for other people's company are defining characteristics of attachment. However, this long-lasting emotional connection involves a variety of feelings that include not only happiness but also relief after a reunion and anger, grief, longing, jealousy, ambivalence, and resentment after separation. The quality, intensity, and duration of these feelings change with age and because of other factors, such as the behavior of the other person.

The emotional connection or tie between child and adult implies special characteristics. The concept of attachment focuses primarily on the child's emotions and internal working model of social relations. The attachment tie involves the child's preference for the adult's company and the wish to be cared for by the adult. However, the nature of the tie, the child's expectations, and the child's experience of emotional interaction with the adult depend, in part, on the adult's feelings and behavior. Unless the adult also has some positive feelings toward a particular child, the child is not likely to have the caregiving and social experiences that create a long-lasting tie. The relationship is not in fact one-sided, but the study of attachment tends to emphasize one side—that of the child.

Though a long-lasting emotional tie is determined in part by the adult, it relies even more strongly on factors internal to the child. According to Bowlby's attachment theory, infants bring to social relations a set of built-in, hard-wired instinctual behaviors toward the environment and the caregiver. These are essential for the formation of attachment, and they include a readiness to prefer familiar rather than unfamiliar people and demonstrate behaviors like looking at and following them. As age and the internal working model progress, however, the instinctual behaviors become less important. They are replaced by the set of emotions, memories, and beliefs that maintain the attachment tie after early childhood—often into adulthood—and that allow early attachment experiences to influence other, later emotional connections.

Attachment is thus, in part, an emotional tie, but it is also the developing of a set of motivations, behaviors, ideas, and feelings. These cause our different responses to familiar people and to strangers, especially when concerning our expectations that others will care for us or that we will care for them. The details of attachment feelings and behavior change drastically from early to later life, but the internal factors seem to be consistent as an individual matures.

Is Attachment Good?

The short-term advantages of an infant's attachment are evident. In early childhood, the major behavior linked to attachment involves staying near a familiar adult, especially in a strange place, or when anything unusual is happening. The wish to stay near acts as an invisible playpen and has enormous safety value for creepers and toddlers. Unexpected events or strange people send the child scurrying to the caregiver's side. Although adults always need to monitor young children carefully, normal attachment behavior means that the adult does not have to spend all of his or her time retrieving a wandering child.

Whether attachment is desirable over the longer term is a question frequently asked by young parents. Parents in the United States place a high value on independence and are concerned with the idea that attachment in early childhood might culminate in a weak, dependent adult personality. The idea that parents should be sensitive and responsive to infant's signals, and should let the child stay close, arouses in many American parents the fear that the child will be spoiled, demanding, selfish, cranky, and undisciplined. American parents often prefer the idea that their children will grow up into independent, self-sufficient, friendly people. They may be concerned that long-lasting emotional ties will somehow make these characteristics impossible to achieve. Some have even expressed the wish that their day care center frequently change children's caregivers to prevent attachment,[17] or they have rejected breastfeeding because they feel it may cause a baby to be too attached to the mother.

As we will see in later chapters, however, there are probably no grounds for the concern that attachment will cause harm, especially in the form of clinginess and dependency in later life. On the contrary, there is a good deal of evidence that secure attachment provides an excellent foundation for personality and social development. A securely attached child has a better chance to be both independent and friendly than one who has had poor early relationships. Adults who have had good early attachment experiences have advantages in marriage and parental relationships, although it is certainly possible for people to overcome moderate early attachment problems.

Why Don't Children Show the
Same Attachment Behavior All the Time?

If attachment involves an internal working model, we would surely expect individuals to show the same attachment behavior at all times, but they do not. Likewise, we might expect children growing up in the same family to have similar internal working models of relationships and attachment behavior, but this does not necessarily happen. Why is this? Do these facts indicate that the idea of an internal working model is wrong?

When we think about the way attachment changes with age, it's obvious that a particular child will show changes in attachment behavior over months or years. It is also true that a child can show urgent, intense attachment behavior on one occasion and seem quite nonchalant about separation on the very next day.

Situational factors are important triggers of attachment behavior. Securely attached children do not show much concern about staying near familiar people until something happens that is construed by the child as a threat of separation.

Here is an example of a change in attachment behavior that depended on circumstances.[18] An unusually tall, male college student observed toddlers and preschool children walking with their parents in a shopping mall. If allowed to walk by themselves, the children lagged as much as twenty feet behind their parents. The children were capable of keeping up with the parents, but if the parents stopped to let them catch up, the children also stopped, maintaining their chosen distance. When the large student observer approached the parents to ask some questions, the lagging children at once closed the gap and stayed close to the parents while the conversation continued.

Did these children suddenly experience an alteration in instinctual processes or in their internal working models? No, of course not. What they did experience was a change in the environmental situation in which they and their parents were functioning. A stranger approached, and he was unusually big, as well as being personally unfamiliar. The children's reaction tells us something quite important about attachment behavior: ordinarily, circumstances must stimulate the occurrence of the behavior. Internal processes alone are not enough to cause observable attachment behavior.

The circumstances that trigger attachment behavior involve fear of strange people or unusual events, especially those that imply separation. No actual threat need be present, and there need not be any potential for real harm to child or parent. The triggering events are different for human beings at different ages and developmental stages. For babies, at the end of the first year, attachment behavior—crying and following—may be caused by ordinary events an adult would find quite unthreatening. For instance, a mother is sitting on the floor playing with her baby. About to sneeze, she jumps up and rushes across the room to get a tissue. The baby wails and scrambles after her, as if there is a genuine threat of abandonment. Similarly, the garbage truck that has come twice a week all the baby's life makes a loud noise, and the child rushes to be near a familiar person.

In the temporary absence of triggering events, these children might show very little behavior characteristic of attachment. They may wander far in their explorations and cry very little, but should a strange event occur, all the behavioral evidence of attachment is displayed.

In older children and adults who are less easily threatened, we often see that illness or injury brings back attachment behavior common to babies. Stress or fear of any type seems to bring out the longing for familiar people. Most of us feel that we would rather die at home with those we love than with strangers in the hospital, and this is not just because we think we will receive better care. One elderly lady, bedridden at home after a stroke, wanted to have photographs of all her children and grandchildren placed by her bed so she could spend her days gazing at them.

When children in the same family have different attachment behaviors, there are at least two factors that may be at work. First, there is no guarantee whatsoever that children in the same family will have had the same attachment experiences. Each relationship is unique, so even identical twins may experience different interactions with their caregivers. Second, each child's emotional life is influenced by *temperamental* factors. Temperament is an individual's biologically determined tendency to react to the world in certain ways. Each human being has a unique set of reactions to life events, and these help determine how attachment behaviors and emotions are displayed. For example, a toddler who is temperamentally calm, mild, and cheerful is less likely to show intense attachment behavior than a brother or sister who is easily distressed and negative in mood. This difference between two children does not mean that one child is less securely attached to a parent than the other.

Differences in attachment behavior between children, as well as differences in the same child on different occasions, occur because such behavior is not just a simple reflection of an emotional tie. The internal working model, temporary circumstances, and other personality characteristics work together to produce a child's reaction to separation.

Is Bowlby's Theory the Only Attachment Theory?

Many careful studies have described attachment behavior, and there is little question about the facts of attachment. The theory created by Bowlby and Ainsworth is the most elaborate and fully realized effort, of those attempted thus far, to understand why human attachment behavior exists. However, Bowlby's theory of attachment is not the only explanation of attachment behavior. Freud's suggestions have already been described in an earlier section of this book. More recently, attempts were made to discuss attachment according to the behaviorist perspective, a view quite different from that of Freud or Bowlby. This approach suggested that mothers and infants provided positive reinforcement for each other's attention, thus, mutually shaping mother-child attachment behavior.[19] As psychology changed over the years, it left the behaviorist approach behind, although the idea of mutual influences has remained important.

As the field of psychology continued to develop over the last twenty or thirty years, the innate, unlearned characteristics of human beings became an important focus of study. Bowlby's view that attachment began with instinctual processes fit well into this approach. As psychologists concerned themselves with innate human characteristics, they returned to an old idea: that the inborn nature of humans is caused by genetic factors, and therefore could have been shaped by evolution. The characteristics best suited to survival in the ancient environment of early adaptation, would be the characteristics selected for, and passed down to, modern humans. These could include mental and behavioral tendencies, as well as physical structures.

Ideas about the inheritance of human characteristics have become an organized viewpoint called *evolutionary psychology*. Without denying that human beings can and do learn from experience, evolutionary psychologists concentrate on the inheritance of behaviors that would have helped in the survival of our remote ancestors. Such inherited characteristics include emotional responses, like anger and jealousy, that may be maladaptive or dangerous today, but were useful in the distant past. Social emotions, social behavior, and emotional relationships are important to evolutionary psychology because human beings ordinarily live in groups and depend on each other for survival.

Evolutionary psychologists have not proposed an attachment theory that is different from Bowlby's, but they have seen the Bowlby theory as congruent with their viewpoint. (Bowlby himself was deeply interested in evolutionary concepts and wrote a biography of Charles Darwin.)[20]

Attachment theory assumes that certain important human tendencies are inherited, and that an infant's responses to caregivers are instinctual in nature. The existence of these inherited characteristics is connected with the survival needs of our ancestors, as well as with the needs of modern humans. Attachment is, of course, an important example of the human social relationships that are essential for the survival of the individual and the species. Bowlby's attachment theory is, thus, very much in the mainstream of modern psychological thought, making this an important reason for continued interest in this approach.

Present-day work is beginning to ask some questions about attachment that differ from Bowlby's. It may be that attachment will soon be seen as only one aspect of developing relationships with others. Chapter 8 will summarize some of this new work.

CONCLUSION

Our growing understanding of attachment has involved the interweaving of measurement techniques and theoretical changes. Modern demands for systematic evidence encouraged the formulation of measurement procedures that made it possible to test aspects of attachment. The data produced by those techniques was fed back into theory and stimulated new ways of thinking. Attachment theory developed in step with attachment measurement, but at the same time was influenced by and instrumental in the growth of evolutionary psychology.

chapter 4

Attachment, Age, and Change: Emotional Ties from Birth to Parenthood

Our struggles in the last chapter with the definition of attachment made it clear that this term has different meanings when applied to people of different ages. Attachment is not a thing inside a human being or a permanent change that is exactly like a duck's imprinting, but a whole pattern of behaviors, feelings, and ideas that change gradually as the individual develops. The great importance of this pattern is that it continues to influence our social relationships throughout life.

The study of developmental changes in attachment gives us essential information that helps our understanding of groups (adopted children, for example) and of individuals (such as children who seem unusually clingy and concerned with their parents). René Spitz, writing more than half a century ago, prefigured this statement when he urged

> ... establishment of norms and regularities in the unfolding of the infant's mental and emotional development. Such norms have to be understood as representing broad generalizations of a statistical nature. They provide chronological age zones within which the emergence of certain behavior patterns, of certain emotional responses and of certain qualities of emotion can be expected with regularity. ... With the establishment of such ... regularities we gain a basis for comparison between various groups, which is indispensable for ... further scientific investigation.[1]

Since Spitz's day, much information has been collected about attachment as it manifests at different ages. Researchers and clinicians have generally focused on age periods that correspond roughly to particular, predictable attachment events. These rough age periods are (1) birth to around six to eight months; (2) from about eight months to two and a half years of age; (3) the preschool period, from about two and a half to five years; (4) the elementary school years; (5) the adolescence and adult years; (6) periods when adults are caring for young infants; and (7) periods in adulthood when new attachment patterns emerge (falling in love, for example, or becoming a caregiver to an elderly parent). This chapter will describe attachment-related events in each of these age periods.

SOME ESSENTIAL ISSUES ABOUT THE DEVELOPMENT OF ATTACHMENT

Some readers will notice that prenatal life has not been mentioned as a time when the infant experiences attachment processes. As far as our current evidence can show, unborn babies are not forming attachments, and children are not born with a preference for their birth mothers. In fact, in the course of evolution, it would have been a serious problem if babies had been born attached; so many mothers died in childbirth that a great proportion of babies would have been traumatized by separation. However, beliefs about prenatal emotional development were at one time put forward in the scholarly world.[2] (Today, they remain a part of popular ideas about attachment, as we will see in a later chapter.)

It seems that the development of attachment depends on a type of event that can occur only after the baby is born: a *transactional process*. Transactional processes involve many interactions between individuals and cause developmental change in a complex way.

We tend to be used to thinking about simple events causing development. (For example, a parent might do something to a child, like wipe her chin.) We also are used to the idea that things might get a little more complicated when a parent and child interact, when one does something to the other and the other responds or reciprocates in some fashion. (Perhaps the father wipes the toddler's chin, and the little girl playfully does the same thing back to him.) A transactional process goes another step beyond the interaction. A transactional process involves many interactions carried out over a period of time, with many small changes in each partner, which occur with each event. The father may struggle only slightly to wipe a ten-month-old's chin, but he probably does not receive much cooperation. By the time she is twenty months old, the daughter may come when she is called, hold up her face to be cleaned, participate by holding the cloth herself, or resist with play or anger. The way the father approaches her has changed too. He would now be very surprised if she fussed in a babyish way as she used to do. Both people have changed very gradually as a result of the many occasions when they have affected each other, and the child, of course, has also changed as a result of maturation.

Attachment develops as a transactional process between the child and a caregiver. Over time, caregivers change their behavior patterns and emotional responses, just as children do. However, the research information we have about attachment is primarily about the child's contribution to the process. To look at both partners at once is exceedingly difficult. To whatever extent it is possible, this chapter will examine both sides of the transactional process, though most often it will be necessary to concentrate on one side or the other. As Donald Winnicott so famously declared, "There is no such thing as a baby"—a baby alone, that is, and we need to remember this at all times.[3]

THE EARLY MONTHS

From a time soon after birth, human babies are responsive to human beings. They imitate facial expressions before they are a day old, and they watch faces and show special interest in people's eyes. It is clear they recognize human beings as something different from inanimate objects. Many of a young infant's actions are attractive to adults, especially the social smile that appears at six to eight weeks in response to another person. When we adults see a baby respond to us like this, we become interested and gratified, and we want more of that interaction. Such attractive baby responses may be called *engagement behaviors*, because they help us become more and more emotionally involved with the baby. Although the baby's engagement behaviors make us feel special, however, they do not actually mean that the baby is concerned with us as individuals.

Early Fearlessness

During the first six months after birth, human beings do not show the preference for familiar people or the fear of unfamiliarity most often associated with attachment. There is plenty of evidence that little babies can tell the difference between familiar and unfamiliar adults, but little proof that they actually prefer one to the other. (An adult who is familiar to the baby, however, is also an adult to whom the baby is familiar, and it may be that a person who knows the baby well can comfort or play with the baby more effectively than a stranger can.)

When abruptly separated from familiar people, young babies show little disturbance in sleep or eating. They do not seem frightened of strangers, and this is not surprising because they are not frightened of the dark, loud noises, big dogs, or anything else on the usual list of childhood fears. Small babies may well respond with distress to a new caregiver who is clumsy or fails to understand the babies' signals, but this is not the same thing as being afraid.

Dyadic Self-Regulation

The youngest babies are characteristically more concerned with their internal processes than they are with the people around them. Infants of a few months may be very responsive to our social overtures at times— because of their own needs and interests and because we just happen to do something that gets their attention—but their responses occur on their own schedule. Most of the time, they ignore us, cry, or fall asleep. If they are crying, they may need a great deal of help calming down, and they may not reach a happy, quiet, alert state until they have again gone through a sleep cycle.

One of a parent's major jobs during this period is soothing or comforting the baby—a task as important in its own way as feeding and cleaning. Skillful, prompt comforting helps a baby establish a first step in emotional development, a step on which attachment probably depends.

This first step is called *dyadic self-regulation*, and it is the ability the baby has to be soothed and to recover from distress with the help of a caregiver. The baby begins to attain calm when in a *dyad*, or couple relationship, with another person who is helping. The ability to calm down without this help is not achieved until much later and is perhaps never totally mastered, even in adulthood. Most adults still need and appreciate sympathetic comforting when we are seriously upset.

It is critically important to understand that an infant of less than six months does not have much ability to calm down alone from real distur-bance, such as a painful experience. He or she may cry frantically and even-tually fall into an exhausted sleep, but this is not the same as attaining the quiet, alert state that permits play and learning. After three or four months, however, most caregivers have figured out ways of offering effective com-fort, such as holding the baby in a certain position, rocking with a particu-lar rhythm, or offering a pacifier. The babies also have discovered some understanding of things that make them feel better; they settle into posi-tions of comfort fairly easily, even beginning to calm as soon as help is of-fered. When they are older, they may imitate a caregiver's strategy by singing to themselves or climbing into the rocking chair on their own.

Dyadic self-regulation is a major step toward attachment, because it helps the baby experience much more quiet, alert time than it did before. These quiet periods are a time for looking at and listening to people, and as they get longer, new transactional processes take place. Not only is the baby quiet and interested in other people, caregivers, who are pleased that they can make the baby happy, are more inclined than ever to be sociable and communicative. From about the age of two months, the baby's smiles reward the caregiver, and within a few more months, the baby's laughter follows the caregiver's playful approach.

Caregivers who have learned good comforting tricks now begin a period of courtship, working hard to get babies to show pleasure. They concentrate on social play. Even during feeding or diapering, the adult's energy goes into keeping the baby attentive and happy.

In the next months, the baby's pleasure and interest become more and more evident to sensitive caregivers, and the caregiver finds more jokes and simple games that please the adult and child. Strangers can manage to make the baby laugh, too, but nothing is really as good as the familiar play routine developed by the play-partners through transactional processes.

EIGHT MONTHS TO TWO YEARS

The toddler period is the stage of life most clearly associated with attachment behavior and emotion. As children of this age become more capable of moving and communicating, they reveal new concerns about separation.

Reorganization: Attachment Behavior, Attachment Emotion

By about the seventh month of the baby's life, a number of factors are in place, preparing for the behavior and feeling changes that reveal the attachment process. If the baby has had the opportunity to learn from interactions with a few consistent caregivers, he or she has some ideas about how those people act. The baby can read the adult's signals and anticipate what is going to happen: the mother's unbuttoning of her shirt is a preparation for nursing; a certain way the father moves means being picked up for play. The baby also comes to expect that his or her own signals will be read, understood, and acted upon, most, if not all, of the time.

By about seven months, most babies become wary of strangers. They are not actually frightened, but seem serious and suspicious at first, checking out the stranger carefully. If the stranger is friendly, the seven-month-old soon warms up and is ready to play. It is clear from the baby's behavior that he or she knows the difference between familiar and unfamiliar people and that the difference is important.

By about eight months, a new emotional reaction enters the picture, and the baby's social world is transformed and reorganized. The new emotion is fear, a response that we do not see in the younger child. Now—and sometimes rather suddenly—the infant signals that he or she feels frightened by loud noises, sudden movements, strange events, and, especially, strange people. Fearfulness becomes part of the developing internal working model of social relationships, as strangers become sources of fear, and familiar people sources of comfort and security. The behaviors associated with strangers and with familiar caregivers are our clues to the development of the child's internal working model, and we may call them *attachment behaviors*. The child's facial expressions and vocalizations tell us that attachment behaviors are accompanied by *attachment emotions* of fear and discomfort or pleasure and security.

The eight-month-old characteristically begins to show stranger anxiety (fearfulness around unfamiliar people) and separation anxiety (fear in situations where familiar people may or do leave). The Strange Situation, described in the last chapter, uses both these situations in mild forms to trigger a child's display of attachment behavior and emotion.

Avoiding strangers and avoiding separation from familiar people are the behaviors most often considered to indicate that a child's internal working model of relationships now involves emotional attachment to one or a few caregivers. Many parents have vivid memories of this stage of child life—the toddler who persistently hid his face when approached by friendly strangers at the grocery store (or even by a grandmother who had not visited for a while) or the child who cried with fear when her mother jumped up to answer the telephone. Some parents are unfortunately disturbed and worried about these behaviors, recalling their friendly, outgoing baby of a few months earlier. If the baby is in child care, outside the home, the parents may begin to fear their child has been abused or harmed in some way that has brought on this new behavior. In fact, moderate social fearfulness at this age is an excellent indicator of good development; it shows that the caregivers have been doing something right. As we will see in the next chapter, though, all children are not equally expressive about their fears, and some who are developing well will display only mild concerns about strangers and separation.

Attachment behaviors and emotions also depend, in part, on situational factors. The presence of a stranger or the threat of separation is less frightening in the child's own home and more troublesome in a strange place. How the stranger acts is a factor that helps guide the child's reaction; a staring person with a serious or fearful face generates more distress than a smiling stranger who is careful to make eye contact brief and flirtatious. If a parent is present, his or her actions also prompt the child's response. Seeing a stranger, the child looks at the parent's face in a pattern called *social referencing*. If the parent looks happy, the child is less likely to act frightened; a parent's expression of anxiety confirms and intensifies the child's fear.

In addition to fearfulness, other negative emotions are characteristic of this period and give rise to the terrible twos. Toddlers seem torn by the conflict between attachment and the need for autonomy, and they express their feelings through resistance and negativism. Temper tantrums, so typical of this period of development, are most often triggered in attachment-related situations—a mother who is shopping refuses to pick up the toddler, for example, and the child responds by throwing himself on the floor, and thrashing and screaming. An examination of this situation shows us important attachment issues at work: the child is in a strange place, possibly near strange people, and he seeks to be near the mother in reaction to this experience. She, however, does not cooperate, and intent on her shopping, does not even offer the eye contact and friendly facial expression that might help the child tolerate this level of distress. The child's loss of emotional control shows the intensity of his or her fear of separation in a threatening situation.

From about eight months to two years or so, babies show a very important form of attachment behavior, in addition to the ones just described. This is a much more subtle behavior than stranger and separation avoidance, and can be observed only in certain situations, so parents often do not notice or remember it. Secure base behavior is an essential indication of attachment, however.

Children show secure base behavior when in a strange place or situation with a familiar caregiver. The child essentially uses the adult as a base from which to make exploratory forays. He or she stays near the adult for a while, and then moves away to explore the interesting, but worrisome new environment. At first the baby moves only a small distance; then he comes back to the adult, perhaps climbing into the lap briefly for what appears to be an emotional refueling. Then another sortie is made, and another, until the toddler has managed to explore the situation thoroughly. As the exploration proceeds, the child may not even return all the way to the adult, but may look back, make eye contact, and find the adult's happy, unfrightened expression enough reassurance for the time being. The adult will often offer emotional support over a distance, by talking to the child, and the child may reply with preverbal jargon or with actual words.

Secure base behavior in the presence of a familiar caregiver is much different from the frightened, depressed stillness of a toddler left alone or with a strange adult in a strange place. When we see the baby can use a person as a secure base, we understand that person plays an important role in the child's internal working model of social relationships. An adult who can serve as a secure base is an adult to whom the child has formed an attachment.

Secure base behavior shows us how children's emotional lives support their ability to learn from the world through exploration. Even when they are not exploring, however, infants and toddlers show us there are connections between their emotional attachment to adults, and their interests in objects and in communication. Toward the end of the first year, babies work hard to accomplish joint attention.[4] They catch the eye of a familiar adult and move their own gaze, signaling the adult to look at something interesting; the two look back and forth at the object and then at each other, enjoying their shared experience just as two adults do. Interesting things seem more approachable when a familiar adult is present; they are more fun too.

Children's displays of stranger anxiety and separation anxiety are often distressing to adult caregivers, especially in modern family life, where maternal employment and non-maternal child care are frequent and economically necessary. The disadvantages of these childhood feelings and behaviors are obvious, and their advantages are hard to see. If we try to see life from the perspective of our remote ancestors, however, it may be more evident that such attachment behaviors have a very positive side. In prehistoric times, a wandering child might easily have been killed or stolen by a neighboring band of adults, and those who feared the unfamiliar were more likely to survive. Children who preferred to stay near adults would also have had more chances to learn social rules by watching adult behavior. In the ancient past (and possibly today as well), adults may have done a better job of child care when they were aware that an unattended child might begin to cry loudly, disturbing adults, and potentially attracting the attention of enemies or predators.

Secure base behavior does not cause the same obvious problems for adults as stranger and separation anxiety may; its advantages may also be less easy to see. But the ability to use a familiar person as a secure base makes it possible for the child to learn and explore, and, at the same time, stay safe. This is a more desirable outcome for human beings than safety alone. One modern difficulty connected with secure base behavior involves the toddler's need for familiar people, without whose presence even the best-designed preschool education may be valueless. Young children who are cared for in their own homes almost automatically have a secure base. Young children in child care outside the home may have no familiar caregivers unless special efforts are made to encourage good relationships with consistent child care staff. The secure base issue makes excellent early childhood care a highly labor-intensive enterprise.

TODDLERS, SEPARATION, AND LOSS

The period from eight months to two years is thus characterized by specific attachment-related emotions and behaviors, and these need to be taken into account as we try to understand all young children's experiences and plan their care. In addition to these almost universal attachment-related concerns, however, there are other situations that arise for some young children.

These have to do with the child's short- and long-term reactions to abrupt, lengthy separations from familiar people. These reactions, aspects of what René Spitz called hospitalism,[5] are fortunately not part of every child's early family life, though they do occur for far too many toddlers.

A toddler who has achieved attachment to one or a few caregivers will respond with serious distress to a separation that lasts for more than a day or two. Far from being too young to be affected by the loss of a parent, these children are at their most vulnerable age. Their responses to loss are completely parallel to the grief and mourning response of a bereaved adult. (In fact, the idea of stages of grief, so popular today, initially came out of work with orphaned young children.) Playing, learning, and other developmental processes may be put on hold for a period of months, and physical health too may be affected.

In the nature of things, of course, a young child may suffer an abrupt separation lasting days or weeks for reasons that are not very serious: the parents may have decided that their marriage needed a second honeymoon, or a new baby may have been born. A reunion with the parents eventually occurs, but children under two years do not understand what is happening and cannot always accept it with grace. The child's behavior during the separation shows distress, and when the parents return, they may be ignored, greeted coolly, or even hit or pushed away by the angry toddler. The child's angry or aloof behavior soon gives way to intense concern that the parents will leave again, and there may be weeks or months of clinginess, anxiety, and sleep problems before the child's worries resolve.

In some cases, of course, there has been a serious reason for the separation, and there will be no reunion. The child's distress is great and prolonged. Given an emotionally supportive caregiver, young children may recover completely from a serious loss and are then able to form a new attachment. In the course of recovery, however, the child will show deep unhappiness, crying, eating and sleep disturbances, failure to play, and, often, a regression from recently achieved goals, such as toilet training. This profound disturbance gradually gives way to a depressed withdrawal and a lack of interest. If the lost person returns, the child shows no recognition. Finally, a new attachment and a new interest in life can occur. (For some children, such as the mutilated orphans of the Congo, there is no sympathetic caregiver to offer a new life, and the experience of loss becomes the central organizing feature of life.)

Adoption and Breastfeeding: Connections with Attachment?

In a later chapter, we will be examining in detail some popular beliefs and misunderstandings about attachment. This may be a good point to touch briefly on two common ideas at odds with the material we are discussing in this section. First, we need to realize that the experience of adoption does not necessarily cause problems of attachment, or of general development. It is important to understand that children adopted early in their first year proceed through the same developmental steps with their adoptive parents as non-adopted children do with their biological parents. Because attachment is based on social experiences that adoptive parents usually provide, there is no reason that the early adoption of children should have negative effects on attachment. (Later adoption, of course, may involve a different set of social experiences, especially if it occurs after the point when attachment is usually evident.)

A second common misconception has to do with breastfeeding. Breastfeeding, or any other type of feeding, has in itself no known effect on the child's internal working model of social relations (nor, as we will see later in this chapter, is it known to influence the mother's feelings toward the child). Ordinarily, of course, the person who feeds the baby most is also the one most likely to play and interact socially in ways that connect to attachment, playful communications being a real part of the feeding interaction. Breastfeeding mothers usually have a bit more leisure or flexibility of schedule, they are healthy themselves, and they have healthy babies. These factors encourage both breastfeeding and attachment, whereas sick mothers with sick babies and overwhelmingly demanding schedules are more likely to have problems with nursing and attachment. We might see better attachment in breastfed babies than in some bottle-fed babies, but the feeding method would not be the direct cause of good or poor attachment development.

THE PRESCHOOL PERIOD

As we have seen, the social behavior of the four- or five-month-old gives way to much different attachment-related behavior by the end of the first year. It appears that this first stage of attachment forms the core of the internal working model of social relations, which will continue to develop for many years. The intense, anxious emotional concern the toddler shows for the caregiver will change again and again, until in his own late adulthood, the grown-up, former toddler becomes the concerned caregiver for elderly parents as well as for children or grandchildren. To prepare for this series of changes, the individual has to stop expecting to be the one who is nurtured. He or she has to become capable of negotiating or compromising with respect to other people's needs and of developing close relationships with new people. Without such developmental changes, the individual would remain a big, self-centered baby.

The preschool period features a child's first steps away from the emotional egocentrism of the toddler. Preschool children in most cultures are likely to experience more separations from their parents than babies do. If they were breastfed, they have generally been weaned by this age. Most are at least beginning to handle their own toilet needs. They walk and talk well. Sometimes their own interests in play and in their peers draw preschoolers away from their parents' sides. But the parents too seek separation. A mother may have a new baby to care for, and her work at home or away may require her to arrange that someone else care for her preschooler.

Like older human beings, preschoolers do not mind an unpleasant event like separation so much, if they can control when and how it occurs. Preschool children may protest vigorously against separation from their parents, but they also seek separation themselves, or accept it calmly after some negotiation has occurred. For instance, the preschooler may agree to be left at the day care center when she has received the number of kisses equal to the time on the clock, when the coat and lunch have been put in the cubby, or when the parent reads one story.

Separations and reunions are a fact of life for most preschool children, but their effect on the internal working model depends on the child's experience of predictability and control. Ideally, the preschool child's internal working model of social relations will involve a trust in compromise with others, and will thus move the child past the belief that safety and security exist only in the presence of a familiar caregiver. Experiences of caring negotiation are an important way to begin to trust compromise. Without these developments, the later experience of school and independent play with peers can only be frightening and difficult.

Parents have their own goals for their preschool children's development, and these involve compromise too. Most parents want the child to develop greater independence, but at the same time they want family rules to be obeyed. Though a few parents want to exercise complete authority over the child, most are committed to the development of a *goal-corrected partnership*, a relationship in which both the parent's and the child's needs will be considered, using mutual communication and planning as negotiating tools. An important issue at this time is the parent's skill at communication; careful communication is a major way to help the preschool child maintain a sense of security when the parent is absent, and, as well, it is an essential model for the child to follow.

Negotiation, bargaining, and compromise are thus aspects of the preschooler's attachment relationships. They bring about a step toward maturity in the internal working model. We can recognize attachment at work at this stage of life when the child attempts to negotiate separation from familiar people. Parents or child care providers may recall negotiations of this type, such as the lengthy proceedings at bedtime requiring more and more extended rituals before the final good night. Preschoolers are often said to be better or more obedient with less familiar people. Of course, there is no need for them to negotiate separations with people of little emotional importance to them.

Especially if they are sick, tired, or distressed, preschoolers can also show some of the same attachment-related behaviors as toddlers do. The preschooler still seeks a familiar person when frightened and has trouble feeling secure when alone or with strangers in a strange place. Preschoolers go off on their own sometimes, but like younger children they will quickly close the distance from their parents if they feel any threat.

Abrupt, long-term separation from a familiar caregiver is still a blow to the preschool child, but its effect is somewhat buffered by a developing part of the internal working model: language and symbols that represent attachment relations. A four-year-old whose parents have gone away for a month can be helped to cope with verbal reminders that they will be back or even by crossing days off on a calendar, whereas a twelve-month-old has no equivalent way to symbolize events and reassure himself.

Preschool children in industrialized countries today are more likely to find themselves separated from a familiar caregiver due to divorce than to death. Family breakup is a particularly difficult type of separation to work through with negotiation, because parents can rarely tolerate the compromises the child wants: that Daddy or Mommy will live at their house half the time, or that the divorce can happen, but no new partners may be brought into the picture.

However, the most important issue for this age group may simply be that some negotiation and joint planning take place, with the child's wishes and feelings being considered, if not entirely gratified. Even if the child is only offered the choice of a visit on Friday or one on Saturday, he or she needs to have some input in the decision-making. It is also important for the parents to affirm the child's choice by complying with the child's decision, rather than changing plans unilaterally. Grief and sadness will always follow serious losses in the preschooler's life, but the family's handling of the situation probably has a more powerful impact on development than does the loss itself.

SCHOOL-AGE CHILDREN

By the elementary school years, children generally have a social circle outside the immediate family. School, teachers, neighborhood friends, clubs, and religious groups all form part of the child's internal working model of social relations. Children of this age may leave home for periods of time, for a sleepover birthday party, a lengthy hospital treatment, or even to go to boarding school. They may experience periods of loneliness and homesickness, but on the whole, they are ready to include new situations and relationships in their internal working models.

Although friendships with age-mates are an important aspect of attachment for school-age children, parents remain at the core of the child's emotional life. As was true of preschoolers, schoolchildren's behavior may not reveal this fact unless there is a threat, or in cases of illness or injury, when they desire the security of nearness to the parent. Talking on the phone or even daydreaming about a reunion may be enough to help the separated child—although we should note that having to use these expedients takes the child's energy away from work or play. The internal working model of attachment still designates the parents as the ones who make you feel safe—this is the case even when a parent has been unpleasant, unreliable, or overtly abusive.[6]

For most parents and children, the elementary school period is one of lessened negative emotion. Both adults and children have improved negotiating techniques, and parents are less likely than before to assume that the child's wishes are just silly whims. Parents also have more confidence that yielding to a child will solve a problem rather than create incessant demands. Children's improved command of language enables them to communicate in situations where they once would have dissolved into tears and had tantrums. The attachment relationship with the parent still involves negative as well as positive emotion, but this is likely to be expressed with sulking, dawdling, and forgetting rather than with direct anger.

Parent and school-age child are generally continuing to work toward a goal-corrected partnership. In order to manage this, both must recognize how the child's changing needs and abilities affect their relationship and their ways of making decisions. If a boy of twelve says he wants music lessons and promises to practice, for example, a parent will generally assume that he knows what he is talking about, even though the same promise made at age six was not kept. The parent gradually encourages the child's initiative and autonomy, thus moving toward a more mature, flexible relationship between parent and child. As the parent systematically modulates the roles each plays in the attachment relationship, he or she also helps the child build flexibility into his internal working model of all social relationships.

ATTACHMENT, PEERS, AND POWER

Internal working models of social relations cannot be built on parent-child relations alone. Parent-child relations involve considerable differences in power, whether it is in physical strength, knowledge, or financial resources. This is much less true about many other relationships, especially as the child's age advances. Whereas preschool children had large power differences in many of their important relationships, school-age children have more connections with siblings, friends, and classmates, in which power is likely to be more equal than it is in the case of parent and child.

To have a complete, mature internal working model of social relations, the individual needs to have experiences with a variety of power differences. Children's experiences with siblings usually involve some level of power difference, whether based on differences in age, skills, or relationships with parents. In some families or cultures, the child who belongs to the more favored sex has extra power, in spite of youth or small size. Sibling relationships often seem to share the formidable emotional power characteristic of attachment to adults. The conflicts and sibling rivalry that emerge from this emotion can be very provoking to parents, but with help, children can use these situations to learn about negotiating and to extend their internal working models.

School-age children's peer relationships outside the family should also be considered an aspect of attachment. They provide an addition to the internal working model of social relations, an addition that stresses the fine-tuning of negotiation when power differences are very small. The simpler internal working model of the early school years directs the child to get an adult to solve disagreements with peers, but as the model becomes more complex, children offer each other compromises, often deciding that one will give up what he or she wants, rather than be separated from the friend. Sometimes an adult can facilitate compromise simply by asking, "Well, do you *want* to play together?"

THE ADOLESCENT YEARS

For all families, the management of attachment concerns in adolescence can have a critical impact on the teenager's later success in life. A fine balance between independence and emotional connection needs to be maintained, while the family serves as a secure base for the teenager's first exploration of the real world.

Events in the teenager's modification of attachment to parents are in many ways parallel to those of toddlers. This does not imply that adolescents are babyish, or so incompetent that adults must manage their lives, but like toddlers, they are in the process of finding ways to use their family attachments as support for coping with new tasks. One of the tasks for which they need family support is, paradoxically, *emotional separation* from the parents. The aspects of this confusing situation include ambivalence, frustration, increased emotionality, and irrational responses to people and events. Like toddlers, adolescents need responsive, supportive parents to help them achieve emotional and social growth, but, again like toddlers, they resist being guided against their wishes; to comply easily with parents' desires brings on the fear of lost autonomy and developmental regression.

During the adolescent period, boys' and girls' attachment relationships to their parents alter in somewhat different ways. Part of the difference is determined by the timing of puberty (occurring on average two years earlier for girls than for boys). The physical changes of puberty are a powerful impetus for emotional separation, as they make it obvious that the old relationships no longer work.

Families with a history of goal-corrected partnership have a relatively easy time transmuting the old attachment relationships into models where parent and teenager play nearly equal roles. Each may offer the other some degree of secure base (adults need this too), but both have important goals that are independent of their relationship. When this is the case, parents can remain available as guides, consultants, and supporters throughout their offspring's teen years and early adulthood, a period when good advice and help can be most useful.

If a family has never thought a goal-corrected partnership desirable, it is likely that the parents and the teenagers share a problematic internal working model of social relations—a model based on power, not on preference for a familiar person. The family may have succeeded for many years in managing children by threat or by force, but this strategy no longer works when the children themselves become powerful. A power-based internal working model does not allow for negotiation and compromise, but assumes the complete capitulation of the weaker participant. Adolescence in this power-oriented family involves a series of showdown struggles, eventually won by the teenager who then has no recourse but to leave home. Premature separation of this type means that the adolescent must enter immediately into adult responsibilities, without guidance or a secure base to which he or she can return. Such teenagers are often correctly described as "throwaway," rather than "runaway," children. In addition to the obvious problems, the youth who has shared the power-based internal working model will expect others to have the same model, and he or she will view offers of negotiation as weakness rather than as a useful social strategy. His or her capacity to develop a more mature, complex model of social relations will be limited, though not completely absent.

An important and complex developmental issue for adolescents and their families is the intensification of sexuality at puberty. Although much early sexual behavior is solitary, eventually sexuality needs to be incorporated into the internal working model of social relations. Adult sexuality usually involves a social context and a relationship with a partner, even if only a brief one. Like older people, adolescents fall in love, or at least feel that another person is attractive. They experience sexual interest in connection with other people, in reality or in fantasy. They do not simply experience sexual desire as an event within the self. The desire and the object of desire go together. Even masturbation involves the fantasy of a partner.

The process of bringing sexuality into the model, the choice of partners, and the whole matter of gender identity are outside the scope of this book. These events are related to attachment but involve many other complex components as well. We can briefly compare falling in love to some early steps in attachment, but although the degree of emotionality is similar, there are some real differences. An obvious difference is in the erotic aspect of adolescent or adult romantic love, something that is absent in the young child's attachment to a familiar caregiver. Another difference is in timing; falling in love or falling out of love can happen quite quickly, but attachment usually takes some months to develop. It does not disappear spontaneously; instead it diminishes painfully and gradually, if there is a separation. When threatened, a teenager or an adult does not necessarily seek the romantic love object as a child seeks the familiar caregiver. The internal working model of social relationships probably does a great deal to help shape ongoing romantic relationships, but this does not mean that the first steps in romance are parallel to the first steps in attachment.

PARENTHOOD

Mothers love their children because of their natural instinct, don't they? Or do they? The idea of maternal instinct is one way of explaining the change in their model of social relationships that most women experience after a child is born. Like many uses of the instinct idea, however, this explanation becomes less satisfactory when it is examined carefully. Neither mothers nor fathers know automatically how to care for a newborn baby. Different cultures have different infant-care practices, a fact that suggests infant care is not instinctive for humans. If it were, everyone would behave in exactly the same way.

Because the word instinct does not seem to describe human parental behavior very well, investigators in this field at one point turned to "bonding" as a substitute. In an earlier chapter of this book, we referred to the term bonding as a description of an emotional connection between human beings, and we noted that this was a nontechnical use. Technically, the word bonding is used only to describe the development of an adult's positive feelings toward a child. There is no question that the feelings we call bonding can be extraordinarily powerful; they preoccupy and motivate parents in ways almost unimaginable to people who have not experienced this part of life. Particularly in the early months of the baby's life, bonding involves constant thinking of the baby, intense feelings of love, as well as some of anger and hatred, and the motivation to care for the infant's needs at all costs. Parents experiencing these feelings are literally more comfortable with their own hunger or pain than with the idea that the baby is hungry or suffering. Yet, at the same time, most human parents feel occasional flashes of anger and the temptation to attack the infant; some parents neglect, abuse, or even kill their children. Obviously this process of bonding is not a simple one. It requires explanation.

The awkward word "bonding" makes an already complex situation more confusing than it might otherwise be. The word seems to imply somehow that each member of a bonded pair is in some way equally attached to the other. But the development of the adult's positive feelings (bonding) and the child's (attachment) are on quite different schedules. The adult's sense of connection to the baby may, and usually does, exist for months before the baby shows any behavior that suggests attachment to the adult. Eventually we see the child and the adult function as a pair; they watch for and concern themselves with each other, and they each bring some powerful feelings to their emotional connection. The period of intense connection is short-lived, however, for the child begins to move toward negotiating separation, and the adult may then have a new baby, a new romantic interest, or any of the many emotional concerns with which adults need to deal.

For a period of time in the 1970s, some authors wrote about bonding as if it were an instinctively determined form of rapid learning, much like imprinting.[7] Researchers working in this field thought that bonding was a change in a parent's thoughts and emotions, most easily created shortly after a child's birth, and triggered in part by the physical appearance and behavior of the newborn baby. Early experiences with seeing and touching the young infant were thought to cause a long-term emotional change in the parent, much as following an adult duck causes a change in the duckling's response to other ducks.

Because of the comparison with imprinting, some researchers investigating bonding thought that early contact between mother and newborn might be a powerful factor influencing the mother's emotions. In modern times, as more babies were born in hospitals rather than at home, mothers became less and less likely to see and hold their babies right after birth. The babies were customarily taken away, weighed, cleaned up, wrapped, and—since they were often chilled by this time—taken off to the newborn nursery to be warmed. Hours often passed before mother and newborn were reunited. (In hospitals whose policy required that the baby be checked by the staff pediatrician during his rounds, the delay could be as much as twenty-four hours.) When the baby was finally brought to the mother, she might feel timid about unwrapping her child and bothering the nurses; the visit might be brief, and usually there was little privacy.

Researchers working on bonding were concerned that these hospital policies might be interfering with bonding, or at least that the conditions were less than ideal. They proposed that mothers and babies be given a period of early contact within a short time after the birth. The father was to be included, if possible, and he and the mother were to be given privacy and encouragement to undress and examine their baby. When parents had this experience, they were usually engrossed with the baby and thrilled with the sense of doing something very important.

The evidence from the reports of the parents was not enough to prove any real advantages from early contact. Did the parents' early contact create a bond that helped them care for the baby, who in turn developed particularly well? This was the kind of question that is essential but so difficult to answer experimentally. How was it even possible to create a situation where one group of parents had early contact, but another comparison group did not? And what about ethical concerns? What if it should prove that early contact actually did some harm to the family, rather than giving the antici-pated benefit?

Fortunately, a situation allowing research did arise, as one hospital changed its policy from delayed to early contact for healthy babies and their mothers. A comparison was made between the development of the delayed-contact babies, born in the last week of the old policy, and of the first week's group of early-contact babies. The babies' development was followed over several years, and significant advantages were reported for the early-contact group.[8]

The researchers proposed the following chain of events: (1) Early contact brought mother and baby together when the mother was most ready to bond, soon after giving birth. (2) The newborn was at that time more alert and responsive than the baby would have been the next day, and its appear-ance and behavior affected the mother emotionally, causing her to form a bond to her particular baby. (3) Bonding was an internal emotional and cognitive change that made the mother more aware of, and more con-cerned with the baby's needs, so she became more sensitive, responsive, and receptive to the baby's signals than she would otherwise have been. (4) The mother's increased sensitivity helped her do a better job caring for the baby. (5) As a result, the baby's condition was improved; bonding led to good child health and development.

The idea that early contact could accomplish so much was eagerly welcomed. Programs to encourage early contact were established, and hospital policies altered to allow this. The idea was generally accepted that bonding—and therefore good development—depended on early contact. (Even today, nurses sometimes speak about bonding when they are simply helping mothers with early contact and encouraging mother-child interaction.) Some parents were concerned and distressed about bonding, when health problems delayed contact with their newborn.

A More Recent View

As the excitement about bonding died down, more unanswered questions surfaced. The mothers in the initial bonding study had been poor, educationally deprived teenagers in unplanned pregnancies. Would affluent older women respond the same way? It began to appear there might be many factors at work in the determination of a mother's attitude and a child's development. Of course, this was far from the first time social science research had come to this conclusion.

We now know that it would be more useful to think of bonding as a change in an internal working model rather than an instinctually determined process such as imprinting. This view does not diminish the powerful emotions and motivations that are part of bonding, any more than attachment should be considered less emotional because of its function in the internal working model of social relations.

It is probably correct to say that bonding, like other aspects of the internal working model, may be best understood as part of a *dynamic action system*. In such a system, many factors work together to determine an outcome—in this case, the parent's feelings and behavior and the child's good or poor development. An important characteristic of a dynamic action system is that a small change in one factor may bring about a large change in the outcome, though even a large change in a different factor may affect the outcome very little.

Bonding—both the parent's feelings and the parent's responsiveness to a child—may be much easier to disturb than the child's attachment to the parent. Attachment processes are robust and hard to shift, but changes in the many factors that determine bonding are more likely to occur.

The baby itself supplies many of the factors that influence bonding. A healthy, alert baby responds easily to parents and gives clear signals about its needs, so the parents are able to feel satisfied that they are doing the right things. A frail or premature baby is less responsive. Parents are deeply gratified by the sense of communication with their baby. Serious birth defects do not necessarily interfere with bonding, but those that affect the eyes and facial expression make it harder for the parent to have that sense of communication.

Factors in the parent also influence his or her emotional response to the baby. Fear and grief seem to interfere seriously with bonding. A parent who is mourning the death, during the previous year, of a loved one may have difficulty feeling an emotional connection to a newborn. (This applies to grief about an earlier miscarriage or stillbirth, too, and the death of one twin is especially problematic.) Anxiety about a baby's health seems to trigger a sort of premature mourning that interferes with bonding. Maternal depression lasting for more than a few months causes problems with the infant's emotional development, putting the relationship more and more at risk.

Situational factors can also distort bonding. A difficult, unwanted, or frightening pregnancy leaves the mother less prepared than she should be for beginning a new relationship. If a mother can see her sick newborn only through a nursery window, she may feel that the child is not her own.

Most new parents bring to their situation some factors that could interfere with bonding. Many do not experience their first contact with the baby as a thrilling moment of falling in love. But days or weeks of interaction with the baby cause an emotional reorganization which changes the internal working model, and results in powerful positive emotions and a deep preoccupation with the child. Although early parenthood can involve fury and frustration, most parental feelings are strongly positive, enabling them to provide enough sensitive, responsive care to support the child's good development.

Do the hormonal changes of childbirth really cause bonding, or at least make it more likely to occur? Probably hormones play only a small role, if any. Fathers and adoptive mothers, who have no dramatic hormone changes, show bonding to the same degree as biological mothers. We need to remember that the hormonal changes of pregnancy and childbirth are also accompanied by important experiences that can occur in the absence of pregnancy. A biological mother has normally known of her pregnancy for six months or more and has had plenty of time to focus her thoughts and feelings on the person she expects her baby to be. This experience—which is shared by fathers and adoptive mothers—may do as much or more to prepare her for bonding as biological events do. A pregnant woman also experiences much social guidance, as other people tell her of the ups and downs of birth and motherhood, treating her as a prospective mother and helping her prepare to be one. Fathers may receive this type of guidance mainly from their wives, their own parents, and intimate friends. Adoptive mothers may receive it through the adoption agency, but they do receive it just as pregnant women do.

A persistent myth about bonding is the belief that breastfeeding causes it to occur. (As we saw earlier, it is also common to assume, and equally inaccurate, that breastfeeding causes attachment.) People who have this belief often offer an unlikely picture of a mother gazing into a very young baby's eyes as the child nurses. This very old idea certainly goes back at least to Shakespeare's time as we see from Lady Macbeth's line, "I have given suck, and know how tender 'tis to love the baby that milks me." In the early twentieth century, just as Freud was suggesting the gratification of needs was a source of attachment, one writer proposed that lactation is the cause of maternal love.[9]

Of course, it is not practical or ethical to try to test the role of breastfeeding in an experimental fashion. In order to do so we would have to make sure that certain mothers breastfed and that others did not, a most difficult task, as well as one involving potential dangers for some children. What we know about the effects of breastfeeding comes from our observations of self-selected mothers who have chosen breast or bottle-feeding on their own, or at least without any researcher's advice. However, observations of breastfeeding and bottle-feeding mothers give us no reason to think that one group loves their babies any less than the other. Adoptive mothers, who rarely breastfeed in this country, ordinarily experience bonding, and their children have excellent developmental outcomes if they have been adopted early in their lives.[10] If breastfeeding were necessary for bonding, the extreme popularity of bottle-feeding in the 1940s and 1950s should have created catastrophic developmental problems, and this did not occur. In addition, the necessity of breastfeeding would mean that no father could ever bond to his child.

It may well be that mothers who have bonding problems may also be less likely to breastfeed. It is also the case that a sick newborn, especially one with facial birth defects, may be too weak to breastfeed, and bonding problems may occur. However, what we are seeing in these cases is the effect of other factors on both bonding and feeding, not of feeding on bonding, or vice versa.

THE STOCKHOLM SYNDROME

A rare and little-understood form of adult attachment is sometimes called the Stockholm Syndrome after the city in which it was first clearly described. This syndrome occurs in situations where an individual, usually a woman, is threatened or held hostage in a case of genuine danger. The hostage-taker negotiates for the woman's safety with the authorities, using the captive's life as a bargaining chip. Rather than hating and fearing the captor, as might seem logical, the hostage falls in love and does not want to be rescued or separated from the captor.

The situation occurs so infrequently that it has hardly been studied in detail, but the characteristic emotional changes seem to have much in common with normal forms of early attachment. Studies of concentration camp inmates during World War II describe some individuals as admiring and imitating the guards in ways that seem parallel to both early attachment and the Stockholm Syndrome. Sigmund Freud also referred to a similar process of identification with the aggressor in adults. It is not known whether the Stockholm Syndrome actually involves the same emotional processes as normal attachment, or whether this is a pathological process made possible by some vulnerability in the hostage.

REVIEW AND SUMMARY

Attachment and bonding both have to do with attitudes and beliefs about specific people. Neither could develop in a social vacuum, for each requires the participation of at least two people. We focus on the feelings of the child when studying attachment and those of the adult when studying bonding, but it would be ideal if we could look simultaneously at the steps of both partners in their interpersonal dances. Perhaps we can manage a little of this if we simply examine which events are happening at which given time.

Shortly after a baby's birth, the parents are interested in and attracted to the baby, and they respond happily if they can feed their child or get the baby to look at them. The baby cannot do a great deal, but does sometimes look at faces and eyes, and may even imitate facial expressions, giving the parents a sense of gratification. As parents bond, they become more preoccupied with the baby, and more sensitive and responsive to signals. This helps to comfort and soothe the baby, who becomes gradually a little more able to regulate his own emotions, enabling him to spend more time quiet, alert, and responsive to adults. The parents are aware of this change and are encouraged to try more and more playful communications. The parents now strongly prefer their baby to other babies and know how to play with and soothe her, but the baby does not yet particularly prefer the parents.

By about eight months, the child becomes capable of fearfulness and begins to stay close to the parents, especially if there is any threatening or unfamiliar event going on. Parents respond to this new behavior with mixed emotions and often with some anxiety. They change their behavior toward the child in anticipation of the fear and distress the child may express. Some parents are supportive and comforting, others punitive about the beginning of attachment behavior.

During the later toddler and preschool period, child and parent begin to move apart emotionally and socially. The child can tolerate more separation, but wants to negotiate it in order to keep some sense of control. Parents at this point may have reason to encourage separation; a new baby may be on the way, or parents may be turning toward work, school, or other adult activities. The child's negative emotions may make the parents ambivalent, both longing to be with the child at times and repelled by tantrums and irritability.

School-age children and their parents ideally have arrived at a goal-corrected partnership. While parents retain the greatest power and authority, they can also respect their children's maturity and ability to make decisions. For both parents and children, the relationship may seem casual and low-key—until there is a threat to one person, which brings the other in haste.

The adolescent years again involve a focus on separation, but this time it is the parent who may be reluctant and want to negotiate, while the teenager wants to move toward independence. However, the teen will do better with emotional support from parents than she will if abrupt separation occurs. In the teenage years, as well as later, close emotional connections to friends form an essential part of the individual's internal working model of social relationships.

Families, Experiences, and Outcomes: What Difference Does Attachment History Make?

Astartling news story in early 2004 revealed a strange family history and raised questions about the effects of experiences on children's emotional lives. At a children's birthday party, a young mother named Luz Cuevas encountered a former friend with a six-year-old girl who was identified as the friend's daughter. This was not particularly unusual, but Ms. Cuevas immediately wondered whether this child might possibly be her own daughter, Delimar, who had disappeared as a week-old infant, apparently having been consumed in a blazing house fire. Unnoticed, Ms. Cuevas obtained a clipping of the child's hair and managed to get a DNA analysis. The result? It was Ms. Cuevas' own child, who must have been kidnapped as a tiny baby by the woman claiming to be her mother, the fire having been set deliberately to cover the kidnapping. When these facts were discovered, Delimar was taken by the state child protective service agency and eventually returned to Ms. Cuevas.

Delimar, thus, experienced two abrupt separations: the first at one week old and the second at six years of age. What would we expect to be the results of these experiences? Chapter 4 has already answered this question with respect to the earlier separation. As devastating as the event was to her mother, the infant Delimar would have had no difficulty with the change of caregiver at one week old, as long as she was treated well.

What about the separation at age six though? This question opens up many issues. Are there short-term or long-term consequences of relationships and of losses at different ages? How do early experiences influence the individual as he or she matures and develops? Does the individual's personality show the influence of attachment experiences from any time in the past?

WHAT, WHEN, AND WHY: ASKING QUESTIONS ABOUT ATTACHMENT AND PERSONALITY

The questions in the previous section could be answered in a wide variety of ways, for they have more than one implication. To do that, we need to define what we mean by "influence" more carefully.

What

In asking about the influence of attachment events, we might be inquiring about serious psychopathology. In Bowlby's early study of the forty-four boys,[1] attachment was thought to be a major factor determining antisocial behavior. (Bowlby's later work did not stress this idea as much as his earlier writings.) Some writers have speculated on whether attachment problems might be factors in autism or even adult serial murder. This question is a complex one and will be addressed in Chapter 6. At this point, we can say that attachment alone is probably not the cause of major emotional disturbances of the types mentioned above.

For our present purposes, the influence of attachment experiences may be best defined as the extent to which attachment events shape an individual's emotional and behavioral reactions to other people—the unique characteristics that we refer to as *personality*. Such influences could change from one stage of life to another, but for our purposes, they would only include feelings and behaviors within a normal range. The focus is on individuality—normal personality differences—and on the minor emotional disturbances that may be troublesome but do not interfere severely with education, work, marriage, and parenthood. Because attachment involves an internal working model of social relationships, we tend to look for the effect of attachment experiences on relationships, rather than on, say, memory or athletic prowess.

When

If attachment experiences have long-term effects, they could crop up at any time during life, and they might not be equally evident at all times. There are many points in life when these effects might occur, and we must search throughout the life cycle to find evidence for and against long-term effects.

There is another kind of "when" to deal with, too: if attachment experiences have a long-term influence, at what point in life might the most important attachment experiences occur? We need to handle this question carefully and open-mindedly and realize that more than one answer is possible.

Most of us assume experiences in early childhood have powerful effects on personality development. Freudian theory and its derivatives (including Bowlby's attachment theory) have impressed this idea on us and stressed *infant determinism* as an almost unquestioned principle of development. Though we do not have very good evidence that this principle is correct, we just assume it is. Developmental psychologist Jerome Kagan suggests that infant determinism is one of the seductive ideas about which we should remain cautious—ideas that seem self-evident but that may be wrong.[2]

It is not necessarily the case that the attachment experiences of early childhood are paramount in an entire lifetime of social relationships. We will find, though, that most existing research focuses on early childhood. There is not much work that looks at later experiences as essential, but this does not mean they could not be as important as early events.

Why

What leads us to ask this kind of question in the first place? Why should attachment events have a real impact, when some other early experiences do not? Part of the answer involves the enormous significance of emotional relationships and social behavior in human lives. From childhood and beyond, our success and happiness are linked to emotional connections with others. The preschooler who fights other children and resists his teacher will be punished, deprived, removed from the group, and prevented from having many satisfying experiences. The schoolchild who is sullen or quarrelsome is not chosen to go on a special trip or be in the school play. Although some adults may achieve professional success through intellectual abilities, most of us need to use good social skills and cultivate personal relationships to be successful at work and home.

Fortunately, we can pursue the question of attachment and personality because we have the tools to do so. Chapter 3 described techniques for assessment of attachment in children and in older people. No one would claim that our tests of attachment are perfect, but they have been used for many years by large numbers of researchers, both to collect new information and to make comparisons with much older work.

Tests like the Strange Situation have shown us the continuity or stability of the measurements we make of attachment behavior. This is an essential factor in our understanding of the links between early attachment experiences and any later impact on personality. To a considerable extent, we can expect that a twelve-month-old, categorized as securely attached using the

Strange Situation, will show related, similar characteristics years later; another child, classified as insecure-avoidant will develop along different, but equally predictable lines.[3] When they are years older, the children will not behave in just the same ways they did as toddlers, of course, because all their ways of acting will have matured; however, the differences that once existed between the one-year-olds will resemble the differences that now exist between the five-year-olds.

This continuity or stability of attachment behaviors tells us that some characteristics were already established at an early age; this means it is possible that the characteristics were actually caused by early attachment experiences. Another fact that suggests that personality may be shaped by early attachment experiences is that some children show different attachment behaviors toward their mothers and than they do their fathers.[4] These differences imply that attachment is not altogether in the child, but is instead in the relationship, and thus arises, at least in part, from early experiences.

CONFOUNDED VARIABLES: CONFUSED AND CONFUSING DATA

A word of warning is in order before we discuss attachment experiences and personality development. It is extremely difficult to sort out causes and effects in this matter. There are some individual personality characteristics that clearly do not come out of attachment experiences. These traits, called temperamental or constitutional differences, apparently result from genetic or other biological factors. It may be all too easy to confuse these with the child's actual attachment emotions, behavior, or even, memories and thoughts.

Take, for example, a temperamental quality called "intensity of reaction." Infants and toddlers show individual differences in their emotional expressiveness. Some cry loudly and vigorously when unhappy, yet are equally vehement in their expressions of pleasure, laughing and shouting when tickled or chased. On the other hand, young children who are more mild in their reactions may frown or look sad instead of crying, and smile or chuckle instead of shrieking when amused.

These temperamental differences affect attachment in two ways. First, adults may notice a child's concerns about separation when they are so loudly and vociferously expressed, but may pay less attention to the milder signals from the less intense child. Second, having noticed the child's unique behaviors, the adults may provide different types of experiences to a child who was already different. Temperament can cause children to have different kinds of social experiences.

A parent of an intense toddler may plan to handle separations carefully in public so unfavorable attention is not attracted by the child's cries. Some parents may try to sneak out, when leaving the child with a sitter or at a day care center, in an attempt to avoid hearing the child's loud distress. Others may decide that care outside the home is impossible for their child, who seems so terribly upset when left. Still others may punish the crying child for disobedience or willfulness.

Parents of milder toddlers may feel relieved and proud of their child's independence when little distress about separation is displayed. They may go ahead with day care arrangements and concern themselves very little about the moment of parting. On the other hand, some parents of mildly reacting toddlers may be disturbed by their child's relative calm, and they may fear that he or she has not formed an attachment.

The important point here is that children's different emotional expressiveness—their mild or intense reaction to separation—can cause the parents to handle separations differently. The child's attachment experiences are directly affected by the parent's actions, and indirectly affected by the child's own temperament. Which contributes most to the child's developing personality characteristics? It is extremely difficult to tell.

A final source of confusion is connected with the question of the importance of early experience. Is the child's individuality shaped primarily by early experience, or is it gradually molded over years of growing up? To answer this, we would have to look at children whose infant and toddler years were spent in one sort of emotional situation, and who then went to quite different households. There are, of course, some children who are adopted by new families or who live in foster families for years; with any luck, these children go from poor emotional situations to good ones. We do not see many who have reversed this order, so we do not have very good material for examining the two potential formative periods. And most children in industrialized countries live in the same families from birth through adolescence. For the average child, chances are that the basic environment of infancy and of later years will be the same. The parents who encouraged attachment in infancy with sensitivity and responsiveness will continue to provide appropriately sensitive, responsive care for their older children. If we look at the average ten-year-old, then, we have no way of knowing whether her personality was completely determined at age two, or whether the ensuing years did the real work of making her who she is.

SHAPING ATTACHMENT AND INDIVIDUALITY: INFANTS AND TODDLERS

Whether we are considering early experiences or early displays of attachment emotions and behaviors, much of what we know about attachment focuses on early life. The first two years of life have received the most attention from researchers interested in the outcomes of individuals' attachment experiences.

Mothers' Attitudes and Experiences

For most babies, their mothers are the major sources of social and emotional experiences. The mothers' attitudes and expectations about their babies might well cause differences in their babies' emotional development.

As we discussed in an earlier chapter, the 1970s and 1980s produced a great deal of work on mothers bonding with their babies. This research, though difficult at best, was especially complicated because no one was able to offer a good independent assessment of bonding. Many parent behaviors and emotions seemed related to this concept. For instance, *engrossment*, the adult's profound attentiveness to the baby, might be a step in the bonding process and a way to measure emotional change. However, there was no clear-cut way to say that one mother was bonded to her baby, and another was not. It was even less possible to determine that one woman had bonded a little, as opposed to someone else who had bonded a lot. Human behaviors toward young infants are enormously influenced by cultural expectations and by situational factors, such as a lack of privacy in the hospital. A new mother may act very differently when in a room alone with her baby than when she has a roommate whose mother, mother-in-law, and cousins are all visiting and chatting.

Although the idea of bonding has not been abandoned completely, researchers have now started to look at other, related aspects of mothers' attitudes. *Maternal depression* is one of the most important factors determining a mother's ability to show sensitivity and responsiveness to her child and thus to work toward secure attachment. Depressed mothers lack the energy and attentiveness needed for sensitive detection of a baby's signals, and they may feel too tired, preoccupied, or irritable to respond, even if they do get the signal. Drug and alcohol use have similar effects on maternal behavior.

Grief over personal losses also has an impact on parents that interferes with responsiveness to infants and thus potentially with attachment. The recent death of an older baby or loved one plays a significant role here. Early work on bonding stressed this problem, emphasizing the difficulty of forming a new emotional connection to a baby while simultaneously having to let go of another connection through mourning.

Grief may result from a loss of personal identity or a change in expectations about the world, as well as from a death or other separation. For example, couples that have had children through Assisted Reproductive Technology (ART), after years of infertility, are sometimes happy. But they have also been described as "unexpectedly... depressed, exhausted, and ambivalent."[5]

They may fear losing the child and they may try to avoid conflict with that child, a difficult task with respect to the negotiation of separation we discussed in an earlier chapter.

When grief and fear are overwhelming, mothers' attitudes, feelings, and behavior are powerfully affected. A fascinating and disturbing account of this is given in *Death Without Weeping*.[6] Nancy Scheper-Hughes describes the dire poverty in Brazil and its impact on mothers' caregiving. Hungry and sick themselves, the poor Brazilian mothers suffer many emotional and material losses. After giving birth, they may identify a child as one who does not want to live. They fail to feed or care for the baby, who eventually dies of malnutrition and disease. This decision would certainly mean these mothers have failed to bond, if we could define such a category at all. However, when a baby survives and becomes stronger, the mother's interest increases. Such mothers then describe the children as attached. One interviewee said,

> The little one never lets me out of her sight. [She] hangs onto my skirts, and she cries whenever I leave the house. I can't take a step without her. What kind of children are these, so afraid to move without their mama? So I yell at them to toughen them up.[7]

This mother seems to dislike the child's signals of attachment and preference, but it may be that she is concerned about the child becoming independent enough to survive in their very harsh environment. A mother's own *attachment status* seems to be of major importance in determining the outcome for her child. Mothers whose attachments are secure, as assessed by the Adult Attachment Interview (discussed in an earlier chapter), are far more likely to have securely attached children.[8]

Mothers' Behavior and Children's Attachment Status

Mothers' feelings and attitudes help to determine their behavior toward their children, but it is the behavior itself that influences the child's development of attachment. What kinds of behavior are relevant here? What events shape early development so that toddlers show individual differences in their attachment behavior and emotions?

Generally speaking, small children are strongly inclined to become securely attached to their caregivers, and most do so, despite parental illnesses, marital disagreements, and less than ideal day care arrangements. They seem to have had enough sensitive, responsive adult interaction to be secure, even though life has not all been absolutely perfect.

Smaller numbers of toddlers behave in ways that place them in the A and C categories discussed earlier in this book, with one or another type of insecure attachment relations. They may avoid the mother when she returns from an absence, or may go to her but not be able to be comforted by her.

Most studies of mothers' behavior and children's attachment status have focused on the small number of toddlers whose behavior is in the D category—disorganized or disoriented reactions to the mother's return from a brief absence. These children have often experienced many changes in caregiver or inconsistent relationships with their parents. Parents who are depressed or who habitually use drugs and alcohol are particularly likely to create inconsistent, unpredictable experiences for their children. Parents who themselves experienced early losses, or were physically or sexually abused, may also lack sensitivity or responsiveness to their children.

In addition to the past experiences that may cause D-category behaviors, it is possible that a parent's behavior at the time of the reunion serves as a direct trigger for disorganized/disoriented-child responses. When children respond with fear or freezing on a parent's return, their actions may be cued by the parent's own facial expressions. The parent may appear frightened and thus be frightening to the child, and may also show sudden, unpredictable behavioral changes, like abruptly moving a hand across the child's face.[9] A "natural" source of comfort and security for a toddler, the parent, also acts in this situation as a source of fear. The child looks at the parent's face for information about the parent's emotional state and finds there is indeed a reason to be frightened. Freezing or collapsing may be a logical response to a puzzle where no solution is really right.

Many Caregivers: The Effects of Change on Attachment

Human births most commonly involve a single child, and the simple arrangement of one child—one mother is what most of us have in mind when we think about attachment. For practical reasons, however, most babies have more than one caregiver, and this has been the case throughout human history. In traditional societies, grandmothers, neighbors, and child nurses took turns at caring for the baby, giving mothers time for other work. In modern industrialized groups, formal day care arrangements are common. The experiences of some babies are additionally complicated by a permanent change of caregiver— the mother may die, or law or custom may take the baby, following neglect or abuse.

Few babies are cared for by a single adult at all times, and it is possible that having one adult caregiver is not an ideal arrangement when it does occur. Generally, two or three adults are greatly involved with a given baby, and secure attachment can and does readily develop in this situation. But what happens to attachment when the circumstances are quite different?

Boarder Babies. The *boarder baby* is an unfortunate modern phenomenon: an infant born in a hospital, abandoned by its mother, and prevented, by legal or practical considerations, from going to a family member or to a foster home. Boarder babies are cared for in the hospital for many months, fed, rocked, and talked to by an ever-changing roster of nurses and volunteers. Adults who pass by are attracted by the infant; they pop in to say hello, then quickly leave to continue their work—the baby learns a mirror-image form of social response, smiling quickly, but failing to sustain the interaction. The boarder baby's behavior is quite different from that of a family child, who from an early age learns to sustain a conversation and to communicate in ways that are probably the foundation for attachment. Whether the boarder baby's oddities are entirely due to experience with too many caregivers is hard to say though, because the child's situation is often connected with the mother's alcohol or drug use, which might have also affected development.

Foster Care. Change of caregiver is a major feature of foster care for infants and toddlers, with many babies in foster placement experiencing frequent reassignments. Foster care may be planned as a temporary measure while parents find appropriate housing or solve medical problems, and infants may go back to their biological parents when difficulties have been solved. However, it is not uncommon for the same or new problems to arise. Then the baby is likely to go to a new foster (or "resource") family, perhaps because the old one has taken another child. Visits with biological parents may be encouraged, but they are usually infrequent, awkward, and filled with anxiety, especially for parents who know they are being watched for evidence of bonding or attachment. Transitions may be handled very poorly, as in the case of a one-year-old boy who was taken from a now familiar foster home while he was asleep, only to wake up at the house of his prospective adoptive parents, whom he had never seen before.

It is common for children who have had many early foster care changes to be impulsive and aggressive in personality, and it is easy to blame this outcome on the lack of opportunity for attachment. However, in the interests of genuine understanding, we should remain aware of potential difficulties that might have existed before the child ever went to foster care. Behavior problems and other personality differences can be based on genetic factors, or on health problems and drug or alcohol exposure before birth. It is also true that some foster homes unfortunately model aggressive behavior, either in the form of maltreatment by foster parents or the examples of older children placed in the home.

Adoption. Children may be adopted in a variety of circumstances— straight from the delivery room, after many foster placements, after traumatic experiences, or in later childhood, when we would expect attachment already to have occurred. Studies of adopted children seem to show little or no unusual emotional development when adoption takes place in the first few months, though there are some differences in the types of problems shown by early adopted and non-adopted children. Children who are adopted between eight to twelve months and three years of age are more likely to show general developmental problems in language, attention, and cognitive ability, as well as trouble dealing with frustration. Children adopted at age five to six, or older, after having lived in a consistent, well-functioning family up to that point, may be sad or depressed. Though they may continue to mourn their loss for years, they otherwise do not show serious developmental problems. (Delimar Cuevas, whose case introduced this chapter, would be an example of this.) The most important factor for these children is not the fact of adoption, but whether they received consistent, sensitive, responsive care during their infant and toddler years.

Separations and Losses. Babies who are less than six months old generally show little real distress about separation, as long as they are well cared for by a responsive caregiver. It is only when clear attachment behaviors, like staying near, occur that separation becomes a painful matter. Brief separations from familiar caregivers result in protest, often followed by calming, and then a renewed brief complaint, as the familiar person returns. Protest is less intense if the child is in a familiar place (his or her own home, ideally) and if the substitute caregiver is somewhat familiar. Divorce and separation from one parent is responded to like any other separation from a familiar person.

Long-term separations are extremely distressing to the older infant or toddler, especially if they occur abruptly or involve being in an unfamiliar place with unfamiliar adults. A film made by one of Bowlby's colleagues, James Robertson (*Nine Days in a Residential Nursery*), shows a toddler's loss of emotional control, difficulty eating and sleeping, and development of physical illness.[10] Continuing separation triggers a grief reaction that eventually enables the child to forget the lost person, perhaps over a period of a year. The extent to which a severe separation experience like this has long-term effects (such as a tendency toward depression) probably depends on incidental factors, such as the availability of sympathetic, comforting adults or the possibility of entering a stable situation with a supportive new family. Infants and toddlers benefit greatly when adults can serve as buffers against the experience of loss.

Infant and Toddler Day Care. When young children are cared for in groups outside their homes, their social experiences are rather different than they might be within the family setting. How does group child care affect infants and toddlers? Do they lose their attachments to mother and father? Do they have to try to function without a secure base? Is their emotional or communicative development harmed?

These questions were asked repeatedly during the so-called "day care wars" of the 1990s, when psychologists struggled to understand whether non-parental care was harmful or helpful. Insecure attachment was reported as being associated with babies' longer hours in day care, and insecure toddlers were described as playing less and crying more.[11] Other researchers sought explanations with a more positive message about day care.

There is no question that infant and toddler day care is here to stay. Few families can manage financially without some form of non-maternal care. But not all day care centers are alike; it is possible to find attachment-friendly child care. Paradoxical as it may seem, day care centers can help toddlers develop and maintain attachments to their parents, both through support to the parents and through encouragement of children's attachments to child care providers. Children generally have several caregivers, and good attachments to all of them are possible. Attachment to a day care provider does not remove or diminish attachment to the parents.

To encourage the formation of secure attachments, day care centers need to use assigned caregivers, each staff member having a small number of children for whom she is the consistent and familiar caregiver. Because children are apt to be at the day care center for periods of time that overlap shifts, a second group of providers needs to be assigned in the same way. Attachment-friendly day care also reduces turnover in staff, allowing children to go for many months without having to adjust to a new face (staff salaries are usually at the heart of the turnover problem). Attachment-friendly day care centers can also train their staff to help children transition at the beginning and the end of the day. They can be supportive of parents who have trouble saying goodbye and encourage children to use "blankies" or a favorite stuffed animal to comfort themselves. Day care centers that encourage attachment in these ways are likely to be among those accredited by the National Association for the Education of Young Children.

One additional point about attachment and day care has to do with the child's developmental status. Infants and toddlers who are in a period of intense concern about separation are not likely to adapt very readily to a new care arrangement. However attachment-friendly a day care center may be, it cannot easily overcome the anxiety about strangers and separation that are so characteristic of the end of a child's first year. Parents should be aware that a toddler's protests about day care are probably due to separation concerns; they are not likely to be a sign that he or she has been abused or molested at the day care center.

Marital and Family Separations and Divorce

Infants and toddlers can experience separations and loss as a result of their parents' occupations and relationships. The Iraq war, for example, has forced both mothers and fathers to separate from their young children, causing distress, anxiety, and possible changes in attachment. For many other infants and toddlers, marital disagreements, separations, and finally divorce may disrupt attachments to parents.

Such separations certainly have short-term effects on many young children between six months and two years of age. Far from being too young to notice, they are strongly affected because they are too young to understand anything that is happening. Anxiety and clinginess are common responses to family separations. Sleep problems, depression, and temporary behavior changes are also common in these cases, there being an obvious parallel to the child's reaction to the loss of a familiar person through death.

Paradoxically, infants and toddlers often show what appears to be increased distress when they have a visit with a parent who has left the household. For instance, an eighteen-month-old may have settled a bit (meaning he may be sleeping better and appearing less disturbed) in the month following his father's departure from the marital home. Then the father reappears for an afternoon visit, and the child responds with renewed sleeplessness, clinginess, and restlessness. The custodial parent may read this as a signal that visits had better be avoided, or may even believe that the visitor treated the child abusively—a belief that may culminate in a charge of sexual abuse so frequent today.

Handling this situation is a delicate task, especially in light of the emotional distress of both parents and its negative impact on their coping skills. It is difficult for people in this situation to see beyond the present discomfort to the long-term goal of maintaining a positive relationship between the child and each of the parents. Nevertheless, it is clear that most parent-child relationships have real value for the child's development, and that such relationships are preserved by staying the course through the early years of separation.

To maintain attachment to an often-absent parent, infants and toddlers need visits that are as lengthy and as frequent as it is possible to make them. These visits may—indeed, often will—be followed by increased expression of distress by the child, but the distress is caused by the absence, not by the visit. In these circumstances, tantrums or other displays of emotion should not be punished, but accepted as what they are, a reaction to family disruption.

Ideally, the conditions for visiting should be as familiar as possible to the child. Allowing the absent parent to come to the young child's home is the best approach, allowing the child to deal with the situation in an environment of maximal security and familiarity. However, such home visits may be agonizing for both parents, reminding them of matters they want to forget. If the child shows distress, it may be extremely hard for the custodial parent to stand back and let the other parent work to mend the relationship.

Of course, if other adults—grandparents, sisters, boyfriends—have come into the picture, home visits may involve disagreements or even violence.

For reasons such as these, visiting parents often want to take infants or toddlers onto the adults' own turf and deal with the relationship in a setting with some degree of privacy and leisure. The problem with this approach is that the parent may be frightened of unanticipated problems and may decide to avoid visiting rather than risk having the child screaming in distress. Young fathers may be particularly in need of guidance here.

Take, for example, a situation in which an eighteen-month-old girl has been sleeping in her mother's bed after a marital breakup; both mother and child have found the physical contact comforting in a time of anxiety and loss. Now the child is scheduled for an overnight visit with her father in his new apartment. He does not know what the child's sleeping arrangements have been and plans to put her in a crib in the guest bedroom. The little girl screams with fear at this. She tries to get out of the crib, calls repeatedly for her mother, and finally falls asleep exhausted at 4 a.m. This leaves the father to ponder whether he is an acceptable parent and whether his former wife has abused the child, spoiled her, or in some way turned her against him. This father may well begin to avoid visits even though, in truth, he loves his child and wants to maintain the attachment relationship. We should note, by the way, there is a double whammy of consequences at work for this father. Given our society's present concern with sexual abuse, if he were to take the sobbing child into his bed, he would risk serious accusations, perhaps followed by a declaration there could be no contact and even imprisonment.

The early months and years of a parent and child's visiting relationship may be difficult to handle for all concerned. Perhaps the real key to success is understanding the visit as a step toward a life-long attachment relationship, and, therefore, toward the child's development of a positive internal working model of social relationships. This means the visit needs to be focused on parent-child interaction that is developmentally appropriate for the child. Constructive visits will not usually include the parent's romantic partner; if the romantic relationship is a serious one, the partner can wait to form a connection with the child until parent and child are doing well together. Similarly, grandparents need to wait their turn, unless they are already very familiar people who have their own secure relationship with the child. It is especially inappropriate for a parent to arrange an adult social activity and to leave the child in someone else's care in the course of the visit. It need hardly be said that habitual lateness or failure to arrive for a planned visit is not a way to establish a secure attachment.

Does the short-term distress of the divorced child also cause long-term personality effects? This is a most difficult question to answer because the child who experiences parental separation will usually live for years in a household shaped by that separation. The circumstances may include financial uncertainty, the need to move to a new house, distress and depression for the custodial and perhaps the non-custodial parent, and possible new relationships with stepparents and stepsiblings, all in addition to the continuing difficulty of balancing a visiting relationship.

It is possible for parents and children to maintain strong, developmentally appropriate attachment relationships, in spite of early marital separation, and for children in these circumstances to continue on a trajectory of positive personality development. However, this desirable outcome requires care, energy, and a certain amount of good luck, and may occur a good deal less frequently than we would like.

SHAPING ATTACHMENT AND PERSONALITY: THE PRESCHOOL YEARS

As we discussed in an earlier chapter, preschool children show their emotional attachment in different ways from those typical of toddlers. Preschoolers often initiate separation themselves, and they can accept it well, just as they can be appropriately sociable with friendly strangers. In cases where they are disturbed about separation, preschoolers may show their feelings by squabbling with the mother when she returns.

The child who does this seems to be trying to re-establish important aspects of the relationship with the returned mother rather than just trying to be close to her, as a toddler would do. The internal working model of the relationship is in need of adjustment, and the child is seeking to readjust it.

The preschool child's existing attachment relationships seem related to other aspects of mood and behavior. Secure attachment in the past seems to accompany the preschooler's willingness to comply with rules and her trusting acceptance of adults as legitimate authorities. Such children also tend to cooperate with their peers and do not need a lot of control by adult caregivers. Less securely attached preschool children can be deliberately disobedient, and may behave provocatively in order to get the attention of an unmindful parent.[12] For example, in one family where the father was physically ill and weak, the preschool children responded to his withdrawal by acting up until he took off his belt to punish them.

Both serious loss and everyday stress have potential effects on children of preschool age. Separation from familiar people and adoption or foster care placement at this age can lead to long-term sadness and irritability, although these are less likely when the new family is effective in helping the child's adjustment. Even holidays, birthday parties, and vacation trips can trigger negative responses in preschoolers, presumably because of unfamiliar events and the withdrawal of the parent's normal attentiveness to the child. Using time-out discipline techniques may simply worsen these situations if the real problem is a sense of unnegotiated separation. Time-in, where the child stays quietly with the parent until calmer, may work better.

Marital separation and divorce are still difficult for preschoolers to deal with, although preschoolers have the advantage over toddlers of better language skills and a more realistic concept of time. Children under the age of four have much trouble with the long, hard task of letting go emotionally, and, even if they will continue to see a parent on visits, they must let go of their old picture of family life. Preschoolers are still immature, in emotional reactions and in thought processes, so they are likely to persist in mourning their loss rather than coming to terms with it. They have difficulty understanding that the loss is a permanent one, and they lack the clear awareness of their own feelings needed for resolution.[13]

When divorce occurs, it is hard for preschoolers to accept the reality of the parents' estrangement, especially if there are repeated trial separations followed by reconciliations, or if one parent often voices the belief that there will be a reunion. It is also quite difficult for the preschooler to disengage from the parents' conflict and go on with developmentally appropriate tasks; preschoolers are not yet adept at separating their own feelings from those of others. Preschoolers' reactions to divorce make it difficult for them to put their energy into their normal developmental processes.[14]

The preschooler's reaction to loss is of a different nature from that of the infant or toddler. Rather than the devastating withdrawal of security, the preschool child experiences loss as an occurrence strongly contrary to his need for joint planning and negotiation of separation, the foundation of his present sense of trust and confidence in a parent. Neither death nor divorce is negotiated with a child—and he or she may not even be informed about what is happening until presented with a *fait accompli*. In addition, parental reactions to either form of loss involve shock, anger, depression, and withdrawal, reducing their capacities for negotiating and buffering any aspect of the child's situation. Many non-custodial parents exacerbate the situation by continuing to treat the child as he or she was treated when the divorce occurred, rather than negotiating and fine-tuning the relationship.

THE SCHOOL-AGE CHILD: ATTACHMENT, EXPERIENCES, AND OUTCOMES

Teachers and Parents

By the time they reach school age, children have expectations about people's interactions with each other. These expectations usually have evolved from the early attachment relationship between parent and child, a relationship that has its parallels in other relationships, such as those between teacher and pupil, older and younger person, or a more powerful person and a weaker one. First-graders are well known for their tendency to call their teacher "Mommy" and address their mothers as "Mrs. Brown" by accident. This does not mean that schoolchildren of any age think the teacher is their mother, but it does show the child is considering the parallel aspects of the relationships. The child is thinking about how teacher-pupil relationships can be expected to work, given the extent to which they resemble parent-child relationships. The internal working model of relationships, developed in the early years, may thus help determine how the child acts toward teachers, who in turn will behave in ways that influence the child's attitudes toward school.

For good or ill, however, parents remain at the core of a school-age child's emotional life. How this works varies from family to family, class to class, and culture to culture, but it is generally true that parents are at its center, even for children who go to boarding school or who leave home for other reasons.

The nature of the child's attachment to the adult continues to shape his or her relationship. Of course, school-age children display much less attachment behavior toward their parents than they did when they were younger, and they may seem to take the parents for granted much of the time. When the parents go on a trip or the child goes to sleep-away camp, however, the child may show concern about the separation. For example, one ten-year-old went to Girl Scout camp for the first time, when her parents were leaving for a long-planned cruise; she cried every day, and finally disclosed her terror that there would be a shipwreck and her parents would drown.

When there is an apparent threat, the child tries to feel more secure by getting closer to the parent, talking to them on the phone, or even just daydreaming about a reunion. Under these circumstances, it becomes harder for the child to do schoolwork or even play constructively. It does not matter whether the parent is an unpleasant, unreliable, or even abusive person; the child still turns to him or her when feeling threatened.[15] The desire for contact with the parent can be set off by threats other than separation, too: being bullied on the playground, getting sick at school, or being punished in the classroom. The child's internal working model still includes the idea that relief from anxiety can be obtained through contact with the parent.

School-age children regularly experience separations from teachers who have become familiar, either when the teacher leaves the school or when the child passes to a new grade level. Because American families tend to be geographically mobile, many children experience separation from teachers, schools, and classmates as the family moves away. The practice of having the child's home address determine which school is attended is another common source of separation experiences, for even a move to a new house may put the child in a new school district. Most difficult for the school-age child is the family disruption following divorce. It often means a new house and a new school, the transition coming at a time when the child is least able to tolerate it.

Just as the school-age child is continuing to construct new mental categories and to learn new problem-solving skills, he or she is also constructing new ways of thinking and acting toward parents and similar adults. In the course of doing so, school-age children move toward behaviors and emotions that allow some autonomy, as well as gratifying the wish to cooperate and be on good terms with the parent. A school-age child may comply with a parent's requests incompletely, but just enough so the parent is not actively angry or punitive. (For example, the child puts her clean clothes in the dresser, but leaves one sock hanging out or in the laundry basket.) Although such behavior is annoying to parents, its goal is not actually to irritate them, but to build toward a future relationship in which the child achieves greater independence and the parent relinquishes responsibility and authority. Whether the parent is relaxed and tolerant, or intrusive and authoritarian, about these matters will help shape the child's understanding of later social relationships.

Sibling Relationships

As children get older, their relationships with siblings also add to the internal working model of relationships, which is becoming more complicated. Attitudes and relationships of school-age children with siblings are determined by complex interactions among many factors. Power differences are almost always present (even between twins) because there are differences in age, specific skills, or relationships with parents. In some families or cultures, the child belonging to the more favored sex has power in spite of youth or small size. The internal working models of sibling relationships have not been studied much, but they probably have considerable influence over other intimate relationships in later life. Especially when children are near in age, sibling relationships seem to share the emotionality of parent-child attachment relationships with an even greater display of anger and frustration at times.

Although school-age children are able to do some negotiating in their relationships with siblings and peers, they still need parents to provide some scaffolding, or support, allowing the children to bring their social skills to bear on emotional conflicts with other children. Because neither child in the relationship is a very mature negotiator, they cannot do as well together as each could do with an adult. Conflicts and rivalry between siblings can be terribly provoking to parents, but it is likely that with parental help, children can use these conflicts to understand more about social interactions.

Models of Relationships with Babies

The relationships of school-age children with infant siblings are especially interesting for two reasons. First, they let us focus on the early stages of an individual's development of parenting skills, and second, they let us focus on the older child's own social abilities, there being a relatively small contribution from the baby.

Some, but not all, school-age children show behaviors indicating their emotional involvement with a baby brother or sister, and they may even have been fascinated during the mother's pregnancy. Older siblings may get close to the baby and work to get eye contact. They notice cues given by the baby's behavior, such as pushing a bottle away, and they speak for the baby as adults do, stating what they think are the infant's feelings and wishes. The older child may express pleasure in the baby and practice rhythmic turn-taking and initiation of communication.[16]

Some older siblings, of course, do not do any of these things. They may appear oblivious or actively hostile toward an infant sibling in the early months. Affectionate interest in the baby seems to result from some family characteristics.[17] The older child has to be interested in the baby to begin with—an older child who is unduly stressed by the birth may not feel interest, and, of course, some babies are more responsive and interesting than others. The older child also needs to have chances to hold and interact with the baby without being directed by the parents, and not all parents feel comfortable with this. The development of a mutual relationship between older child and infant is also more likely if the parents have modeled this tie in their sensitivity and responsiveness to the older child. If the parents have included the older child in planning and taking responsibility for the baby (feeding, for example), but have not gone beyond the child's interest level, the relationship is encouraged. Finally, it can be helpful if the parents remark on the way the baby is responding ("I'm not sure he likes that.") rather than telling the older child what to do. There is little research showing whether this family activity helps the older child parent when he has grown up and had his own family, but the experience would seem to be an effective way of elaborating the internal working model of relationships to include infant care.

Divorce and Death during the School Years

Just as responses to separation told us about infants' emotional attachment, family transitions like death and divorce may reveal important aspects of school-age children's emotional development. Loss of a parent through death or divorce creates a painful and stressful transition period, which has a real impact on children's mood, school performance, and general adjustment. Loss of a grandparent can have a similar impact, but the less close the relationship, the less the child will be affected. In the case of Delimar Cuevas, her abrupt separation from the woman she had thought was her mother was no doubt exactly parallel to the death of a parent.

The death of a family member is more possible for school-age children to understand than it is for preschoolers. Nevertheless, the process of grieving for a deceased parent and returning to reorganized emotion is a matter of at least a year. During the mourning period, children are likely to cry more than usual and to have trouble concentrating in school. Some also have difficulty sleeping. While these problems decrease by the end of a year, bereaved children, at that point, are more likely than others to have some health problems.[18] Many children also dream and think about the parent, often treasuring objects that belonged to the parent.

Though it has become a normative, statistically common, and socially acceptable experience for school-age children in the United States, divorce is nevertheless a family transition with major impact. Remarriage solves some practical and financial problems for families, but the emotional adjustment of children is about the same in divorced, single-parent, and divorced, remarried families; in both cases there are more difficulties than in non-divorced families.[19]

Both death and divorce trigger the need for change in the child's internal working model of social relationships. It may actually be more difficult for children to adjust to divorce than to the death of a parent. In both situations, the internal working model must alter to take in the fact that a person to whom the child has been attached has simply gone away, but this does not necessarily mean the adult did not love the child. The model has contained some assumptions about negotiation and about the child's skills in maintaining relationships, and now the child knows there are at least some situations where these assumptions do not work. Human death becomes more familiar to the child at this age, and it is possible for her to understand that death is beyond human control. When divorce occurs, however, there are some cognitive and emotional tasks forced upon the child; these tasks are difficult and they are also highly relevant to the elaboration of the internal working model.

The emotional tasks of adjusting to divorce take years, and they may not even be possible until adolescence.[20] First, the child must simply accept the fact that the parents' separation is real, not a joke or a mistake. Second, the child needs to disengage from the parents' conflict and learn to ignore it; the school-age child is better at this than the preschooler. School-age children have more trouble if *parentalized* by a custodial parent who turns to the child for companionship and comfort. If the child does not disengage, though, she will become more and more lonely for her peers and have more difficulty in school, and the increasing stress will be problematic. The internal working model will go through some confusing and inappropriate alterations, if the child becomes the parent's caregiver, reversing the normal parent-child roles.

The child's third emotional task, in terms of adjusting to divorce, is *resolution* of the loss—the act of giving up the wish for the lost family life, and moving toward the future rather than longing for the past. This entails a sense of powerlessness and humiliation in the face of the immovable obstacles presented by the parents, who are both beloved and apparently indifferent to the child's feelings. Again, the internal working model of social relationships must take in the complexity of the divorced family's relationships. The same is true for a fourth task, the resolution of anger toward the parents and the self-blame the child may experience, if he believes he has been the cause of the divorce in some fashion. And, as a final step in dealing with divorce, the child needs to accept the situation as permanent. There is no going back, even though only about 25 percent of divorced parents achieve a new, cooperative, co-parenting relationship with each other in a way that a child can accept as an adequate permanent arrangement.[21] These steps need to become part of the child's internal working model; otherwise, in the child's later view of relationships there will be a sense that there can be no positive relationships in the future, that anger and blame are major parts of important relationships, and that there can be no stability or continuity in intimate relationships.

ADOLESCENCE: EXPERIENCES
SHAPE THE INTERNAL WORKING MODEL

Most adolescents and their parents have to work out ways of negotiating separation after they have long shared a close relationship that evolved from early attachment ties. Usually parents have developed some family patterns that worked when their children were younger. Now, the dramatic changes of physical maturation make some of the old patterns ineffective or even destructive. Parents have to do a great deal of fine-tuning to maintain the relationship while the teenager is changing so rapidly. The adolescent, too, has to alter his or her internal working model of relationships, no longer can a teenager think of the emotional connection with the parents as a younger child does.

The way a family works together to change relationships depends on their history together, and as well, on their present circumstances. For example, in one study, girls who saw their mothers as affectionate and accepting were more capable of expressing their emotions than girls with less accepting mothers.[22] The girls who could explain their feelings well used their skill to help others to understand them. Thus, they could contribute in a mature way to the reworking of family relationships, as well as using the ability for a realistic remodeling of their internal working models.

We discussed earlier how important it is for preschoolers and parents to participate in negotiation of separation. At that point in development, of course, it is the parents who have reason to want to separate; the children are the ones who generally like the parents near. During adolescence, when negotiation of separation comes to the fore again, it is the teenager who wants to move toward independence, while most parents cherish the child's last years spent in the heart of the family. Ideally, negotiation can produce a gradual separation; unfortunately some parents demand that the adolescent remain a child to the point where he or she seizes independence prematurely. In each situation, there is a different impact on the teenager's internal working model of social relationships. A preferable model would include the idea that people are able to work together, trusting in a mutually agreeable outcome. A less preferable view is that the support and care of others comes only with complete compliance and dependence. Just as parents of toddlers tend to use the time-out method of discipline—raising more separation concerns—it is common for parents of teenagers to use grounding, which increases the adolescent's anxiety about independence.

Negotiation of rules with adolescents can be a very effective parenting technique. However, it requires time, energy, patience, and acceptance of the idea that rules should change as a teenager matures. Parents who negotiate also need to admit their side of the negotiation usually involves their own needs, rather than some absolute standard of behavior. This admission may be humiliating for some parents, who may feel as if they have revealed a personal secret to the adolescent. For example, a recently divorced mother may condemn a teenager's dating as disgraceful, rather than disclose her anxiety about her own sexuality.

Negotiation of separation may be most difficult when the family history has positioned the teenager as a *hurried child*.[23] This term has been applied to a child who has become parentalized into a parent's friend and confidante following divorce. A divorced mother, for example, may tell her job and relationship troubles to a preteen child, asking the child's opinion and advice. The child may experience adult-like responsibility for household tasks and adult-like authority for decision-making about clothing, companions, bedtime, and so on. When the hurried child arrives at adolescence, however, the parent becomes frightened by the autonomy the child has been exercising. The possible dangers to an inexperienced adolescent become

apparent to the adult, who knows how other people may interpret sophisticated clothing on a thirteen-year-old girl or the freely chosen video of a
thirteen-year-old boy. The parent tries to reduce the teenager's power below what it used to be, although the teenager knows that the teen years are
supposed to be a time of increased independence. Negotiation of rules will
not be possible for this family unless parent and child can explore the mis-
takes of the past, which will probably require the help of counseling.

The Adolescent Parent

Adolescent parenthood is often seen as a problem in industrialized countries. Teenage mothers are generally unmarried, uneducated, and unem-
ployed, and their lives do not give adequate support for a baby's development.
Although even schoolchildren may have begun to make a place for babies in
their internal working models of social relationships, most adolescents have
not yet achieved a model that takes infants' vulnerability into account. One
young mother, for example, said her two-week-old son was "just like his
father" and would hurt women. She complained that the baby had scratched
her face while waving his hands and declared he "knew it hurt" because she
had said "ouch." Another shouted at her baby to stop making "disrespect-
ful" noises and slapped him when he persisted with the sound. The adolescent parent's immature internal working model can cause an insensitive,
unresponsive approach that fails to acknowledge how babies differ from
adults. The parent's immaturity thus fosters poor attachment in the baby.

ADULTHOOD: THE EFFECTS OF PAST EXPERIENCE

By the time adulthood is reached, every individual has had a wide experience of events related to attachment and has constructed the pattern of
thoughts, emotions, and behaviors that we call the internal working model
of social relationships. Although it is possible that events during adulthood—
like divorce or the death of a child—could influence a man's or a woman's
view of emotional ties, most studies in this area have concentrated on memories of the past.

An obvious question has to do with the effects of past attachment experiences on marriage. Certainly, adults whose early lives featured neglect,
abuse, and abandonment would seem unlikely to trust or cooperate with
anyone, including their spouses. However, the importance of attachment
issues in marriage may be overwhelmed by other factors, such as cultural
and religious variables, economic considerations, childrearing needs, and so
on. It may be easier to see the effects of past attachment experiences on
other social relationships, and particularly on the relationship of the adult
with his or her own children.

Pregnant women usually have a mental image or description of the future nature of their yet-unborn babies. Because the mother cannot really know much about the individual baby, it is possible that her ideas are shaped largely by her own past attachment history and her current internal working model of social relationships. In one recent study of pregnant mothers' beliefs about their babies, the women's descriptions of their babies were linked with the babies' actual attachment behavior at one year of age.[24] Mothers whose descriptions were complicated, rich with detail, and coherent, and who expressed sensitivity toward the baby and a sense of competence, were likely to have babies who showed secure attachments at twelve months. These mothers were also likely to have gratifying memories of their own childhood attachment experiences.

Though interesting, this study was not able to show exactly how the mothers' beliefs and memories had effects on the babies' development of secure attachment. (Certainly, there was no implication that the infants picked up their mothers' prenatal thoughts.) The mothers' memories and expectations somehow influenced their caregiving, and the caregiving pattern in some way affected the babies' emotional development, culminating in secure attachment. It was also true that some other factors in the mothers' lives appeared to play a role here. It seems, however, that the mothers' internal working models of social relations, derived from their own childhood experiences, were an important factor in shaping that most adult relationship, parenting.

SUMMARY AND CONCLUSION

Differences in early attachment experiences apparently help to shape personality differences, especially those that have to do with social and emotional relationships. Rather than a direct connection between infant experiences and adult personality, however, we see a long series of gradual steps toward development of the adult internal working model of social relationships. These steps involve experiences with other people, but they also depend on maturation of the individual's intellectual and emotional abilities. Six-year-old Delimar Cuevas, whom we met at the beginning of this chapter, would have responded very differently to her change of homes than a twelve-month-old. Many children and adolescents experience family situations that can distort the development of ideas about social relationships, but they can benefit from positive guidance by adults who are aware of the attachment issues characteristic of particular age groups. By adulthood, internal working models of social relationships should be complex and many-faceted, allowing for appropriate social and emotional relationships and behaviors with a variety of people, including infants.

Attachment, Mental Health, and Psychotherapy: Emotional Ties and Emotional Disturbance

Does attachment have any connection to serious mental illness? Many people have a vague idea that it does, but they are not very clear on the details. One child care provider at a training conference questioned a speaker who had alluded to attachment: "Isn't there a disease about that? Stranger anxiety or something?" Another member of the audience, a nurse, spoke of a fifteen-month-old who was equally friendly to all adults: "I just thought he was really nice and well-adjusted." Talking about older children, people may describe a child as too clingy or demanding or as a Mommy's boy. There may be general comments about adults, concerning attachment issues or attachment problems.

This chapter will focus on connections between attachment and mental health, focusing on the part attachment concepts play in psychotherapy and the use of psychotherapy for attachment problems. Though there are many unanswered questions in this area, the attachment concept gives us a useful approach to the understanding of mental health.

ATTACHMENT AND MENTAL HEALTH

A repetitive theme in this book is that attachment plays out differently at different ages. An infant or toddler shows characteristic attachment behaviors, and seems to have characteristic attachment emotions and expectations about other people. Preschoolers, school-age children, and adults have age-appropriate characteristics related to their attachment history. Individuals in these different age groups also have their own forms of mental illness, which are displayed in age-typical ways.

What Is Mental Illness?

The term mental illness refers to unusual and disturbed emotions, thoughts, and beliefs, generally troubling the rest of us, as well as the afflicted individual. When these factors are only mild or intermittent, they may interfere with the person's education, work, friendships, and love relationships, causing loneliness and other difficulties. At a more severe level, mental illness can make the individual dangerous to himself or to other people.

For over a century, one focus of those who study mental illness has been to construct diagnostic categories, or descriptions, of types of mental illness. This task was formalized in the *Diagnostic and Statistical Manual* of the American Psychiatric Association (DSM), a volume that has gone through a number of revisions.[1] The DSM takes into account not only the degree of disturbance of a behavior but also its social acceptability. (For example, homosexuality was, at one time, a category of mental illness in DSM, but as social attitudes changed in recent years, the category was removed.) Revised editions of the DSM discuss and list criteria for different diagnoses. These reports are generated by working committees that must make sure empirical evidence exists before adding a new category to the manual. From a practical point of view, DSM provides diagnostic codes that are used by private and public health insurers.

Mental Illness, Experience, and Genetic Factors

To begin this discussion of mental illness, we should remember there have been many serious changes in thinking on this subject. In mid-twentieth century, mental illnesses were commonly believed to have been caused by the patient's past experiences. A patient's experiences as a child were carefully scrutinized as possible causes of emotional disturbance, and the mother's role was considered to be especially relevant, even perhaps blame-worthy. Autism, for example, was attributed to the harm done by an overly intellectual, so-called "refrigerator mother" who could not give her child warmth and love. Schizophrenia was thought to result from early experience with contradictory, double bind communications, in which the child could not safely discover exactly what an emotional message meant.

This stress on experience as the major cause of mental illness is far less common today. Serious explanations of mental illness generally assume an important genetic component, either one directly causing the emotional disturbance, or one that makes the individual unusually vulnerable to certain harmful experiences. Because of this emphasis on genetic factors, it is unlikely that modern psychologists or psychiatrists would count attachment experiences, in and of themselves, as the cause of serious disturbance. However, this does not rule out the possibility that attachment experiences work with other factors to cause mental illness.

Infant Mental Health

The term infant mental health may sound unfamiliar or even a bit bizarre. Can there be crazy babies? Can tiny children in some way parallel the adult schizophrenic who hears voices, or the violent, paranoid patient? No, of course not—and, in fact, infant mental health generally refers to good physical, cognitive, and emotional development. These tend to go together in infants, rather than dividing into clearly separated categories as they do in older people.

Infants (and this term properly includes children up to about three years of age) can show early symptoms of mental illness, however. A *pervasive developmental disorder*, such as autism, may begin to affect the child very early in life, even at birth. These disorders, which have genetic factors as their primary cause, interfere with communication and therefore, with social relationships.

Does attachment play a role in disorders of infant mental health? This is a very difficult question to answer because many causes are linked with many outcomes in early development. Sensitive, responsive parents are likely to encourage attachment in a child, at the same time that they foster good physical health, nutrition, growth, and language development. The child who shows good attachment development is likely to be better off in every way, not because he or she is attached, but because the experiences that improve attachment also improve everything else. Factors like maternal depression create insensitivity and unresponsiveness, which in turn interfere with the development of attachment and of other behaviors and abilities.

Children, who spend their lives in brutally neglectful foreign institutions, like the Romanian children studied by Sir Michael Rutter,[2] have little or no opportunity to form emotional attachments. But this is not a complete explanation of their developmental problems. They are also poorly nourished, receive little health care, get little exercise (or may actually be physically restrained), and experience little in the way of speech or other communication. They may even have been placed in the institution because of existing physical or mental problems. It would be a great mistake to assume that attachment is the single, causative factor in these unfortunate children's problems.

An important consideration for infant mental health is the fact that the attachment behaviors and feelings that would indicate emotional disturbance in an adult may be quite normal and healthy in a child. The child care provider's question about stranger anxiety being a disease shows how infant behavior may look when we mistakenly use an adult context. Anxiety about unfamiliar people and places is a normal part of infant development, as is the need for a secure-base person to make exploration possible. These anxieties should almost never be considered indications of infant emotional disturbance. On the contrary, as we will see later, it is the absence of anxiety that might be an indication of mental illness.

Mental Health after Infancy

Pervasive developmental disorders, such as autism, are usually diagnosed by the end of the infant period; the parents are alerted to the problem because the child fails to talk. During the preschool and early school years, the problem most likely to emerge is that of impulsive, aggressive behavior, which can verge on conduct disorder. *Oppositional and Defiant Disorder* (ODD) is one syndrome characterized by this kind of behavior. During the school years, some children are diagnosed with depression or with *bipolar disorder*. Both ODD and bipolar disorder involve emotional disturbances that impact social relationships and thus have a connection with attachment (although they are probably not directly caused by attachment experiences).

In the late teens and early twenties, some individuals' thinking, emotions, and behavior become so disturbed that a diagnosis of schizophrenia is made. Schizophrenics' social relationships are severely distorted; these problems are thought to be largely determined by biological factors and not by previous attachment experiences.

DO ATTACHMENT EXPERIENCES CAUSE MENTAL ILLNESS?

Attachment is a robust process, and most children make a clear emotional attachment to familiar caregivers. For a sizeable minority of the world's children, however, attachment-related experiences do not follow a smooth path. In industrialized countries, children may have caregivers who are depressed or physically ill and who cannot provide the sensitive, responsive care that is ideal. Domestic violence, alcohol, or drug use may lead to a child being placed in foster care or adopted by a new, unfamiliar caregiver. In the developing countries, the death of a mother from AIDS, or in civil or other warfare, may leave a child who receives a minimum of care from virtual strangers. Do these experiences cause actual mental illness? It is possible that a resulting *disorganized attachment* can be serious enough to be considered a mental illness, but the answer to this question is not simple.

Disorganized Attachment Status

In a previous chapter, we looked at the Strange Situation and found that a small proportion of toddlers responded in an unusual way to their parents' departure and return. These children were classified as having a Disorganized/Disoriented type of attachment, characterized by strange, contradictory behaviors and emotional expressiveness.

One study of Disorganized/Disoriented toddlers gave a detailed description of the children's unusual behavior. Some of these children showed a sequence of contradictory behaviors, moving rapidly from one type of emotion to another. Some children moved suddenly from what appeared to be strong emotion to a much less emotional state. For instance, "[i]mmediately following proximity seeking and a bright, full greeting with raised arms, the infant moves to the wall or into the center of the room and stills or freezes with a 'dazed' expression." For other children, the sudden change was from calm to anger, as in a case where the "[i]nfant [was] calm and undistressed during both separations from the parent, but becomes extremely focused upon the parent, showing highly distressed and/or angry behavior immediately upon reunion." Other Disorganized/Disoriented toddlers managed to express simultaneously their desires to be near the parent and to stay away. An example would be children for whom "[m]ovements of approach are repeatedly accompanied by movements of avoidance such as the following: (a) infant approaches with head sharply averted; (b) infant approaches by backing toward parent; (c) infant reaches arms up for parent with head sharply averted or with head down."[3]

Another characteristic of Disorganized/Disoriented toddlers is their use of undirected or incomplete movements. The authors described situations where the child moves her hand toward the parent, then stops and pulls it away without touching. There are also very "slow or limp movements of approach to [the] parent, as though the infant is resisting the movements even while making them ('underwater' approach movements)."[4] These underwater movements, which are less obvious than freezing, are defined as "the holding of movements, gestures, or positions in a posture that involves active resistance to gravity,"[5] such as standing with the arms held out waist-high. These odd movements may be accompanied by a "dazed or trance-like facial expression ... [a] tense, smooth closing of the lids or ... [a] lifeless stare."[6]

The researchers also saw these children acting frightened of the parent, and acting confused when reunited with the parent. For example, the children sometimes looked frightened when picked up by their parents, or a child would be seen "flinging hands about, over, or in front of face, or over mouth, with fearful expression."[7] These toddlers sometimes turned suddenly and approached the stranger (Strange Situation) with their arms raised. This happened when the parent reentered the room after the standard separation. As a final indicator of confusion, the children would sometimes fall to the floor when they approached the parent or the parent reached toward them.

Do Parents Influence Disorganized Attachment Behavior? Do these descriptions of odd behavior mean that inside these children there is a strange set of ideas and feelings about people—a bizarre internal working model of social relations? That is one of the possibilities, but it must be remembered that any social interaction takes place between two people. Both parent and child had roles to play in the Strange Situation, and further research showed that the parents of these children were not behaving normally either. Parents of Disorganized/Disoriented toddlers may be frightening to their children, and they may be frightened themselves.[8]

For example, the parents showed unusual voice patterns in talking to their children. They used a "breathy, extended, falling intonation" that sounded "ominous" or "haunted," especially when greeting or touching the child.[9] The parents also used voices that dropped suddenly to a deep pitch, which was described as "startling, especially when the speaker is a woman whose pitch and intonation suddenly seem to belong to a male."[10]

The parents of Disorganized/Disoriented children in this study also made strange and unusual remarks to the toddlers. Sometimes their comments suggested that real harm could come as a result of the child's actions. One said, "You'll kill that little [stuffed] bear if you do that!" Another responded to the toddler pushing a toy car across the floor, "Gonna have an accident! Everybody's gonna get killed!"[11] The parents also would suddenly begin "chase" games, using the common "I'm gonna get you" pattern, but with a frightening voice and movement style. Sometimes they showed directly that they were afraid of the infant; one backed "away from the infant while directing the infant not to follow in a stammering, apprehensive voice— 'Don't follow, d-don't.'"[12]

Why would parents or toddlers behave in these very unusual ways? The authors of the descriptions above felt there were several possible reasons. Among them was the chance that there might be neurological problems in some Disorganized/Disoriented toddlers. More importantly, however, they felt these parents had had traumatic experiences, which were attachment-related—for example, the death of one of their own parents.

Why would the loss of a beloved person make the mother's behavior so strange and confusing to her own child? For one thing, the child may remind the mother of her own, early emotional ties and losses. She may then actually be frightened when she looks at the child, and she may want to get away from, what is in her mind, a frightening situation. The child looks at the mother's face and then looks around, trying to figure out what is so frightening to her—he sees that he must be a source of her fear. This is in itself disturbing to the child, but in addition, the mother cannot offer effective comfort, because her fear is increased when she is close to the child. The child has frequent experiences of alarm, but, in the end, he must cope with them alone, even though his impulse is to rush to the mother for security.

Is Disorganized/Disoriented Attachment a Mental Illness? The Disorganized/Disoriented classification does not seem to match our definition of a mental illness (although it is unusual behavior and does involve emotional disturbance in the form of frightened behavior). It does not involve problems of development as serious as some seen in twelve-month-olds, such as autism. The Disorganized/Disoriented child still manages to communicate with others, to develop language, and to play. If the child has attachment relationships other than the one with the mother, they may be more normal, as long as the behavior of the other adults is more normal than the mother's.

Children with Disorganized/Disoriented attachment do have the potential to develop later disturbances of social interactions, both with peers and adults, especially if they have few opportunities for early interactions that are emotionally healthy. No one would deem this status a sign of good mental health or positive future development. However, as so often happens, it is hard to know whether later problems result directly from the early attachment status itself, from the fact that these children often have been maltreated, or from the experience of having to live with a traumatized and anxious parent.

Reactive Attachment Disorder and Alternative Diagnoses

Historically, one of the earliest concerns about attachment and mental illness dates back to John Bowlby's reports about the forty delinquent boys whose past attachment experiences he studied. Bowlby and others initially felt that children who failed to form attachments had a strong potential for criminal behavior. However, after further work, Bowlby and his colleagues then reported they did not think that children who have been institutionalized or emotionally deprived would commonly develop psychopathic characters (a conscienceless personality, possibly associated with attacks on others who seem to be interfering with the person's wishes).[13]

Reactive Attachment Disorder: The DSM Category. The 1994 edition of the *Diagnostic and Statistical Manual* of the American Psychiatric Association (DSM-IV) included a category called *Reactive Attachment Disorder*. This disorder, often

abbreviated to RAD, was considered to be a result of inappropriate early social experiences. DSM categories present a set of criteria to help clinicians
make a diagnostic decision, and in this case the criteria included both behavior
symptoms and the child's past history. Here are the diagnostic criteria for diagnostic category 313.89, Reactive Attachment Disorder of Infancy or Early
Childhood.[14]

A. Markedly disturbed and developmentally inappropriate social related-
   ness in most contexts, as evidenced by either (1) or (2):
   1. Persistent failure to initiate or respond in a developmentally appro-
      priate fashion to most social interactions, as manifest by excessively
      inhibited, hypervigilant, or highly ambivalent and contradictory re-
      sponses (e.g., the child may respond to caregivers with a mixture of
      approach, avoidance, and resistance to comforting, or may exhibit
      frozen watchfulness).
   2. Diffuse attachments as manifest by indiscriminate sociability with
      marked inability to exhibit appropriate selective attachments (e.g.,
      excessive familiarity with relative strangers or lack of selectivity in
      choice of attachment figures).
B. The disturbance in Criterion A is not accounted for solely by developmental delay ... and does not meet criteria for a Pervasive Developmental
   Disorder.
C. Pathogenic care as evidenced by at least one of the following:
   1. Persistent disregard of the child's basic emotional needs for comfort,
      stimulation, and affection.
   2. Persistent disregard of the child's basic physical needs.
   3. Repeated changes of primary caregiver that prevent formation of
      stable attachments (e.g., frequent changes in foster care).
D. There is a presumption that the care in Criterion C is responsible for
   the disturbed behavior in Criterion A (e.g., the disturbances in Criterion
   A began following the pathogenic care in Criterion C).

Reactive Attachment Disorder is referred to as the *Inhibited Type*, if the
child shows more of Criterion A1, and the *Disinhibited Type*, if more of
Criterion A2.

The RAD diagnosis continues to be included in DSM and has been used
in courtrooms and other public discussions. However, the category has
been severely criticized, and alternative suggestions have been, and continue to be, made. RAD has been described as "not a particularly clear or
coherent diagnostic entity."[15] The same authors note that not all children
who receive poor care develop symptoms of RAD, and some develop such
symptoms even though their care has been good.

The DSM criteria for RAD do not make it clear how serious the symptoms are, although many of them seem related to the disturbed behavior categorized as Disorganized/Disoriented attachment. It is hard to know whether excessive familiarity means conversing eagerly with, or climbing into the lap, of a friendly stranger. And how unfamiliar is a relative stranger—is it the child's mother's friend who comes unexpectedly to pick him up at the day care center, a new child care provider, or the mailman?

The RAD criteria also assume knowledge of the child's early social experiences, which may be difficult or impossible to know accurately. The child in question may have been abandoned, without any identifying information, or, equally problematically, the story told by a noncustodial parent or child care provider might be seriously biased.

Finally, the RAD criteria are confusing because they do not define developmentally appropriate behaviors, consider cross-cultural issues, or deal with the effects of context, such as the behavior of the unfamiliar person or characteristics of the environment. Because the criteria require more than a brief observation of the child's behavior, decisions may be subject to distorted reports by adult caregivers. It is possible that these factors will produce a diagnosis of RAD when some other diagnostic category would be more appropriate.

According to one commentator, empirical studies of Reactive Attachment Disorder are quite rare, and there have been difficulties with the definition of the syndrome.[16] The DSM description is unusual in that it includes the background causes and attachment history of the child, as well as his present symptoms. Most DSM categories focus on criteria related to the individual's present situation.

ICD-10. Attachment disorders are also listed in the International Classification of Diseases and Related Health Problems, commonly called ICD-10.[17] ICD-10 is the European version of DSM. ICD-10 lists two separate disorders: Reactive Attachment Disorder of Childhood and Disinhibited Attachment Disorder of Childhood, and these are parallel to the two types of syndrome combined in DSM. One difference between the classifications is that ICD-10 does not include the background and history as criteria for the disorders.

Alternative Ideas: Five Types of Attachment Disorders. The well-known child psychiatrist Charles Zeanah and his colleagues have suggested five possible outcomes of poor early attachment experiences.[18] These categories can be used with children from age one to four or five. The criteria are based on behavior alone, with no attempt to depend on the child's early life history. In addition, the category can be assigned even if the child shows the behavior with only one adult caregiver—an important point, because as Zeanah has shown, children can have very different relationships and behaviors with different familiar adults, as well as with strangers.

Zeanah's list of possible attachment disorders begins with Type I: *Nonattached Attachment Disorder*. In this condition, the child develops no preference for a familiar person and appears detached and uninterested in people because he or she has had no opportunity to form attachments. As we have seen elsewhere in this book, infants do not need a great deal of help forming an attachment; they do need the chance to experience the responsiveness of a small number of attentive people and to have time to become familiar with them. Children with a Type I problem may have been in institutions or had many changes of caregiver, and perhaps were also badly neglected. They are able to form attachments but have not had the chance. Their internal working models of social relations do not link comfort or security with the nearness of familiar people.

Boarder babies, who are sometimes cared for in hospitals for months, their mothers having abandoned them, typically have lives that can lead to a Type I disorder. They spend a good deal of time alone, with staff members occasionally popping in, getting the baby's attention, and leaving again. With this kind of social experience, the baby develops a quick, superficial social reaction; he or she does not persist in interactions or seem upset when the interactions stop abruptly. (Hospitals sometimes post notices in these babies' rooms, requesting people to come in for fifteen minutes or not at all.)

Zeanah and his colleague Alicia Lieberman gave a case description of a child who fit the Type I category. He was twenty months old at the time and had been with the same foster family for nine months. He was aggressive and he bit himself and others, but he would stay for hours in the place where he was put down. He did not reach for toys, preferring to stare at spinning objects—often considered a symptom of autism. When moved to a new living situation where he was favored, nurtured, and given much attention, however, he improved greatly and began to show a preference for one of the staff members. Apparently he had needed the much-increased, responsive and interested interaction.

Zeanah and his colleagues have also proposed the diagnostic category Type II: *Indiscriminate Attachment Disorder*, which resembles the disinhibited type of Reactive Attachment Disorder described in DSM-IV. This group of children will go to anyone, are overly friendly, and do not show the usual secure base behavior, or run to a preferred caregiver when frightened. Any adult seems to be equally comforting. (We should note the potential dangers here, as these children are easily approached by molesters.) Children who show these behaviors are likely to have been in institutions early in life, but by no means do all institutionalized children fall into this group.

Zeanah has suggested that children in Type II may not simply be indiscriminately friendly; they may combine that characteristic with accident proneness and excessive risk-taking. Zeanah described one thirty-four-month-old, risk-taking child, who was living with his mother and who was hard to manage because of tantrums, aggressiveness, and other behaviors, like running into the street. Put into the hospital for assessment, this little boy did not behave recklessly. He played quietly and was unusual only in his tendency to ask total strangers for hugs and kisses. When his mother visited, however, he again took risks and went out of control. The risk-taking behavior was part of the disturbed relationship with the mother, not a characteristic of the child.

Zeanah's proposed Type III: *Inhibited Attachment Disorder* involves a very different kind of behavior than described above. These children want to stay near their familiar attachment figures, even at times when they might be expected to play and explore.

Zeanah described two subcategories of a Type III disturbance. In the *Excessive Clinging* category, the child shows an extreme and continuing desire to stay near the caregiver (beyond the usual initial shyness that wears off with time), as well as a tendency to show an anxious mood when around unfamiliar people. One little girl described by Zeanah had apparently developed this behavior pattern as a result of her mother's ongoing fears about the child's congenital heart ailment. The mother had a very different relationship with another daughter.

A second Type II subcategory is *Compulsive Compliance*, in which the child obeys the caregiver immediately, a pattern he or she has developed in order to avoid physical abuse. The caregiver may practice serious maltreatment or simply use excessive punishment. The symptoms of this disorder are most obvious when the child is with the caregiver; the child is likely to be subdued, wary, and unspontaneous. (Although normal caregivers do try to establish some habits of quick obedience for safety reasons—"Hot! Don't touch!"—an excessive amount of this interferes with negotiation, which is a healthy part of the developing internal working model of social relations.)

Zeanah described one little boy named George, as he played in the foster home and was then taken to visit his natural mother. Thirty months old, George had been with the foster family for ten months. In the foster home, he played freely and loudly and was somewhat resistant to the foster mother. When a caseworker appeared to take him on a visit, "George screamed in a terrified manner and attempted to hide," having to be carried bodily to the car, where he cried throughout the trip. He stopped crying at the mother's door.

> He looked soberly at his mother when she opened the door, but he did not greet her.... [He] walked in silently and stood in her living room. The natural mother told George to sit down, and he did so immediately.... George did not move from where he sat down initially unless his mother directed him otherwise.... He watched her constantly, maintaining a vigilant and anxious expression.... He cringed slightly when she spoke to him, but he always complied immediately with her directives.[19]

While this was going on, George's brother, who was visiting from another foster home, ran around and vocalized.

The difficulty George was having clearly emerged from the relationship he had with his mother—he did not behave this way with other adults— nor had his mother developed the same relationship with the other child.

Type IV: *Aggressive Attachment Disorder* is another possible outcome of poor attachment experiences proposed by Zeanah. This category involves a persistent, pervasive level of anger and aggressive behavior toward the parent, but can also include symptoms of anxiety, such as sleep disturbance. The child may hurt himself (by head-banging, for example), may have lengthy tantrums, and may hit, bite, or shout, "I hate you!" These children have often been involved in, or seen, domestic violence. They may have received inconsistent care and unpredictable physical punishment.

Zeanah and Lieberman suggested one more type of attachment disorder called Type V: *Role-Reversed Attachment Disorder*. In this pattern, the child behaves parentally toward the caregiver, both nurturing and acting bossy or punitive.

As an example, Zeanah described twenty-four-month-old Beth, who was brought in for an examination because of sleep problems. Her mother was depressed and cried during the interview.

> Beth played with [toys] only in the first 20 minutes, ... when her mother seemed more animated. Her mother looked sadder and began to cry as she described her frustration and hopelessness.... Beth walked over and signaled to be picked up. She remained in her mother's lap.... Beth began to stroke her mother's hair gently. She continued caressing her mother's hair and back intermittently for about 20 minutes. At times, however, she pulled her mother's hair vigorously and provocatively.[20]

Is Aggression Part of Attachment Disorder? Although statistics do not show an increase in child and adolescent violence, Americans are very concerned about aggression among children. The mass media have emphasized killings by the young, and a topic of recent public discussion has been whether very young killers should be tried and executed as adults. Are there connections between attachment experiences and youth violence? As we will see, clinical psychologists and psychiatrists say one thing, and popular opinion says something else.

We do have some empirical evidence about the connection of aggression and attachment. Some degree of aggression is a part of normal development. How much is acceptable, and what kind, depends on family and cultural standards. But excessive violence is also part of a number of early emotional disturbances. As for its connection with attachment, Zeanah's Type IV attachment disorder involves aggression, but the DSM category of Reactive Attachment Disorder does not. Aggressive behavior is described as a problem in several early childhood emotional disorders. Oppositional and Defiant Disorder (ODD) is characterized by aggressive responses to adults. Autistic children may react with severe tantrums when an adult attempts to guide or manage their behavior.

Serious psychotic illnesses, such as early onset schizophrenia, can also involve intensely aggressive behavior. In a case that received much publicity a few years ago, Malcolm Shabazz, the then twelve-year-old grandson of Malcolm X, set the fire that killed his grandmother, Betty Shabazz. The boy had shown serious emotional disturbance since early childhood: he had set fires and spoken of an imaginary friend called Sinister Torch. He and his mother had had physical altercations that left them both bloody. Although this case and others undoubtedly involved disturbed relationships, attachment issues were by no means the direct cause of the violent behavior.

Children who have had poor attachment experiences are also likely to have experienced violence and to have modeled their behavior on others' aggression. As Zeanah noted in his analysis of Aggressive Attachment Disorder, these children were likely to have been involved in domestic violence. When children are institutionalized, too, chances are all too great that they will undergo or see some violence perpetrated by their peers or staff members. Children in the foster care system are often there because of domestic violence, and they may encounter still more violence within the system. However, this source of aggressive behavior is parallel to the experiences that cause disorders of attachment, not a direct result of those experiences.

Some beliefs about attachment and violence are without an evidence basis. A section in Chapter 7 will discuss a popular theory of attachment disorders that is advocated by some practitioners and parent groups. We can refer to this belief system as the Attachment Therapy (AT) philosophy. Adherents to this set of ideas stress a connection between rage and disorders of attachment, but they do so without any evidence basis. This group agrees with the view so succinctly stated in *West Side Story*: "He's depraved on accounta he's deprived." The depravity in question is considered to begin with disobedience and cruelty to animals and then develop into serial killing, a characteristic expected of all adopted children who are seen as suffering from attachment disorders.

The AT belief system emphasizes the idea that complete control over children's actions is the only way to eradicate the intense aggressiveness expected to result from a poor attachment history. All adopted children are considered to be full of rage and to direct their anger first at younger children and pets, and later at their adoptive parents. A treatment intended to neutralize rage is advocated by this group and will be discussed later in this chapter.

Again, there is no systematic evidence to support this belief system. It is clear from both the DSM criteria for Reactive Attachment Disorder and from Zeanah's categories that aggressiveness is not a hallmark of disorders of attachment, although it may be present in some cases.

Assessing Attachment Disorders in Older Children. The descriptions of attachment disorders given above show a good deal of variation. There does not seem to be a single, invariable form of attachment disorder even among preschool children. Although poor attachment experiences have a real potential for causing poor emotional outcomes, their consequences can be different for children in different situations, and can be influenced by individuals' basic temperamental characteristics. By the time children reach school age, they have developed along individual lines to such an extent that early attachment experiences are only one factor among many that determine emotion and behavior. Assessments of Reactive Attachment Disorder at that point may not be possible, as leaders in this area of research have stated.

Teachers and parents need to be cautious about claims that Reactive Attachment Disorder can be diagnosed by means of checklists or through observations by mental health counselors. One group of counselors, for example, has suggested that they can diagnose RAD in three to seven controlled five-minute observations, but the evidence presented is quite questionable.[21]

ATTACHMENT, DISORDERS OF ATTACHMENT, AND PSYCHOTHERAPY

Serious disorders of attachment need treatment. Not only do they cause unnecessary stress and fear in early life, but as development progresses, they distort the child's experiences and beliefs about other people. This section will examine therapeutic interventions that seem to help compensate for a poor early attachment history. In addition, this section will consider the fact that even people with mild attachment problems may benefit from having these considered during psychotherapy in adult life. And therapists themselves need to take their own attachment experiences into consideration as they work with patients.

In the discussion of therapy below, the reader may see what seems to be peculiar language. Interventions that are intended to deal with disorders of attachment or that take attachment issues into account are often called *attachment-based therapies*. Why not simply attachment therapy? As we will see below and in Chapter 7, the term attachment therapy was preempted some years ago by a group of quasi-professional practitioners, who use it to mean a treatment of their own design. This treatment is diametrically opposed to the ones we will stress; it is based on a completely unorthodox set of beliefs about attachment. In order to clarify the differences between the unvalidated attachment therapy and evidence-based treatments, it has become important to use terminology that shows what type of intervention is being discussed, and the term "attachment-based" indicates treatments generally accepted by clinical psychologists, clinical social workers, and psychiatrists.

Therapists and Other Interveners

Therapeutic interventions for childhood attachment disorders are far from the simple talking therapy model used in adult counseling and similar clinical work. Instead, many types of professionals employ a wide range of interventions. These can include parent education, foster parenting techniques, residential treatment, medication, and individual or family psychotherapy. The people performing the interventions may be teachers, social workers, psychologists, psychiatrists, and foster, biological, or adoptive parents.

What Do Interveners Bring to the Table? We saw earlier in this chapter that a child can show disturbed attachment behavior with one adult caregiver, but behave quite normally with another. The adult brings something to the situation, and the child responds to it. Similarly, we see that adult interveners can influence a child's attachment-related behaviors through their own emotions and expectations.

It is by no means a new idea that both patients and therapists bring their emotional histories to the treatment room. The patient's emotional background has long been thought to provide a unique responsiveness to and relationship with the therapist. The feelings that result from past emotional experience are termed *transference*, and are considered a refocus on the therapist of some beliefs that stem from early relationships with parents. For example, the patient might feel angry with the therapist, not because of the therapist's own actions, but because of a pattern of feelings toward authoritative, caregiving people, a pattern that developed in interactions with the patient's parents. This transference of patterns is like the application of an internal working model of social relations, a model developed early in family life.

Far from being utterly rational, completely neutral observers, therapists also bring their own emotional backgrounds to the therapy room in the form of *countertransference*. The therapist's responses to the patient are shaped in part by the therapist's internal working model. Countertransference has sometimes been a matter of concern, because it can interfere with the therapist's objectivity. Recently, however, some therapists have begun to think about countertransference as an authentic part of the interpersonal relationship between therapist and patient, and one that gives important feedback to the patient about other people's feelings. This may be especially important when the problem to be resolved involves separations, loss, and trauma.[22] Therapists who work with traumatized patients may feel much anxiety and find the intensity of the relationship overwhelming. The therapist wants the patient's attachment to be transferred or refocused on him, but this involves accepting both the patient's desire for closeness and its associated danger. Many therapists find the situation awkward, difficult, and a producer of many contradictory emotions. A great puzzle for therapists is the extent to which they should allow the patient to see these feelings, and the extent to which they should suppress their emotional responses.

As with the relationship between therapist and patient, children and caregivers are affected by their interpersonal interactions. Children affect adults, who in turn affect the children, who in their turn influence the adults again—or, if you want to begin the sequence with the adults, that statement would be equally true. Children have immature internal working models of social relations that help guide their interactions, and adults have much more advanced models that make their own contributions.

As we saw in an earlier chapter, adults' internal working models can be measured by means of the Adult Attachment Interview (AAI). Some research indicates that the most effective foster parents, the ones who best establish a secure attachment in their foster children, are those who are judged autonomous on the AAI. These parents have confidence in emotional attachment and are able to think coherently about their own early attachment experiences. Children are likely to show high rates of disorganized attachment behavior when cared for by foster parents who do not have an autonomous state of mind with respect to emotional ties.[23]

People who foster or adopt young infants are in an excellent position to establish a secure relationship and guide the child to a positive internal working model of social relations. For those who care for older children, however, the relationship may be rockier. This is not surprising when we recall that the older child brings along an internal working model in which adults may be expected to be untrustworthy or even cruel. What is more surprising is that foster or adoptive parents may inadvertently behave in ways that bring out the worst in the children and in the family system.

In one clinical study, a number of problems were cited as characteristic of adoptive parents of older children.[24] All the parents in this study were worried and distressed by the children's behavior, even to the extent of regretting the adoption, feeling anger at the child, and experiencing concern that the child might have inherited the biological parents' problems. These reactions are difficult to hide from children, and are bound to influence the affection, spontaneity, and playfulness that would ideally be part of the children's lives.

The adoptive parents were also unexpectedly oblivious to the child's communication of anxiety or wishes for care. It was as if the parents were so convinced the adopted child could not prefer or care for them, they missed the child's signals. For example:

> A 15-month-old girl looked momentarily worried when the father left the room, and smiled imperceptibly on his return. He remarked: "she did not notice I was gone, did she?" ... Parents also misinterpreted temper tantrums, defiance and noncompliance as signs that the child did not care for them, instead of seeing them as age-appropriate expressions of anxiety and fear of loss.[25]

The adoptive parents observed in this study also tended to discipline children for behavior that was actually an indication of the child's attachment. They often used time-out techniques, which unfortunately fed into the child's fear of rejection, separation, and abandonment. These parents did not usually choose firm but comforting responses such as time-in, an approach in which the child stays close to the parent until calm. The author, Alicia Lieberman, noted that few of the adoptive parents had been well prepared by their adoption agency, especially with respect to the emotional needs of later-adopted children.

Types of Intervention

Treatment of emotional problems today most commonly emphasizes the family system and assumes that every family member influences each of the others. Therapeutic interventions with children are especially family-oriented. Children are not sent to be fixed, nor are children the sole focus of intervention, even when the child's behavior and feelings are the reasons the family has sought treatment. When the child's difficulties seem to be relationship-connected, all the family's relationships need to be considered, and more than one may need serious work.

Unfortunately, this is sometimes unacceptable to parents; some cannot tolerate it well enough to participate in therapy. When the therapist says that every family member has an influence on the child, parents sometimes seem to hear this statement as an accusation of blame for the child's behavior or emotional state. Treatment must involve the parents, as well as the child. It can be quite difficult to convey this message without implying that the parents are responsible for the problems. Families often prefer to bring their child to therapy so that the child can be "worked on," rather than do the complex, cognitive, and emotional work of understanding how the family functions. Indeed, some therapists prefer this approach, too.

When attachment is an issue, however, the therapeutic work must involve relationships, and each person in a relationship contributes to the outcome. It is difficult to imagine how a child could be treated for a disorder of attachment without the participation of a major attachment figure from the child's everyday life. To do otherwise would be like doing marriage counseling with a husband or a wife alone—this is better than nothing, but not nearly as effective as having the couple work together.

Whether or not a child has been diagnosed with a specific attachment disorder, there are a number of different circumstances in which therapy may be sought for problems associated with attachment. Families who have adopted an older child and feel that child is unreachable may want intervention. Adopted or non-adopted children who take risks or disobey frequently may be thought to need attachment-based interventions. Adults who have difficulty with relationships may also seek attachment-related therapy.

Autistic children are no longer considered candidates for attachment-based therapy, although psychologists once thought their pervasive problems stemmed from the absence of attachment. Some parents, unfortunately, are still convinced that the serious developmental problems of the autistic child are relationship-based, and that genetic problems like Tourette Syndrome can yield to relationship-focused treatment.

As we think about attachment-based therapy, we need to consider the treatment of poor children who are diagnosed with serious emotional problems. In many states, unhappily, families cannot receive state aid for a child's needed mental health intervention unless the parents relinquish custody. The parents' rights are legally terminated, the child no longer lives with them, and the parents have no right to visit with the child or even to obtain information about her condition or whereabouts. Whether or not the child's emotional disturbance began on a relationship basis, the effects of separation and loss now become part of the problem. At the same time, intervention with the biological family becomes impossible.

Parent Education. The clinician Alicia Lieberman, whose observational research was discussed earlier, has suggested that parent education is an essential intervention, especially for adoptive families. Adoptive parents need to know what special problems to expect from an adopted child, especially one who has had little opportunity to form attachment relationships, having lived in multiple foster homes or spent months, or even years in a foreign institution. In addition, these parents need to receive "emotionally supportive, child-focused developmental guidance, which allows the parent to become more receptive to the child's often overlooked or misunderstood efforts to obtain reassurance."[26] For children who use and understand language, this reassurance can come in the form of storytelling, having a discussion about what has happened to the child, and naming the child's fears, with an assurance that they are groundless. For children who do not talk, games of peek-a-boo or hide-and-seek may convey some of the same messages—and these games are fascinating to children who are at the point in development when attachment concerns are most intense.

Adoptive parents who have raised their own children are not necessarily ready to deal effectively with the adopted child. They may be sensitive enough to ensure a good outcome in a relatively easy situation, but they have to work harder and think more about picking up the signals of adopted children, who need a particularly strong sense of continuity and communication. These children's communication cues may be easy to miss; the children may miss the parents' cues as well. For example, Lieberman suggests, "Parents need to over-emphasize their response to the children's muted signs of need, marking separations with unambiguous demonstrations of sadness and assurances of a prompt return, and underlining reunions with clear demonstrations of joy."[27] An analogy may be drawn to what we do when speaking to a hearing- and speech-impaired adult; we speak loudly and clearly enough, we give the person a view of our face, and we use gestures and repetitions. To understand the adult, we pay careful attention and try to become familiar with the person's unique habits.

Guidance for Foster Parents. Foster homes are sometimes thought of simply as holding environments—somewhere for children to be fed, sheltered, and protected, before a permanent arrangement is made. In reality, foster care provides a variety of scenarios for children. Some children remain in foster care for years without permanent arrangements being made for them. They may be in placement because the biological parents cannot provide for them, because of parental illness, or for other reasons in which parental rights would not be legally terminated. It may be that the biological parents try again and again to care for the child, but on each occasion are forced to give the child up because of longstanding or new problems. Other children may spend a short time in foster care, but are there because of traumatic circumstances, such as the death of a parent in a car accident, or, worse, domestic violence.

A relatively recent foster care problem is the shortage of foster parents who can be full-time caregivers for the children. In a number of cases, foster mothers work outside the home, and children in their charge are often placed in day care, further complicating their experience with relationships.

Can foster care become an effective intervention and not just a way to keep young children off the streets? There is no doubt that it can and should. Whether this will ever happen is questionable, however, because the steps necessary to make this an effective solution will not be cheap.

Foster care needs to become an experience that can guide children to the development of positive internal working models of social relationships. As we know, the first step toward this accomplishment comes from experiences with a small number of consistent, sensitive, and responsive caregivers. Consistency of caregiving is difficult to achieve if children attend day care and live in a foster home, where there are apt to be too many caregivers. Increased wages for foster parents would be needed to enable one or both foster parents to stay at home with the foster child.

Some specific suggestions have been made about improved training for foster parents.[28] One idea is that foster parents learn how to gently challenge young children to change their expectations about other people and to alter their internal working model, one that predicts rejection and indifference from adults. Foster parents behaving with normal sensitivity are likely to respond by backing away when foster children seem not to want them. However, the children do need care and contact, and foster parents need to be helped to give this care even though from the child the adult gets only mixed or negative signals. Here is one such intervention:

> [C]aregivers [are encouraged] to provide nurturance to these children even though the children are behaving in ways that suggest they do not want or need nurturance.... [If] a child turns away from the caregiver when hurt, the caregiver is encouraged to respond in a nurturing way; for example, at first the foster mother may just pat the child's back gently while the child sits on the floor turned away from her. Over time, the child usually allows the foster mother to come closer, and offer more support and nurturance.[29]

A second point in the same intervention program involves the unusual physiological reactions to distress many young children have when they have been traumatized by separation. Foster parents need to learn to buffer children's stress levels by creating a "very controllable interpersonal world" in which the child knows who will be present and how they will consistently respond to social communications.[30]

Floor Time (DIR). What about *direct individual treatment* of children with attachment–related problems? Are there therapeutic techniques that seem to work? One important approach has been reported to be effective when used by parents, teachers, and therapists, either individually or together. This technique, developed by the leading child psychiatrist Stanley Greenspan, is called *floor time*, or Developmental, Individual-difference, Relationship-based therapy (DIR).[31]

DIR is based on the assumption that cognitive, social, emotional, sensory, and physical development are interlinked. Communicative experience with other human beings creates emotional reactions and a chance to learn what to expect in the world. Floor time involves communicative experiences. It is intended to support the development of capacities much like the internal working model of social relations posited by Bowlby's attachment theory. These capacities involve a set of interwoven feelings, expectations, beliefs, and memories that serve as guides for relationships.

Floor time is, in practice, exactly what it sounds like: an adult gets down on the floor with the child and follows whatever leads the child gives. The adult—whether parent or therapist—does not use floor time to tell or show the child what to do or not to do, but to help support the child in his own ideas and plans. If the child can and will talk, talking can be part of floor time, but nonverbal communication may be all that is used.

Adults who are doing floor time need to be patient, relaxed, and attentive to the child's cues. Otherwise, the rule of following the child's lead becomes impossible to obey. An anxious, impatient adult may also make the mistake of thinking that a child is doing something intentionally, when this may not be true.

Floor time needs to begin with engagement between the adult and the child; the adult becomes attuned to the child's thoughts and feelings by trying to respond to the cues the child gives, even when these are hard to read, as may be the case with foster or late-adopted children. Floor time proceeds with two-way communication, allowing the therapist to understand which responses draw a returned response from the child. In a video recording of Greenspan working with a withdrawn four-year-old, the therapist shows the boy a toy lion. "Can he shake your hand?" The boy indicates refusal with a brief movement of his head. "Can he shake your foot?" Again, no. "Can he shake my hand?" A quick nod indicates the child's agreement, and a very simple form of two-way communication is underway. The child does not speak, but the rudiments of a relationship with the therapist are there.

Floor time can be an effective way for caregivers and therapists to work with a child who seems aloof, withdrawn, indifferent, or out of control in ways that are common among children with disturbed attachment histories. An unusual characteristic of the DIR approach is its stress on children's individual differences, including their abilities for self- regulation and any special sensory processing tendencies that can interfere with communication.

Attachment Therapy and Related Treatments. Earlier in this chapter, we noted that the term Attachment Therapy—the one we would intuitively use in talking about treatments for attachment disorders—was preempted some years ago by a group of practitioners whose work differs vastly from anything we have so far discussed. As we will see in a later chapter, Attachment Therapy (AT) is an unvalidated treatment; it is unrelated to Bowlby's attachment theory and is directed primarily toward adopted children, whether or not they show symptoms of attachment disorders. AT uses physical restraint and emotional intimidation as its primary tools. There is little or no systematic evidence about its effects, and the treatment may accurately be described as "a cure without a disease."[32]

Parents adopting children from foreign countries are especially likely to be advised by their adoption agencies to seek AT practitioners or persons who use similar techniques, but who object to having their work classified as AT. Psychologist Ronald Federici, who specializes in post-institutionalized foreign-adopted children, advises parents to use a *beltloop* technique with newly adopted children.[33] This technique permits the child to go no more than an arm's length from the adoptive parents, except when sleeping, for weeks at a time. In addition, Federici suggests parents use a prone restraint technique when the children are angry or disobedient, a practice that has a higher probability of asphyxiation than other restraint modes. He also advises restraining the child in a cradling position to create an emotional tie between child and adult. None of these practices has an evidence basis, and the techniques Federici recommends seem rather similar to the inappropriate responses of adoptive parents as recorded in Alicia Lieberman's research, which was discussed earlier in this chapter.

Attachment Issues and Therapy in Adults. There are a great many situations in which attachment concerns may affect adult relationships, but attachment is probably most critical when parent-child relations are in trouble. The space limitations of this book will confine us to a few situations of that type and the interventions they require. One fascinating topic, far too complex to be considered here, involves the emotions connected with Assisted Reproductive Technologies (ART), such as artificial and in vitro insemination, or the use of gestational surrogates. ART is increasing as people delay childbearing to an age of decreased fertility, and as more same-sex couples seek parenthood. Couples' emotional responses to a successful pregnancy following ART are by no means simple, and therapists working with these adults and their children need to keep many attachment issues in mind.[34]

More common problems between parents and children have to do with the parent's history of traumatic experiences, such as rape. These parents may have a diminished capacity for sensitive responsiveness to the child.[35]

Instead of responding to the real baby in the here-and-now, they react in terms of an internal working model distorted by trauma. Like the woman suffering from major depression, a mother with a history of trauma has a compromised ability to respond to her baby. Unfortunately, the baby's crying, or her other signals for help, may reduce the mother's responsiveness even more. "When a baby's distress or another feature of the mother's current environment—such as domestic violence involving the baby's father—stimulates negative affect in a mother ... [she] may confuse past traumatic memory with her perception of her baby, and herself, in the present."[36]

In one case, when pregnant seventeen-year-old Marta began to feel her baby move, she started to have memories and nightmares of having been sodomized by her father at age five and raped by her brother about a year before she became pregnant. She said these memories and dreams began when her doctor told her the baby was a boy. When the little boy was born, Marta thought he was "angry" and "manipulative." She found herself so exhausted that she did not wake up if the baby cried at night. Clearly, Marta's perception of her baby was distorted and unrealistic. If she responded to the baby's cry as manipulative, she could not be successful at establishing a good relationship and providing good attachment experiences for the child. Marta had little *Reflective Functioning*—the ability to think about other people's minds and her own—so she was not likely to solve this problem for herself.[37]

What could be done for Marta and her child? She was certainly a person who needed to be shown rather than told, but how to manage this? Her problem does not seem to be the right kind of situation for a talking kind of therapy.

What worked for Marta was a series of video feedback visits, which helped her see the interaction she had with the baby. This procedure began with the videotaping of mother and baby as they played and interacted. The videotapes were reviewed, and four 30-second segments were chosen, including moments of separation and reunion.

Several weeks later, the mother was asked to come back and watch the videotaped segments, together with a clinician. After each video clip, the mother was asked to give her responses to some questions: "What happened? What is going on in your/your child's/the interviewer's mind? Does it remind you of anything?"[38]

This simple intervention is effective in helping mothers reinterpret their children's signals in a more accurate way. For example, one of the mothers who received this treatment, Ms. V., had a three-year-old son, whom she saw as angry and controlling. At the time of the videotaping, he held on to her to keep her from leaving the room. She described this at the time as "trying to get away with something ... trying to have things his way ... and ... feeling angry." After watching the video with the clinician, Ms. V. responded very differently and far more accurately: "I think he was scared.... Oh, my God! That was a scary moment for him. He probably thought that I was leaving and wouldn't come back."[39] Though the video feedback intervention was an experimental one, and the families all received more conventional psycho- therapy, this treatment may prove to be an effective way to help traumatized mothers become appropriately sensitive to their children's communications.

CONCLUSION

When attachment experiences are poor, individuals' internal working models of relationships seem to develop along distorted lines. The early models are based on a few primary relationships, and if those are all diffi- cult, the child's beliefs and expectations about relationships will also be problematic. Because relationship quality depends on both child and adult, even a child with one very poor relationship may benefit from other, better relationships. A very few children have no consistent relationships, but even these children have models of how human beings interact, because they have experienced some minimum care and companionship.

Children with poor experiences, involving interactions with inconsis- tent, unresponsive adults, begin on a developmental trajectory or pathway in which they have less and less opportunity to develop healthy expecta- tions and good social skills. An adopted child, for instance, may turn away from the parent when hurt; if the parent accepts this as meaning the child does not like, or want, care, the child's belief that people are not a source of nurturance will be further confirmed. When the child's development has been affected repeatedly by such experiences, he or she may become so negative in his or her emotional responses and behavior toward others that the question of mental illness will arise.

The term attachment disorder describes an emotional disturbance that is the outcome of poor early social and emotional experiences. However, complete agreement among psychologists and psychiatrists does not exist on the behaviors and feelings associated with disorders of attachment, and a number of possible types have been described. Aggression does not seem to be a major feature of attachment disorders.

Because attachment disorders arise from experience, treatment focuses on experiences that can change the individual's understanding of the self and of relationships with other people. The most effective treatments in- volve improvement of communication between adult and child; they re- quire the adult to increase his or her sensitivity and ability to respond to the child's communications, especially those about fear of separation.

chapter 7

What Everybody Knows: Popular Views of Attachment

As the first chapters of this book have shown, the concept of attachment is complex, and it remains the subject of much discussion in professional child development and psychotherapy circles. This fact does not prevent simplified views of emotional development from becoming popularized. Indeed, the idea of attachment is broadly accepted in the United States, although not necessarily with the definition we have used in this book. Decisions and practices that claim to be based on attachment are readily accepted by the media and the public, even though attachment has a variety of definitions. In our Age of Attachment, statements about emotional ties may go unquestioned.

The present chapter will examine three major popular ways of thinking that use the term attachment, but fall outside the realm of professional psychology and psychotherapy. Two of these belief systems involve parenting practices and treatment of children. The third involves ideas that have been developed in the courts and have strongly affected child custody and visitation decisions.

ATTACHMENT PARENTING

New parents seeking advice about childrearing may come across books and Internet sites that counsel the use of *attachment parenting*, an approach developed by a physician named Dr. William Sears and his wife.[1] Attachment parenting stresses the need for parental sensitivity and responsiveness.

Although much of the attachment parenting material is directed toward parents of very young babies, there is also advice about school-age children and adolescents.

Sources, Definitions, Evidence

Attachment parenting advisors refer occasionally to John Bowlby and Donald Winnicott, another British theorist of the 1940s and 1950s. They also allude to some research on prenatal reactions of babies, and to behaviors soon after birth. Although the basic concepts of attachment parenting are rooted in theory and research, the actual, practical recommendations to parents do not necessarily share this foundation.

Attachment parenting sources do not define attachment the way we have in this book. Rather than applying the term to the child's early emotional development, it appears to apply to the mother's feelings for her baby. For example, one attachment parenting Web site states:

> Attachment is a special bond between parent and child; a feeling that draws you magnet-like to your baby; a relationship that when felt to its deepest degree causes the mother to feel that the baby is a part of her.... Attachment means that a mother and baby are in harmony with each other. Being in harmony with your baby is one of the most fulfilling feelings a mother can ever hope to have. (http://www.askdrsears.com)

Harmony appears to be equated with the mother's sensitive reading of the baby's cries and signals, and her effective comforting. (Fathers do not get much mention in discussions of attachment parenting.)

Attachment parenting advocates also seem to consider attachment to be apparent in the mother's mood and feelings. "You will know when you get that attached feeling for your baby.... When your baby cries and you respond with a feeling of rightness about your response, you are well on your way to becoming an attached parent." Mothers are advised to check their "sensitivity index." They are considered to be "becoming attached" if they become increasingly sensitive to the baby. For example, increasing sensitivity may be revealed by the mother's distress when the baby cries, by her anticipation of crying when the baby's facial expression changes, or by a sense of the intuitive rightness of responses to the baby.

Attachment parenting advocates thus see attachment as a change in the parent—particularly the mother—rather than in the child. However, the ultimate goal and desired long-term outcome is related to the child's development. It is claimed that families who use attachment parenting techniques are able to shape positive emotional development in the child, enabling the child to develop trust in others and positive self-esteem. The child will learn to "bond to persons, not things," have "meaningful attachments with peers," and, in adulthood, achieve a "deep intimacy with a mate." Other positive outcomes are said to be better discipline, a healthy conscience, and less need for punishment.

Not surprisingly, there is no systematic evidence basis for attachment-parenting claims. The assumption that more sensitive mothers guide babies to better development is well substantiated, but the other statements are really impossible to test in any controlled way. The attachment parenting recommendations described below are particularly difficult to confirm through systematic investigation.

Attachment Parenting Recommendations

Attachment parenting sources emphasize that their recommendations are tools, rather than absolute requirements, and different choices may be needed for babies or families with different characteristics. A strict set of guidelines is not advised; instead attachment parenting counsels individual choices based on what works.

For parents of young babies, however, there is a program recommended as an effective way to begin parenthood. Attachment parenting advocates advise a general approach as well as some specific activities they feel will initiate a positive family life. (It is notable that some attachment parenting Web sites include a variety of commercial offerings such as baby carriers, although these are not presented as essential to good parenting.)

Attachment Parenting and Bonding

Attachment parenting proponents discuss bonding or "birth bonding" as an important issue for new parents. They define bonding as "the close emotional tie that develops between parent and baby at birth ... really a continuation of the relationship that began during pregnancy." In spite of these definitions, however, the emphasis is on what we might call bonding activities rather than demonstrable emotional responses. These bonding activities are rather specific and focus primarily on the first hour or so after birth.

One bonding suggestion is that parents request a delay in routine procedures, such as the eye drops or ointment used to prevent eye infection. A second is that the baby should be kept connected by placing it on the mother's abdomen as soon as possible after birth, pausing only if there is a need to suction, cut the cord, or do more serious medical interventions.

Putting the baby to the breast at once is also advised, with the mother's hormonal response to sucking considered an important guide for her mothering behavior. Similarly, touching, stroking, caressing, and skin-to-skin contact are all recommended as pleasurable and supportive of the baby's transition to life outside the womb. Attachment parenting advocates also suggest that talking to and gazing at the baby are bonding activities.

Advocates of attachment parenting believe the parent-child relationship needs more than a few hours to become established. Rooming-in, the arrangement in which the newborn shares the mother's hospital room, is suggested as a way to continue the bonding activities that have been described, and of course these can go on during the early weeks and months of the newborn's life.

Who Is Bonding? The attachment parenting view of bonding is confused—and confusing to the reader. Most attachment parenting material stresses the parent's emotional response to the child, for example, "staring into your baby's eyes may trigger a rush of beautiful mothering feelings," and one would expect this emphasis to apply most to the baby's first few days after birth. However, attachment-parenting materials imply that something emotional is happening to the baby as a result of bonding activities, even right after birth. One reason given for delaying prophylactic eye treatment is that the baby "needs a clear first impression" of the mother (who is also said to need to see the baby's eyes).

Similarly, it is suggested that the baby needs a person to bond to (or with) in the first hours after birth, and that the father or someone else can be bonding while the mother recovers. The attachment parenting Internet advice says, "One of the saddest sights we see is a newly born, one-hour-old baby parked all alone in the nursery, busily bonding (with wide-open, hungry eyes) with [the] plastic sides of her bassinet." The implication being that there is indeed something the baby needs and does shortly after birth, and that it does not depend on human beings or on specific bonding activities. It is difficult to see what emotional reaction to the bassinet side could occur. But what could the baby be doing, and how would the outcome be different than if the baby were looking at its mother? The difficulty in the logic of this explanation seems to stem from the confusion of parent or baby actions with changes in parent or baby emotions.

Attachment Parenting and Attachment Tools

Attachment parenting recommendations stress the idea that bonding or bonding activities early in life are only the beginning of a developing parent-child relationship. Proponents of attachment parenting recommend a set of child care techniques that have a long human history, but that are far from universal in industrialized societies today.

Breastfeeding, not surprisingly, is first among the attachment parenting recommendations for fostering attachment (and we need to remember that this group is defining attachment as the mother's sensitivity and responsiveness to the baby). Breast milk is described as a diet that promotes brain development, but the major emphasis is on breastfeeding as an exercise in *babyreading* and, therefore, as a cause of increased maternal sensitivity.

As we have noted in earlier chapters, breastfeeding has not been shown to be a factor in the child's development of attachment (that is, attachment as it is usually defined). Whether breastfeeding experience causes an increase in the mother's sensitivity, or whether sensitive mothers more often elect to breastfeed, is a very difficult question to answer. It is certainly true, however, that breastfeeding mothers must pay attention to their babies' signals—for example, so they know when to switch from the left to the right breast. Bottle-feeding mothers may pay attention, but can feed successfully without much communicative exchange.

Babywearing is a second technique or tool said to increase a parent's sensitivity to the baby's needs and signals (http://www.parentingweb.com/ap/babywearing.htm). Although many parents of infants and toddlers carry their children in back or front packs, attachment parenting advocates advise babywearing mothers to use a sling, which is a small hammock with a broad strap that goes around the mother's back and shoulder. A breastfeeding mother can easily arrange the sling to give the infant access to the nipple, while the mother stays discreetly covered.

As well as an increase in the mother's sensitivity, other benefits of babywearing are claimed. Although there is good evidence that carrying babies helps reduce colicky crying, some of the other claims about babywearing are not only untested, but also quite difficult to investigate. For example, the practice is said to produce a secure maternal attachment, but it is not clear what definition of attachment is being used here. Babywearing is supposed to simulate the sensations of pressure, motion, warmth, and security of the womb. This claim would appear to have some accuracy; however, it is not at all clear whether this result is desirable or even developmentally beneficial.

Some other claims about babywearing are questionable and are based solely on anecdotal evidence or generalization. For example, it is claimed that neurological development is fostered by the movement stimulation experienced in a sling. Again, attachment parenting proponents suggest that toddlers who are carried in slings "initiate separation sooner, and become more self-reliant"—a difficult statement to substantiate, and one for which there is no systematic evidence. Co-sleeping is probably the single attachment parenting recommendation most likely to be criticized in the United States. This may simply involve mother and baby sharing a bed, or a larger, family bed with enough space for both parents and several children. Attachment parenting advocates do not insist on co-sleeping, but they do approve it as one of many sleeping arrangements. Concerns that a baby may be suffocated or lain upon by a parent are rejected in light of evidence that child deaths of this type are usually associated with a parent's alcohol or drug intoxication. In addition, some research has shown that young babies' breathing is regulated by physical contact with adults. Attachment parenting advocates see co-sleeping as advantageous both to the parents, who can reconnect emotionally with the child at night, and to toddlers, who may otherwise experience separation anxiety.

What Is the Connection between Attachment Parenting and a Child's Emotional Development?

Proponents of attachment parenting use terms like bonding, attachment, and even separation anxiety—all familiar vocabulary from earlier chapters' discussion of attachment theory. The definitions of the terms are not the same, however. Are there connections between attachment parenting practices and the development of attachment, as the term is used in formal attachment theory and in systematic research on emotional development?

Attachment-parenting materials do not do much analysis with respect to this question. They emphasize the effect their childrearing techniques have on a variety of desirable developmental outcomes: happier families, better sleep, less frustration, less need for punishment, and more compassionate caring behavior among teenagers and young adults.

Some of these outcomes have certainly been related to secure attachment (as the term is used in most of this book). Attachment, in this sense, includes goal-corrected partnerships between older children and their parents, with less use of punishment as a natural consequence of the child's maturation. Secure attachment in childhood is associated with desirable child care behaviors in adult life.

Parents' sensitivity and responsiveness toward infants are the most important factors known to produce secure attachment as the child reaches the toddler stage. If attachment-parenting tools do successfully increase parents' sensitivity, it seems likely that they should be associated with secure attachment as a characteristic of the child's emotional life. However, people who write about attachment parenting do not clarify what they think is happening within the child as emotional development proceeds.

It would be wise to remember that attachment is a robust, developmental phenomenon. Children are likely to form secure attachments in less than ideal circumstances. While rough, insensitive, indifferent treatment may interfere with the growth of attachment, it is doubtful that most families need to use attachment tools in order to ensure their children's emotional development. On the other hand, if parents agree that they want to follow attachment-parenting guidelines, no harm will be done.

Cultural and Religious Issues as They Relate to Attachment Parenting

There seems to be little evidence to support the use of attachment parenting techniques, but a number of parents are very attracted to this approach. The reason for their attraction may be a matter of values rather than systematic evidence.

Attachment Parenting and Values in the United States. Attachment parenting employs childrearing techniques that come from ancient tradition. Breastfeeding and co-sleeping have been used throughout human history as the most effective ways to care for children in the absence of modern technology. They are physically and emotionally intimate actions. As such, they are in conflict with certain values characteristic of the United States since frontier times, though perhaps in line with modern needs.

Family relationships in the United States have emphasized independence over dependence, and autonomy over cooperative social skills. Children have generally received approval for learning to take care of themselves, refraining from crying or expressing distress, entertaining themselves, and minding their own business. Early weaning, early sleeping through the night, and early toilet training have been parental goals. Children who did not cry for their mothers or avoid strangers, and who were seen as friendly, outgoing, and self-sufficient, were especially valued.

These values, important for the success of pioneer and immigrant families, are possibly less important in the modern world. Modern parents want to connect children with families in order to protect them from the crime, sexual molestation, and drug abuse that may threaten them outside the home, as well as from domestic violence within the home. Keeping the child in the bosom of the family can be a way to protect and guide a child to adulthood. Attachment parenting connects with this family protectiveness by stressing the development of mutual affection and cooperation, and the importance of the parent's emotional engagement with the child and that of the child with the parent. In this perspective, crying and requests for help are seen as communications that should be responded to and encouraged.

Religious Issues. The development of the attachment parenting approach is more understandable if we recognize its connection with Christian thought—primarily the ideas characteristic of Protestant groups that are fundamentalist in nature. (Although Roman Catholics and the Protestant liturgical churches, such as the Lutherans, are certainly interested in childrearing practices, they have not been particularly involved with the matters we are discussing here.) Readers who look at attachment parenting web sites will see links to groups described with names such as "Christian attachment parenting" or "gentle Christian mothers." These groups have enthusiastically accepted attachment parenting principles as the positive, child-centered guidelines that lead to the development of close family ties and the rejection of domestic violence in any form.

The fundamentalist Christian interest in attachment parenting has undoubtedly been intensified by the adoption of an alternative-parenting program by some church groups in the United States. This approach, one that strongly rejects attachment-parenting principles, is sometimes referred to as *Babywise*, or *Ezzo*, parenting. Its guidelines are intensely adult-centered and its techniques are parent-directed. For example, breastfeeding at the baby's signal (a cardinal rule of attachment parenting) is replaced with a parent-directed feeding schedule for breastfed, as well as bottle-fed infants. Mothers are instructed to ignore their emotional impulses to respond to their babies' cues, and instead follow a recommended program. Rather than babywearing, the Ezzo approach counsels planned playpen time as an important way to develop independence. This philosophy's primary goal is the child's obedience to parental authority.[2]

It is possible that attachment parenting would not have grown as it has without the obvious contrast presented by the Babywise group and the appeals the two programs have made to people who share many, but evidently not all, of its values.

ATTACHMENT THERAPY: A TREATMENT AND A CHILDREARING PHILOSOPHY

In spite of some differences in vocabulary, the connection between attachment parenting and Bowlby's attachment theory is incompletely realized, but it is genuine. In this section, however, we will discuss another popular belief system. Though it claims connection with Bowlby's theory and shares some definitions and terms, it is almost diametrically opposed in its basic assumptions and goals. This system involves a complete system of parenting principles as well as an intervention intended to be therapeutic. It is commonly referred to as Attachment Therapy (AT), but attachment parenting and AT have no connection whatsoever other than the use of the word attachment.

Attachment Therapy: The Intervention

Attachment Therapy, the intervention itself, is a physically intrusive technique used principally with adopted and foster children. The stated goal of AT is the transformation of a child's emotional life and the creation of emotional attachment to the adoptive or foster parent.

Although some aspects of AT go back centuries, the technique, as recently practiced, dates from the 1960s, when it was formulated by Robert W. Zaslow, a California psychologist whose license was revoked after he injured a patient. Zaslow developed an intervention he called *Z-therapy* or *rage-reduction therapy*. The basis of Zaslow's technique was physical restraint, or holding of the patient by a group of five or six adults, while the therapist in charge prodded the patient in the ribs and under the arms, grabbed the face, shouted, and tried to force prolonged eye contact. Sessions lasted for hours and were intended to provoke the patient to wild anger, shouting, cursing, and tears. Later developments in AT included having the therapist lie with his full weight on the child patient, as well as covering his or her mouth with a hand.[3]

Zaslow himself believed that this treatment caused emotional attachment and related it to Bowlby's work. When the Colorado physician Foster Cline met Zaslow, he worked to bring together Zaslow's approach and some related ideas in a form he called *holding therapy* or Attachment Therapy. Cline's version of the treatment, directed at children and young adolescents, was practiced for ten or fifteen years, but it remained an underground approach, only rarely mentioned in professional child psychotherapy groups. Attachment Therapists essentially trained each other; they were most likely to practice in Western states where there was minimal regulation of mental health practitioners.

Public awareness of AT practices increased sharply with the death of ten-year-old Candace Newmaker in 2000 during an AT session with two unlicensed practitioners and staff members. Candace, who had been adopted at age six in North Carolina, was brought to Colorado for treatment of Reactive Attachment Disorder (see Chapter 6) by her adoptive mother.

Candace received holding therapy, but this technique was not the direct cause of her death. On the day when Candace died, head therapist Connell Watkins (who now uses the name C. J. Cooil) decided to use a different intervention called *rebirthing*. Candace was wrapped in a blanket and instructed to wiggle out in order that she could be reborn as the true daughter of her adoptive mother. During her wiggling, the therapists and helpers pressed down on her rhythmically in simulation of birth contractions. Although Watkins and her group usually limited rebirthing to a period of a few minutes, in Candace's case, they kept her wrapped for seventy minutes, overlooking her cries of distress, sounds of vomiting, and eventual complete silence. When finally unwrapped, the child was dead of asphyxiation. The two therapists were convicted of child abuse leading to death, and sentenced to sixteen years in prison.[4]

Advocates of AT responded to this tragedy in a variety of ways. Some insisted that Candace must have had an unknown medical condition, and that the death was an unavoidable accident. Others spoke of AT as a gentle, nurturing process akin to rocking a baby. Many asserted that the children being treated were saved from lives of violence, and that conventional psychotherapy would make their conditions worse.

A parent-professional organization dedicated to AT advocacy, ATTACh (Association for Treatment and Training of Attachment in Children), developed a set of ethical standards intended to prevent injury, and hired a public relations firm to handle problems related to AT. ATTACh and other groups presently have over eighty Internet sites that either advocate or offer AT in some form that involves physical contact; some groups advise that physical restraint should be carried out by parents rather than by therapists. It should be pointed out, however, that national organizations of mental health professionals continue to disapprove of AT. The professional journal *Attachment and Human Development* dedicated most of an issue in 2003 to the rejection of holding approaches, and support of AT among universities and hospitals is rare indeed.

Attachment Therapy: Parenting Principles

The AT philosophy goes far beyond the use of restraint as an intervention. When a child is in AT treatment, the home and family life are structured according to related principles. AT-structured experiences may be provided in the child's own home, or the child may be placed for a time with AT-trained therapeutic foster parents. Children who are brought for two-week intensive treatments at AT centers stay in therapeutic foster homes when not actually in a therapy session.

The leader of AT parenting training has been Nancy Thomas, a self-designated parent educator and "lay therapist" who is apparently without relevant formal education. Thomas has presented her approach in a number of self-published books, as well as in lecture tours, workshops, and videos.[5]

Thomas' goals for children in AT treatment are that they become "respectful, responsible, and fun to be around." Her recommended first step toward these goals is *German Shepherd training*. This does not involve actual dogs, but works toward having the child automatically and unquestioningly obey a number of simple commands, just as a well-trained pet would do. Obedience is achieved by practice and by insistence on correctness in every detail. For example, the child, when called by name, should not reply "What?" but must go to the adult and say "Yes, Mom Nancy" (or whoever is giving the command).

Obedience and control are also established by the practice of *strong sitting*, or *power sitting*, in which the child sits tailor-fashion, hands in lap, silent, unmoving, looking straight ahead. Power sitting is to be done three times a day, each time for a number of minutes equal to the child's age in years. This does not seem like a difficult demand until one realizes that the clock does not start until the child is completely compliant, which may be a matter of hours.

Obedience is also exacted through physical means, such as locks and alarms on doors. Children may not have night-lights in their rooms, even when extremely anxious. Food is a major form of manipulation, and a child who does not comply or does not show gratitude for a meal may go for weeks on a diet of cold oatmeal or peanut butter sandwiches. It is notable that school attendance is thought of as a privilege rather than a right, so children in AT treatment may have little or no break from these conditions for periods of months.

Thomas and other AT advocates are particularly concerned that children must not have information about what is happening to them. They do not know when, or even if, they will see their parents again, or whether they will be allowed to eat with the family, go to school, or go on a trip. Adults must be in complete authority, according to the AT view, and possession of knowledge is a part of authority.

One mental health practitioner, in an area where AT parenting was more common than AT therapy, gave the following description of what she had observed:

> [A] child in foster care refers to the man living with her mother as 'dad' and her biological father as 'father' ... and [is] given extra chores for telling 'falsehoods' about who she is related to....When the child continues to refer to the men in her mother's life as dad or father, plus slips up and calls the foster mother 'mom', drinking 8 ounces of vinegar while 'strong sitting' is added to encourage connection between the 'lower attachment centers' of the brain and 'higher reasoning,' thus eliminating 'false attachments.' [6]

Our description of AT parenting principles would not be complete without reference to *reparenting* activities. Thomas and other AT advocates believe that positive emotional change takes place when caregivers carry out babying or nurturing activities with children of school age or older. These activities include cuddling, rocking, bottle-feeding, and feeding of sweet foods that are usually denied to the child. These nurturing activities occur only on the parent's schedule or whim, however. The child who asks for a hug will not get one, but must accept a caress when the caregiver decides to give one.

Attachment Therapy: Assumptions and Belief System

Although descriptions of AT intervention and parenting may sound like random cruelty, these practices have a logical foundation in an organized belief system—which, however, is unsubstantiated by empirical evidence. Few underlying AT assumptions have either an evidence basis or a connection with any established psychological theory.

Prenatal Emotion. AT proponents assume that emotional connections between child and mother begin before birth. Not only does the mother have positive or negative feelings toward the coming child, as we know occurs, but AT beliefs hold that the unborn child feels an emotional tie to the mother. This baby's prenatal attachment can be harmed by the mother's negative feelings, such as those involved in considering abortion. If the child is given up for adoption, even on the day of birth, he or she experiences grief and rage, and these emotions continue to be active until relieved by AT intervention. Meanwhile, mourning and other distressing feelings interfere with the possibility of attachment to loving adoptive parents.

Eye Contact and Catharsis. AT proponents assign an almost magical power to eye contact between children and adults. Sustained mutual gaze, of the kind generally seen only between parents and babies or between adult lovers, is considered to be an essential step that causes the child to form an attachment; it also serves as evidence of an existing attachment.

It is also assumed that negative emotions, once engendered, must be expressed in order to be reduced in strength; that is, they must undergo catharsis. Prenatal anger about the mother's rejection, or grief and rage over separation and adoption, cannot soften with time, but must receive vigorous expression, which will eventually have a neutralizing effect.

The Attachment Cycle. If the child does not experience separation and adoption, AT proponents think he or she will continue to form a strong attachment to the parents during the first two years of life. In the first year, the development of attachment is thought to depend on a repeated cycle in which the child experiences need, frustration, and rage, and the parents step in to satisfy the need, causing the child to become more attached to them. Children who are neglected or who have difficult, uncomfortable medical problems do not have good experiences of this kind and do not form good attachments. In the second year, parents strengthen the child's attachment by setting limits and establishing themselves as authorities. Failure to establish control in this way interferes with attachment. Attachment is evidenced by the child's cheerful obedience, according to the AT way of thinking.

Attachment Disorder. When a problem causes difficulties with attachment, the child develops the symptoms of an Attachment Disorder (AD), considered by AT proponents to be a more severe form of the Reactive Attachment Disorder discussed in Chapter 6. AD involves a high level of rage, and has anger and aggressiveness as its most important components.

Just as attachment is indicated by the child's compliance and obedience, AD begins with disobedience and lack of affection toward the parents.

If left untreated, according to AT proponents, the disorder will lead to serious behavior problems, culminating in serial killing by boys and prostitution on the part of girls.

AT proponents offer a questionnaire, the Randolph Attachment Disorder Questionnaire (RADQ), which is intended to diagnose AD. The RADQ is based on parental opinion rather than professional observation, following the AT principle that any family problems have their source in the child alone.[7]

Therapy Principles. The physical restraint treatment described earlier is intended to evoke rage and cause catharsis through the expression of negative emotions. AT proponents consider this step essential because they believe no new attachment can occur until the old rage is gone. Having disposed of the child's rage, the parent can go on to create attachment by repeating nurturing actions normally experienced by young infants, such as bottle-feeding. The new attachment comes about by recapitulating the child's old experiences, this time in a positive, gratifying form. In addition, the child needs to experience the adult's complete authority. Some German authors, who support holding treatment, have proposed the child cannot feel secure unless it has been made clear that it is the parent who has complete control.[8]

An Evidence Basis for AT?

AT is not based on systematic research evidence, but, curiously, its proponents have claimed that it is. AT materials often depend on the implication that if something sounds like biology or mathematics, it must be true. Some web sites offer links entitled "Attachment Therapy Works!" or the like.

There are no experimental studies of AT—studies using the randomized controlled trial design that is considered the gold standard for research. There are one or two studies using the much less rigorous controlled clinical trial design, comparing children who received AT treatment to those who did not, but unfortunately these pieces of work are full of confused variables. It is impossible to know whether emotional changes were due to the treatment or to other factors. Another complicating factor is the poorly designed Randolph Attachment Disorder Questionnaire often used for diagnostic purposes by AT proponents.

Cultural and Religious Issues

Advocates of AT assume that emotional attachment to the biological mother is universal among humans and possibly among mammals. However, there are many cultural differences in relationships between adults and children. In Islamic societies, fostering of children is much approved, but adoption, in the Western sense, is not. In traditional Hawaiian culture, children are assumed to develop a strong emotional attachment to familiar caregivers, and to have little concern with the biological parent, if he or she has become unfamiliar.

In the United States, there seems to be a strong sense that adopted people need to know their roots and need to be able to contact their biological parents in adulthood or earlier. The unfounded belief that newborns immediately recognize and want their mothers is connected to this idea. Both of these beliefs lend support to the AT view that adopted children are emotionally distressed and need to undergo a transformation that will make them the "real" children of their adoptive parents.

Some aspects of AT thought have their parallels in religious and quasi-religious beliefs. An example is the idea that the unborn baby is aware of events and particularly, the mother's feelings. A number of religious systems hold this belief, as do Scientologists. Similarly, the stress on a child's obedience began with the Old Testament, which (among many other things) expresses approval of the killing of a child who strikes or curses a parent. The Puritans of New England shared this attitude; a child's obedience was considered an essential step toward adult compliance with God's will, and, therefore, it was critical for parents to tame a willful child.

ATTACHMENT CONCEPTS AND THE LAW

Legal and judicial thinking today takes into account some ideas about attachment. Because it takes a long time for new psychological or psychiatric information to be incorporated into law, the ideas that tend to be used are actually a matter of popular or traditional belief, rather than cutting-edge research or clinical work. In this section, we will look at some common legal applications of attachment concepts, and we will see how congruent these are with current work on early emotional development.

Laws govern many aspects of human relationships, especially those dealing with property, such as marriage, inheritance, and parental rights and obligations. Until late in the twentieth century, however, neither American nor British law concerned itself much with the emotional aspects of relationships. Family law was focused on possession of property, titles, or status, and the ways these could pass from one person to another. Illegitimate children had no rights of inheritance, unless the father specifically said so in his will, and they could not use the family name or inherit a title.

Parental rights followed the same pattern. Until the later part of the nineteenth century, divorced fathers had a complete right to custody of their children, just as all family property belonged to men. When formal adoption laws were established, they too were based on property law.

If one set of parents had a right to the custody of a child, another person could not also have that right, no matter what might be the complexity of emotional connections.

Family law began to recognize some non-property issues in the late nineteenth and early twentieth centuries, with the advent of the "tender years doctrine." This guideline suggested that infants and young children would be best in their mothers' custody, because their mothers naturally knew more about caring for them. The tender years doctrine was not concerned with the child's and the mother's mutual affection, or with the possible effect of separation on the child.

The door opened to legal consideration of relationships with the first discussion of the principle of the "best interest of the child."[9] This principle suggested that decisions about child custody should consider a variety of factors that could potentially affect the child, not just the parents' property rights to custody. These factors included the speed and method of decision-making, as well as other concerns, but from the point of view of this book the relationship between the child and one or more adults was the most important factor. The principle of the best interest of the child brought the concept of attachment into the courtroom, and attachment soon became a focus of family law.

Psychological versus Legal Terminology

Although courts today take a serious interest in children's emotions and relationships, they discuss these issues in a language different from that of mental health and child development professionals. For example, the term "bonding" is often used instead of "attachment."

Another term common in courtroom usage is *psychological parent*. The concept of the psychological parent has been used in custody decisions as a way of differentiating between biological kinship and an emotional relationship between adult and child, with stress on the importance of the latter factor. The words psychological parent describe the status of an adult who has been in a familiar caregiving relationship with a child, and who has carried out the obligations traditionally ascribed to parents. The use of the term seems to imply a mutually affectionate relationship that includes bonding (parental love) and attachment of the child to the adult.

In recent years, courtroom discussion has used the diagnosis of Reactive Attachment Disorder, a concept that is defined in the *Diagnostic and Statistical Manual* of the American Psychiatric Association (and that was discussed in Chapter 6).[10] However, there have also been cases in which Reactive Attachment Disorder was either confused or deliberately conflated with Attachment Disorder, the diagnosis proposed by advocates of Attachment

Therapy. As was noted earlier in this chapter, the definition of AD includes serious tendencies toward violence. This distinction is a subtle one, but a misunderstanding here may create a real distortion of the facts about a child. Paradoxically, while psychologists and psychiatrists are denying the assumption that violence is a necessary hallmark of disorders of attachment, the courts appear to accept this belief.

The seriousness of this confusion of terms and definitions is evident when we look at cases of child deaths and injuries where attachment disorders are claimed to have been a factor in treatment of the child. For example, in 2001, an adopted Russian child, Viktor Matthey, was brought to a New Jersey hospital in a state of hypothermia and he died the next day. The adoptive parents, Robert and Brenda Matthey, were brought to trial for the abusive treatment assumed to have caused Viktor's death. The defense's arguments included the idea that Viktor had behaved unacceptably, had been out of control, and had harmed himself in a pattern of behavior that indicated an attachment disorder. It was argued that the adoptive parents had been forced to restrict Viktor's food, tape his mouth, restrain him physically, and leave him in a cold room, as ways of treating his attachment problems.

Assessments and Custody Recommendations

Because judges and attorneys are rarely experts on child development issues, they generally seek help when decisions are to be made about child custody or about termination of parental rights, the legal action that frees a child for adoption. Expert testimony in these cases is usually given by a psychologist or psychiatrist who has done a bonding assessment. (In spite of the fact that the term bonding is unusual in professional discussions of child development, legal discussions do not often speak of attachment.) As we will see, the expert's testimony is actually a custody recommendation and does not necessarily deal directly with attachment.

Assessment of attachment for custody recommendation purposes is not as easy as is sometimes implied. In earlier chapters, we saw that measurements of attachment must be different for children of different ages, and that available standardized routines, like the Strange Situation, are inappropriate for this purpose, having been developed for research on groups rather than evaluation of an individual child.

So-called bonding/attachment assessments may be used to develop very general custody recommendations. These recommendations may also take into account past family history, particularly whether a given adult was the child's primary caregiver in the first years of life. Assessments may investigate a parent's knowledge about childrearing techniques, availability to care for the child, and attitudes about education and health care.

Bonding/attachment assessments may also involve observations of parent and child together, evaluating the appropriateness of their interaction, and whether they seem happy to be together. Although such observations could be valuable (does the parent seem to behave abusively or is the child frightened of or unresponsive to the parent?), in reality the conditions of the observation may be so artificial that the information gathered becomes almost useless. For example, a two-year-old in foster care may be scheduled for an assessment of attachment to a biological parent. The child may be picked up by an unfamiliar social services worker in an unfamiliar car, taken to an unfamiliar building, handed over to another unfamiliar person, and placed with the parent in an unfamiliar room where they are watched by another stranger. The child can hardly be expected to behave normally in these circumstances—and neither can the parent. But it is in such situations that many observations are made.

A recent suggestion is that bonding/attachment assessments need to look at *reciprocal connectedness*.[11] Reciprocal connectedness is evidence of the feelings the parent and child have for each other, feelings that are expressed in different ways toward and by children of different ages. Expressions of feeling may range from eye contact and affectionate touching (parent and young child), to cooperation in teaching and play (parent and school-age child), to cooperation in setting rules and limits (parent and adolescent). The idea of reciprocal connectedness seems to be based on Bowlby's principle that goal-corrected partnership is an aspect of attachment.

Attachment Issues and Legal Decisions

Public attention was brought to the role of relationships in custody decisions by two cases: those of "Baby M" and of "Baby Jessica." In each case, parents' wishes took precedence over considerations of the child's emotional attachment, but the attachment question was clearly present.

In the 1986 Baby M case, the child's biological mother, Mary Beth Whitehead, had entered into a contract with a childless couple. She agreed to be inseminated with the husband's sperm, to act as a gestational surrogate or surrogate mother, and to surrender the child for adoption by the couple. After the little girl's birth, however, Mrs. Whitehead was reluctant to give up the child; she delayed for some months, even disappearing with the baby at one point. The childless couple brought a lawsuit asking for compliance with the original agreement and eventually won custody of Baby M. The court's decision was based on the competing rights of Mrs. Whitehead as the biological mother, and the rights of the couple under the contractual agreement. Baby M was approaching an age where attachment to a familiar caregiver was an issue, and although child development professionals pointed this out, concern for this issue seems to have been absent in court.

In the 1993 case of Baby Jessica, the public's attention was captured by the distress of a toddler and her adoptive parents as they became caught up in a net of contradictory state laws and human errors. Jessica's unmarried biological mother had named the wrong man as the baby's birthfather. The actual biological father was unaware of the baby's birth and was never asked to voluntarily give up his parental rights—an essential step for a clear adoption process. Jessica was adopted and reared for two years by a couple in a state that neighbored the one where she was born, the two states having different laws about paternal rights in adoption.

When Jessica's birthfather became aware of the child's existence, he undertook legal proceedings to assert his parental rights and take custody of the child, whom he had actually never seen. The legal battle again concerned the opposing rights of the birthfather and the adoptive parents, with little or no concern about the impact of a decision on Jessica. The birthfather won, and the adoption was disrupted. Jessica was taken screaming from her adoptive mother's arms and given to the birthfather.

Cases like these, together with the progress of the best-interest principle, have encouraged the consideration of the child's emotional needs as one of the factors in child custody decisions. But, as we shall see, legal decisions have made a rather unsystematic use of this factor.

Child Custody Decisions and Attachment Issues

Looking at changes in consideration of relationship concerns in child custody decisions, we can see a gradual evolution of thinking, but there have been many inconsistencies and changes of direction. A review of cases in the state of New Jersey shows some changes that have occurred.

Sorrentino v. Family and Children's Society of Elizabeth, 1976. In this case, an unmarried sixteen-year-old gave birth, but had no home to take her baby to, so she placed the child for thirty days' temporary foster care. She decided to keep the baby, but was talked into agreeing to adoption. Over the next six months, she twice asked for the child to be returned. She married the baby's father and began a suit for custody of the child when the baby was fourteen months old. The court ordered a hearing:

> [It asked] whether transferring the custody of the child to plaintiffs at that time will raise the probability of serious harm to the child. Plaintiffs, who seek to change the *status quo* and to dislodge the child from the only real home she has ever known, will have the burden of proving by a preponderance of the credible evidence that the

potentiality for serious psychological harm accompanying or resulting from such a move will not become a reality.

This decision obviously took into account the emotional development of the toddler and gave it as much importance as the parents' rights.

Sees v. Baber, 1977. In this case, an unmarried mother gave her child up for adoption when the baby was three days old. She changed her mind two days later, and after about a month, initiated legal proceedings to regain custody. The case arrived at the New Jersey Supreme Court when the child was about a year old, a time when she could be expected to be at a peak in her concern about separation. The court refused to apply any principles about attachment, and gave two reasons for this: one, the court considered one year too short a time to create a psychological bond, and two, the child was too young for psychological evaluation. This decision completely ignored concerns about emotional development and about the impact of separation on a toddler, as well as failing to take into account the importance of time at this age, a point particularly stressed by the principle of the best interest of the child.

Hoy v. Willis, 1978. In this case eighteen-month-old twins, a boy and a girl, had been separated from each other at the time of the parents' separation in 1974, and the two had been placed for several weeks at the homes of two paternal aunts. A little later, one was sent to the home of one paternal uncle, the other to the home of a paternal aunt. The mother visited the boy three times in two years. In 1976 she took the girl to live with her.

The paternal grandmother asked for custody of the boy, and this was ordered, but there was also an order for examination and testing to see whether removal from the aunt's home would harm the child's psychological wellbeing. By this time the child was about six years old.

A psychiatrist testified that the aunt had become the boy's psychological parent and that the trauma of separation would create regression, depression, anxiety, and anger, conditions that would take at least seven years to resolve and might not resolve at all. Asked by the trial judge whether he would give the same opinion if the child had been kidnapped, the psychiatrist said he would—whereupon the judge declared that he could not accept that line of reasoning and ordered the child returned to his mother. The Appeals Court, however, reversed the decision, saying, "It is clear to us that the trial judge failed to recognize and apply present-day concepts of psychological parentage in resolving the custody issue before him." This case is an excellent example of the inconsistent use of attachment principles by courts at that time.

Zack v. Fiebert, 1989. The ages of the children in this important case are not clear, but they were apparently in early adolescence at the time of the decision. The mother of the two children had divorced and was remarried to a second husband; he had adopted the children. She became seriously ill and died in 1987; the children spent much of her illness with their maternal grandparents, but because of a quarrel saw little of them after the funeral. The adoptive father remarried and the children lived with him, his new wife, and her children. The maternal grandparents complained that the father was unfit, and they petitioned for more visitation on the grounds of their relationship with the children. The court refused and defined a psychological parent—in this case the adoptive father—as one whose removal from the child's life would cause the child severe psychological harm. The decision commented, "[N]ot even the most liberal reading of the [grandparents'] pleadings would support the conclusion that they stand in a parent-child relationship with their grandchildren."

The *Zack v. Fiebert* decision emphasized the importance of the psychological parent and treated biological kinship as a relatively trivial factor, thus affirming the serious importance of attachment issues. However, the logic of the decision assumed that attachment concerns would be the same for young teenagers as they are for infants and toddlers. Whereas *Sees v. Baber* assumed that a toddler was too young to be badly affected by separation, *Zack v. Fiebert* assumed that teenagers were still young enough—in each case, a conclusion contrary to what is known about attachment and separation.

B.F. v. DYFS, 1997. The mother in this case placed her young child (age unstated) in temporary foster care and eighteen months later contacted the New Jersey Division of Youth and Family Services to request reunion. The child was in a pre-adoptive home, and the Division decided to bring an action for her guardianship, preparatory to adoption by the family. However, it did not do so for another nine months, at which time the child had been separated from the biological mother for twenty-seven months. The mother was not allowed to visit during this time.

The court returned the little girl to her biological mother's custody, on the basis of the following reasoning:

> [B]ecause the psychological bonding between [the child] and her pre-adoptive family during the period following the [Division of Youth and Family Services'] refusal to allow visitation resulted from the improper denial of visitation rights, consideration of that bonding by the trial court would similarly have been improper.

Thus, in spite of precedents for consideration of attachment issues, the court apparently decided that due process trumped the best interest of the child. The *B. F. v. DYFS* decision contributed to the record of inconsistent judicial attention to parent-child relationships.

V. C. v. M. J. B., 1999. In an example of a new type of case, three-year-old twins were the subjects of a second-parent adoption suit. V. C. and

M. J. B., a same-sex couple, had shared parenting from the time the children had been born to one of them until the women separated when the twins were two years old. The biological mother had custody of the children, and her former partner requested visitation rights on the grounds of having bonded with the children. This was refused by the trial judge, who said: "While there is evidence ... of the plaintiff enjoying a bonded relationship with the children, the plaintiff has failed to establish the relationship to have risen to the level of *in loco parentis*." This judge apparently considered the possibility of degrees of attachment or psychological parenthood, an idea that had not appeared in decisions before.

The attorney representing the biological mother argued that the three-year-old children were too young to be affected by separation. "The fact that the plaintiff is a parental figure to the children and has 'bonded' with them is not a sufficient basis.... [T]hese are very young children ... and children form bonds with people such as grandparents, babysitters, [and] nannies."

The Appeals Court did permit visitation by the former partner and referred back to the *Zack* decision, focusing on the history of the adult-child relationship rather than on an assessment of the children's attachment behaviors. "Psychological parenthood is a finding based upon the role the person historically played in the child's life. Neither optimistic not pessimistic predictions of future harm that would result from ending that role can logically define the role itself."

The discussion of *V. C. v. M. J. B.*, thus, included the beliefs that attachments can be rank-ordered, that three-year-olds are too young to have real attachments, and that the nature of an adult-child relationship is understood on the basis of past events only. Relationship concepts and developmental changes played confused roles in this decision.

Watkins v. Nelson, 1999. In this case, a seventeen-year-old, unmarried mother was killed in a car accident twelve days after the birth of her child. The maternal grandparents cared for the baby, asked to be appointed her guardians, and contested the paternity claims of the biological father, who visited regularly. When the baby was nineteen months old, a trial judge gave custody to the grandparents, citing the principle of the best interest of the child.

The child, who had some physical problems, was said to be "developmentally unable" to show attachment. The grandparents were given custody not on the basis of psychological parenthood but because of their advocacy and involvement with her treatment and their experience with learning disabilities. On appeal, a dissenting opinion argued:

> I perceive no great potential for serious harm to [the child] in making the transition [to the father's custody].... Plaintiff has maintained a relationship with his daughter since her birth.... The change in

custody may, for a while, disturb [the child's] peace of mind ... [but] that will soon pass, considering her extreme youth.

This set of arguments again revealed a very mixed bag of beliefs about attachment and separation. Psychological parenthood was indeed seen as one of many important factors, and the long-term relationship with the father was stressed. But once again there was a failure to recognize that the extreme youth of the child made her more, rather than less, vulnerable to changes in relationships.

CONCLUSION

The concept of emotional attachment is not limited to professionals in child development and mental health work, but is part of popular thinking. Unfortunately, nonprofessional use of attachment concepts has not necessarily followed research findings or advances in theory. Popular advice about early emotional development often distorts important principles, or it asserts recommendations that have no basis in evidence. Such recommendations given to adoptive parents have resulted in problems, including serious injuries and some deaths.

Judges and attorneys who deal with child abuse cases generally hear arguments related to popular views of attachment rather than to research or established theory. These views may involve unsubstantiated statements about Reactive Attachment Disorder and necessary treatment.

Over the last thirty years, judges and attorneys dealing with adoption and child custody cases have begun to consider the role of attachment and separation issues in determining the well-being of the child. Although these factors are receiving far more consideration than in the distant past, they are still applied in inconsistent and contradictory ways. The developmental course of attachment seems to be imperfectly understood in the legal world.

chapter 8

New Directions: Parents, Children, and Attachment Concepts

This book has examined a wealth of observations and research directed toward understanding attachment. It may be hard to imagine that there is still much work to be done in this area. Looking at recent publications, however, it is plain that researchers are beginning to take some very new approaches to the study of emotional development and family relationships.

This final chapter will begin by summarizing the facts that have emerged from John Bowlby's original work. We will then consider the possibility that Bowlby's views may no longer fit the attachment experiences of the average child the way we used to think they did. If children's experiences in their families have altered since Bowlby's time, it may be necessary to think of attachment in a different way, ideally a way that would work for many different family patterns. The chapter will conclude with an examination of some new ideas that show promise for an increased understanding of emotional and social life.

ANSWERING BASIC QUESTIONS ABOUT ATTACHMENT

With fifty years of research and clinical work to draw on, we can summarize what is presently known about attachment. A good way to do this is to answer a set of questions posed by the well-known attachment researcher Everett Waters. The questions are a useful way to share the basic facts about attachment and other aspects of development.[1]

What Develops?

What characteristics of a person's emotional life change with age? Emotions, behaviors, and thoughts about other people all change as attachment develops. The newborn baby has engagement behaviors that attract and interest caregivers, but it is not until about eight months of age that we see children trying to stay near familiar people, expressing distress about separation, or showing pleasure and relief when reunited with a familiar person. In the next year or so, immediate, emotional responses to separation become less intense, and behavior begins to include negotiation of separation. During the school years, children's attachment to their parents presents as an affectionate partnership. During adolescence, other people, especially romantic partners, begin to be the focus of emotion and behavior. In adulthood, individuals show intense emotion and characteristic behavior toward their own children. The whole process seems to be related to the development of an internal working model of social relationships—a set of feelings, behaviors, beliefs, and expectations about interactions with other human beings.

What Are the Speed and Pattern of Development?

Do attachment behaviors and feelings change quickly or slowly, predictably or unpredictably? Some aspects of attachment must be in progress before the age of eight months, but the changes that occur at about that age appear to emerge rapidly and abruptly. From that point on, however, most changes in attachment behaviors and emotions are slow and gradual, and these alterations continue through adulthood and even into later life. Teenagers and adults do show some sudden changes, when they fall in love, or develop strong feelings soon after a baby is born or adopted.

What Are the Mechanisms of Development?

What factors make attachment develop? There are really only two categories of mechanisms, or causes, of developmental change. One of the possible causes is the genetic make-up of the group or of the individual. Because human beings—as well as our primate relatives—almost always show attachment behaviors and emotions if they have experienced a reasonably consistent and responsive social environment, we assume that the human genome carries information that makes it easy for attachment to occur. However, there is some research that suggests individual differences in children's attachment behavior are not caused by genetic factors.[2]

The occurrence of attachment, and the type of attachment emotions and behavior that emerge, seem to depend on social experiences, especially the repeated experiences that make others familiar. Consistent, repeated experiences with a sensitive, responsive adult are the foundation for secure attachment. The continued development of the internal working model of social relationships occurs because of an increasing variety and complexity of social interactions, helped along by language communication and by maturing thought patterns.

Experience is such an important mechanism for attachment that psychotherapy or a new family situation can help to alter the internal working model years after the initial attachment experiences have occurred. Some adults manage to pull themselves up by their own bootstraps and to alter their own thinking toward a more positive and secure view of social relations. Some, however, are so strongly affected by their families' past histories of attachment and separation, it is difficult for them to change.

Are There Normal Individual Differences in the Development of Attachment?

Should we expect social and emotional development to be about the same in most normal individuals? There are certainly normal individual differences in young children's attachment behavior and emotional expression. These differences seem to be connected with the child's temperament, or a biologically determined individuality of response to the environment. However, whereas most children are considered securely attached, there are other variations that may not be exactly normal or desirable. There are significant numbers of insecurely attached toddlers, and a small number whose attachment is considered disorganized. Only the latter group is thought of as definitely outside the normal range. Older children and adults have individual variations in their internal working models of social relations because of their ongoing social experiences.

Are There Population Differences in Attachment?

Are there groups of people who become strongly attached to familiar people, or other groups who do not really care who their companions are? Groups of people who have shared traumatic experiences and separations show different attachment emotions and behaviors than those with a good attachment history. For example, families of Holocaust survivors seem to pass separation concerns down the generations.[3] Toddlers who survived the African rebel wars of the last decade were often stunned and unresponsive; older children who were kidnapped and forced to kill as child soldiers also have had unusual emotional responses to others. Even when brought up in peaceful situations, groups of children can show emotional differences derived from their cultural backgrounds. Boys, however, are not different from girls, and there do not seem to be population differences based on differences in a group's genetic make-up (as opposed to cultural differences).

A CHANGING WORLD: CULTURAL AND SOCIAL ALTERATIONS THAT CAN INFLUENCE ATTACHMENT

A wealth of information about attachment seems to exist today. But will it be true in a few years? Can we expect changes in our understanding of attachment? Can we expect events that might actually change the average child's emotional development?

Of course, changes in our thinking and new research are always possible—and to be hoped for. But it is also possible that the way people live may alter, and with it, children's emotional experiences and development.

Mixing Cultures

Attachment theory and research have up until now been based largely on the habits and beliefs of Western European and North American people. Although there has been serious cross-cultural research, this research was formulated on the basis of Western beliefs about the importance of attachment experiences—as indeed any research must be formulated on some foundation of beliefs and values.

As movement from one cultural setting to another becomes more frequent, and as non-Westerners more often live in the United States and European countries, the cultural contrasts among beliefs about attachment become more evident. In a recent case, a Chinese couple, Shaoqiang and Quin Luo He, who lived in Memphis, learned that a judge had terminated their parental rights to their five-year-old daughter, Anna Mae. Mr. and Mrs. He had initially asked to place Anna Mae in temporary foster care at her birth, a time when they were beset by a variety of legal and financial troubles. When Anna Mae was three months old, they agreed to temporary custody by the foster parents. The Hes visited Anna Mae almost every week for the next two years. They then asked to have her returned. They got into an altercation with the foster parents, were ordered to stay away, and did so for several months. The couple's compliance, far from creating the good will they desired, was interpreted as abandonment.

The American and European view of this situation assumes that legal parenthood of a child can be decided on the basis of the parents' actions, and that placement of a child for care by another person or family is on the verge of abandonment. For Chinese families, a more likely assumption is that young children can be cared for others, sometimes for years, without breaking the parent-child connection. For Chinese children in families that have immigrated to the United States, being sent away may be a normative experience, an experience which many other people have and which the individual regards as an acceptable, though uncomfortable part of life. As the separated child grows up, he or she adds this understanding to the internal working model of social relations; non-parental care does not mean rejection or lack of parental love. This internal working model is, of course, different from what might be found in a highly assimilated Chinese family in the United States.

People of American culture tend to believe in some prenatal or genetic connection between mother and child, but they simultaneously accept the idea that parents earn their rights by showing that they care about the child. This genetic assumption stresses that knowledge of the real father and the real mother are important, even when these people may be thought to have forfeited their right to the child. The belief that an adopted child longs for the chance for reunion has produced laws that allow for open adoption and for the availability of information to adoptees when they reach adulthood. Another type of legal change has been the gradual alteration in the cultural view of pregnancy outside marriage. Whereas women once feared unwanted pregnancy, birth, and adoption as potential sources of great social disapproval, precluding later marriage, there is far less secrecy today. There seems to be a social movement to revise our ideas about the parent-child relationship, including the belief that the early relationship is permanent and the assumption that more than one kind of attachment can exist.

It is difficult to know whether changing or differing beliefs about attachment lead to different practices. If they do, however, the eventual outcome may be a change in common attachment patterns and internal working models of social relationships.

Changing Family Patterns

Whether or not altered beliefs are involved, there is much excellent research to show that social and economic changes result in changed family patterns and in the changed experiences of children in those families.[4] Some social factors that have transformed over the last several decades have had the potential for altering both children's attachment experiences and adults' beliefs about attachment.

Divorce, remarriage, and the creation of blended families form a constellation of factors with implications for attachment. The issue is not so much the experience of emotional loss, as the development of an internal working model of *emotional equivalency*, where one father, mother, brother, or sister is expected to be interchangeable with another. A father departs from the family or changes his role dramatically; a stepfather is slotted into the empty spot, and life is supposed to go on much as usual. Stepbrothers and stepsisters enter the picture, and the children are expected to come to terms with each other rather rapidly. The pattern associated with these family relationships becomes more like that of dating than of traditional marriage, especially if the child experiences several divorces and remarriages, as many do.

Another relevant family change involves the rapidly increasing frequency of births to, or adoptions by, same-sex couples. The resulting families have a variety of biological connections, as opposed to the single pattern for a heterosexual couple with non-adopted children; whether the biological relationships make any difference to the children probably depends entirely on whether the parents think they do (and, as we saw earlier, they may think so).

Lesbian couples have the option for one, the other, or both to arrange to become pregnant. (One such couple each gave birth, after being inseminated with sperm from the same donor, so that, as one of the mothers put it, "Everybody's related to somebody.") The degrees of biological relationship may be different for other same-sex couples, and obviously male couples can donate sperm, but they must have a gestational surrogate to carry the baby. (These couples may use a mixture of semen for insemination, so the real father is not known.) All these families can develop attachment through their social interactions, but it is not known whether their beliefs about genetic connectedness make any difference.

One possible disturbing factor for same-sex couples and their children is the fear of separation. Laws about parental rights have been based on a biological relationship or on adoption by a person or couple following termination of the parental rights of another person or couple. Marriage has been the only circumstance where one parent's rights could be terminated and transferred to the new spouse of the other parent. These laws do not work well with the same-sex couple's family. For women partners, only one gives birth to a particular child; since the women are not married under most current state laws, the other partner cannot adopt and share parenthood of the child.

In many states, this situation has cast a shadow on same-sex couples' family relationships, although it is not known whether attachment processes have been affected. The partner who is not the birthmother or father knows that a disruption in the adult relationship might lead to a complete rupture of the relationships with the children. This partner would not have the rights to visitation or joint custody enjoyed by heterosexual couples. Death of the birthmother or father could also have a disastrous effect, potentially giving grandparents custody of the children, whom they may have never seen.

Changes in laws about same-sex marriage can ameliorate this problem and its potential for disturbance of developing parent-child relationships. Meanwhile, a number of states have permitted second-parent adoption, a legal process that allows the non–birthmother or father to establish rights to contact with the children whom he or she may care for and love as much as his or her partner does.

Changes in Fertility and Adoption Patterns

Attachment processes take place within a broad social and economic context. Changes throughout the society can influence family life and thus have a potential for changing attachment patterns.

Delayed Childbearing. As the status of women and their options for professional education have advanced in the United States, the tendency to delay childbearing has also increased. Women, who would have had children in their twenties in the past, are now putting off pregnancy until the late thirties or even forties. But, heard by their owners or not, biological clocks do continue to tick, and reproductive cycles happen less regularly as the years pass. Not only are these older, potential mothers more likely to conceive a child with serious disabilities, such as Down Syndrome, they are a good deal less likely than younger women to conceive.

Although we do not know exactly what happens, it seems possible that women who experience fertility problems will also have some changes in their internal working models of social relationships, especially the aspects that have to do with the woman becoming a mother or with the place of a child in her life. As we saw earlier in this book, the mother's memories of her own attachment experiences appear to affect her child; it is possible that the grief and anxiety of infertility can also do so.[5]

Of course, there have always been infertile couples, and history records many a queen being "put away" for her failure to produce an heir. The modern situation is a bit different, however. We seem to expect to be able to control our fertility. We turn it off; we ought to be able to turn it on again. Our preference is for a small number of children, with whom we expect to have intense emotional relationships. The vagaries of Assisted Reproductive Technology (ART) involve the practice of fertilizing a number of ova, implanting some, and then possibly eliminating some of the implants to assure the success of others; the couple that experiences this must decide to destroy some potential children for the sake of others. Finally, we see women today choosing to become pregnant by ART while unmarried, a step that involves a different model of relationships than in the past. All of these factors can create a perspective on attachment that is different from the historical view, and it may be that the different perspective can itself influence how attachment develops.

Adoptive Families. At the time when the Supreme Court legalized abortion with the *Roe v. Wade* decision, it was thought by some that there might soon be fewer children to adopt. There has been some truth to this prediction, but, as so often happens, the story has not played out exactly as expected.

In the United States, it is not unusual for a married woman to be unhappy when she finds out she is pregnant. Some give birth and some abort, but virtually none surrender the children for adoption. In the past, an unplanned pregnancy in an unmarried woman, especially a teenager, was often terminated by abortion, but adoption was also an option. About half the girls aborted, when the procedure was illegal; 45 percent had the baby adopted; only 5 percent kept custody of the child, usually with the help of their parents. Today, about half of pregnant, unmarried girls abort; 45 percent retain custody of the baby, and 5 percent agree to adoption.

Does this mean that there are now many fewer children in need of adoptive homes? No, unfortunately, this is not exactly the case. But it does mean there are few young infants available for adoption in the United States. The attempts of young, poorly educated mothers to care for their children too often end in neglect and abuse, followed by later foster care placement. Time passes, the mother makes more efforts, there is more trouble, and eventually termination of parental rights occurs. Now the children are free for adoption—but they are three, four, five years, or older, bear the scars of their chaotic emotional lives, and often have special medical and educational needs. To create good emotional relationships in these later adoptions is much more difficult than to deal with a young baby, who often has charming engagement behaviors and readily responds to affection. It is no wonder that many late-adopting parents are preoccupied with attachment issues.

In the wake of these social changes, a foreign adoption industry has grown up. There are many expenses and problems associated with foreign adoption, certainly, but foreign-adopting parents have no worries about whether a mother's parental rights have been properly terminated or whether a birthfather will suddenly appear, as happened in the Baby Jessica case described in Chapter 7. Nevertheless, parents who adopt foreign children may be struck by the artificiality of the situation, and they may wonder how they can possibly become a real family.

The social changes outlined in this section have powerful implications for people's ideas about attachment. These changes may well encourage the view that attachment is a job to be done, rather than the natural consequence of growing social interactions and experience between parent and child. Parents adopting under difficult circumstances may even fear that attachment will not take place and that the consequences may be terrible.

Infant Day Care and the Day Care Wars. Concerns about attachment have been raised by the fact that many children enter day care while still young infants. It is reasonable to ask whether spending many hours each week away from their parents can negatively affect children's attachment. To put this issue in context, however, we should note that non-parental care is a real part of the history of our species. Human parents love their babies, but they have always wanted some respite from taking care of them. In any traditional culture, it makes perfect sense that a young, healthy, capable woman should spend her time in the fields, at the market, or doing weaving or whatever she can to care for her family's needs; baby-minding may be done by little girls or the elderly aunt who can't walk far anyway.

Babies have thrived in that sort of non-parental care and have done so for most of human history. Why, then, are we concerned about day care arrangements? The fact is, of course, they are very different from that traditional care pattern.

Babies cared for by little girls or by elderly aunts or grandmothers had intimate contacts with their mothers many times a day. They had to, because in most traditional cultures, breastfeeding went on until the age of eighteen months or two years. The point here is not the breastfeeding itself, but the occurrence of real mutual attention between mother and child at frequent intervals. Nursing babies in such societies would also have slept with their mothers and had frequent interactions during the night.

Traditional non-parental care also gave the baby the same familiar caregiver every day. A particular child nurse or older relative had the job, and she was expected to know the baby well and to be able to respond to all its needs, except breastfeeding. Child nurses were admonished not to let the baby cry, and they developed ways of soothing, comforting, and engaging a fretful baby. An important aspect of traditional child care, generally, was the existence of one caregiver per infant or toddler.

Modern infant day care stands in some contrast to traditional non-parental care. Although many day care centers would be willing to cooperate with breastfeeding mothers, few mothers have time to make the journey from their workplace, nurse the baby in an unhurried and interactive way, and return to work. Neither, of course, do bottle-feeding mothers have this chance for frequent workday interactions with their babies. Frequent mother-baby contact during the working day is just not an option in the modern infant day care pattern.

Whether or not an infant in day care has a consistent caregiver depends on circumstances. When an infant is in family day care—a more or less informal arrangement in the caregiver's home—there is one caregiving adult, and she may continue as the consistent caregiver for years. (Or, of course, she may for her own reasons go out of business, forcing the baby's family to search for a new caregiver.) In center-based day care—the form familiar to most people—where hired caregivers work with a group of children, a baby may or may not have a consistent caregiver. In a small number of high quality day care centers, an assigned caregiver takes responsibility for no more than three young children and is alone in a room with them. In more common situations, the ratio of children to caregivers is larger; there are floating caregivers who attend to whichever baby needs them at a given time, and many children and caregivers may be together in a large room.

Infants in day care are exposed to two additional, problematic factors. First, day care providers work shifts of eight hours or less, meaning most babies experience a daily changeover of caregivers because they are at the center when the shift changes. Second, infants in day care are likely to experience abrupt changes of caregiver when familiar people leave the job. Staff turnover is a major problem in center-based day care, largely because pay and status are low even though the work is very hard work.

If we consider what we know about attachment, we can see that traditional non-parental care might be expected to have a different effect on emotional development than modern infant day care. The ideal situation for attachment, as far as we know, involves a small number of consistent caregivers who play and socialize with the baby and who are sensitive and responsive to the baby's needs (food, comfort, or social fun). Consistent and responsive care allows the baby to learn to expect good things from familiar people, building trust and the beginnings of a secure attachment and positive internal working model of social relationships. From the adult's viewpoint, consistent involvement with one or two infants allows for a real understanding of each child's needs and ways of communicating. This understanding allows the adult to be more sensitive to the baby's cues and therefore to respond more effectively. As a result, the adult feels gratified by his or her success, takes pride and pleasure in the child, and becomes more deeply engaged in the relationship. The ideal attachment situation creates a *benign circle* in which adult and child are progressively more involved with each other through the first year or two of life. Traditional nonparental care made this benign circle easy to enter.

Modern infant day care, on the other hand, may or may not make the benign circle possible. A family day care provider is very likely to have several other children to care for, although she may have time to get to know and be sensitive to an individual baby. A high-quality day care center will have providers caring for several babies, but may have an emphasis on relationship building, a point that will be discussed later in this chapter. At the other end of the spectrum, relationships between a baby and caregivers may be tenuous when caregivers have too many children to work with or they are not assigned to particular babies, and when staff turnover is too rapid to allow babies and adults to learn about each other. When parents are also overwhelmed and time at home is rushed so that everything gets done, the day care infant may experience very little in the way of the sensitive, responsive social interaction that is linked to attachment.

It is no wonder, then, that the role of infant day care in early emotional development has been the subject of much discussion among students of child development and mental health. Disagreements on this subject at one point reached a pitch sometimes referred to as the day care wars. Research in the 1980s and 1990s suggested that children with more experience of day care in infancy were more likely to show insecure attachment, and that the combination of insecure attachment and more time spent in day care was associated with more negative emotion and less mature play with toys.[6] These results, however, were difficult to interpret.[7] For example, mothers of insecurely attached toddlers, who expressed negative emotion and did not play well, might be more inclined to put their children in day care for extended periods. Mothers who felt incompetent and ungratified by interactions with their children might well feel that someone else could care for the child as well as they could—perhaps even better.

Despite the day care wars, economic and other social pressures have meant infant day care is here to stay. There is, however, a very positive outcome of the battle, that being a much-increased emphasis on the quality of day care, particularly in the attention paid to social and emotional needs. Many initiatives have worked toward improvement of young children's attachment experiences in day care, and although low-quality day care is still common, the average experience of children in day care today may be different than it was at the height of the day care wars. This is a most desirable outcome, but one that adds confusion to our ability to understand the effect of day care on attachment.

CHANGING PRACTICE, CHANGING THEORY: NEW DIRECTIONS IN CHILD DEVELOPMENT AND MENTAL HEALTH PERSPECTIVES ON ATTACHMENT

As more is understood about early emotional development, both practice and theory tend to change. These changes may be providing children with a somewhat different set of experiences than were common either during the day care wars or in Bowlby's day.

Relationship-Based Practice

Current work with parents and children emphasizes the need to form and support good emotional relationships. This includes relationships between parents and children, those between day care providers and children, and the relationships of parent educators and mental health professionals to parents, children, and caregivers.

Cultural Issues in Working with Relationships. Awareness of cultural factors and the role they play in internal working models of relationships is a major factor in working with families. A simple example involves the use of eye contact—mutual gaze—as a method of emotional communication. Americans of European background often seek or even demand eye contact with a child, as a means of play and affection, but also as a way to exert authority and demand obedience. "Look at me, Jimmy" is a way to overcome the child's resistance and get compliance, and is frequently used by white mothers, teachers, and day care providers. In non-European cultures, however, the child who maintains eye contact, when spoken to, is showing resistance and disrespect for the adult; a lowered gaze is considered respectful and compliant. Culturally determined ways to send emotional messages are gradually built into an internal working model of social relationships.

The way mental health professionals work with parents may be defined in terms of a cultural view of relationships. Among Latino families, for example, there is an expectation of *personalismo*.[8] This term refers to the value of warm and individualized attention to others, with some informality and openness, but without being overly familiar. Personalismo requires helping professionals to give respect to parents' beliefs and assumptions, rather than pressing upon the family the messages garnered from child development research. One such belief among Latino families is that family members should be interdependent, an idea that contrasts with the mainstream or standard American goal of making babies independent.[9]

Child Care and Relationships. The improvement of relationships for infants and toddlers in day care has been a major thrust of child development advocates in recent years. A national initiative, the Better Baby Care Campaign,[10] has focused on a number of improvements in the child care standards as they relate to attachment. These include specialized training for infant and toddler caregivers, with a stress on child development and family relationships.

Other groups, such as the National Association for the Education of Young Children (NAEYC), Zero to Three, and the World Association for Infant Mental Health, are trying to bring about changes in child care and produce a more attachment-friendly setting. They are working against the common assumption that infant day care is the same thing as preschool, which in turn is popularly assumed to be essentially the same as elementary school. Such assumptions are shown in the tendency to name day care centers "Kid Academy" or "Learning Center" and to refer to infant caregivers as teachers.

NAEYC emphasizes the use of *developmentally appropriate practice* in all child care settings as well as in the home. This term refers to ways of working with children that support the normal processes of the child's stage of development. For infants and toddlers, the development of secure attachment relationships appears to be the most important of all developmental processes and to be part of the foundation for other developmental events, such as the use of language. Developmentally appropriate practice for infants and toddlers must emphasize the growth of relationships. For three-, four-, and five-year-olds, developmentally appropriate child care needs to take into account the child's growing abilities to negotiate and deal with conflicts with peers and adults. Developmentally appropriate day care is based on relationships, not on instructional techniques.[11]

Attachment-Friendly Day Care Practices. To allow for the development of good relationships, day care centers need to pay close attention to staff-to-child ratios, group size, and staff turnover. For maximum encouragement of attachment, however, they also need to deal with some other specific concerns.

Feeding practices in day care settings are important ways to foster social relationships and emotional development. The issue here is not about breastfeeding versus bottle-feeding, but about social interactions that are part of feeding by bottle, spoon, or otherwise. A caregiver feeding an infant needs to be with one child at a time, holding the baby to bottle-feed or sitting face-to-face to spoon-feed. For children old enough to self-feed, the caregiver needs to be present and attentive, but several toddlers may be helped at the same time; she may steady a cup, hold a bowl still, or talk and smile. The feeding situation is not just for nutrition; it also provides an opportunity for intense, pleasurable social interaction, full of meaningful communication. In order to use feeding in this way, the caregiver must be able to take enough time, she must know the child and be known by him or her, and she must be able and willing to pick up the child's communications about hunger and satisfaction. The attachment-friendly caregiver does not try to make the baby finish a bottle, trick the child into opening the mouth for a spoonful of food, or react to play with food as if it is an act of insubordination.

A day care center's policy about attachment objects is also an indication of attachment-friendliness. For infants and toddlers dealing with separation and anxiety, the availability of a beloved blanket, pacifier, or soft toy may be the secret to comfort. (These objects are not a substitute for the mother, for the child wants them even when in mother's lap.) A common day care practice in the 1970s and 1980s was to prohibit such objects in the day care center, or to insist that the child share them—an idea about as acceptable to toddlers as the proposal to adults that they share a spouse with a friend. Attachment-friendly care encourages the use of attachment objects, recognizing that these provide a way for children to handle separation and also, the exciting stimulation of the group.

Recognition of secure base behavior in the day care center is a way to support both emotional and cognitive development. The toddler's exploration of new people and events works much better when a familiar person is available as a secure base to return to for emotional refueling. The secure-base person needs not just to be available, but to cooperate in the task. She needs to be responsive when the exploring toddler comes back, but also attentive enough to return eye contact from a distance, or to speak to a child who is looking back anxiously. A good secure-base person does not regard the child as clingy or whiny, but recognizes the emotional significance of checking-in with a familiar adult.

The handling of transitions is another factor relevant to attachment. The arrival of a child at the day care center, going to sleep and awakening, and being picked up by a parent at day's end are all transitions which relate to separation and reunion concerns. These times need to be handled carefully and with attention to the child's communications. Arrival and departure are especially problematic times because parent and child affect each other with their emotional communications about their situation. The parent may fear a scene, if the child does not readily accept separation, and may be equally concerned with the child's distress, worries about other parents' disapproval, and anxiety about being late to work. Or, paradoxically, the parent may be concerned that a child who separates quietly is not sufficiently attached. In either case, the child is liable to be affected by the parent's involuntary communication of fear and sadness.

In the late afternoon, many children will express anger about separation, often by ignoring the returning parent and resisting what the parent tries to do. Parents in turn feel anxiety, weariness, and irritation at the complexity of what should be a simple process. Day care centers can help by providing plenty of time for transitions and giving emotional support for parents and children who have trouble with separation and reunion. At the time of arrival, especially, a caregiver needs to greet the baby and help to make the entry a gradual one.

Finally, attachment-friendly day care centers need policies that support families' emotional lives and their connections with their children. Exhausted and emotionally drained, young working parents often turn to their child's caregiver for advice and nurturing, needs that are not the caregiver's real job, nor anything she has usually been trained to deal with. Day care staffs need help recognizing and understanding parents' needs, but at the same time they need to set limits on the demands made of them. The combination of responsiveness and limit setting needs to be done at a managerial level and in a way that provides helpful guidelines for parents. The increasing interest of day care centers in these relationship issues is a real, but very gradual change.

Changing Psychological Theory

Since Bowlby and Ainsworth's day, attachment has become a focus for researchers, clinicians, and parents. Attachment could accurately be described as an imperialistic schema, taking over and subordinating other categories. We have certainly seen how the idea of attachment has become the most important way of thinking about emotional development. However, as we look at changes in psychological and mental health theories, we can see that the concept of attachment is now becoming a part of some broader schemes, hardly thought of in Bowlby's day.

Systems Theory, Transactional Processes, and Attachment. The idea that attachment is a thing inside a person, a state or process that exists independently of other factors, is certainly a gross over-simplification of Bowlby's work. It is not, however, so very far from the ethological view of an imprinting event that happens quickly and can permanently change the direction of development. Nor is this simple view much different from some of the popularized ideas we encountered in Chapter 7.

Modern psychological theory does not deal much with simple ideas. A fact that becomes ever clearer is that human beings are complex creatures dwelling in a complex environment. Like other modern disciplines, psychology has come to respect and to use *systems theory*, and of all aspects of psychology, the study of development has been most drawn to the dynamic systems approach.[12] Concepts of attachment are now often couched in systems terms.

Briefly, dynamic systems theory involves the assumption that many factors work together to create any behavior, emotion, or thought. These factors are coordinated in their effects and function nonlinearly. That is, it is possible that some very large change could have only a small influence on a developmental outcome, but another small change could create a major effect (or vice versa). Systems theory assumes a natural variation in events such as emotions and behaviors and posits that not all changes result from definable causes. The theory also assumes that any group of factors, in the child or in the environment, could begin to combine in a new way just because some small change has occurred. Just as one last degree of heat brings a pan of milk to a boil, a brief experience or small maturational event could seriously alter beliefs, feelings, or behavior.

How do these systems ideas apply to attachment behaviors and emotions? First of all, there are many factors involved in the expression of attachment, and a slight change may have obvious effects. Toddlers may ignore their parents, wander off, and even deliberately keep their distance until a stranger appears or the child gets hurt, whereupon the child makes a beeline for the parent.[13] Children may behave quite differently if they have had similar attachment experiences but different temperaments (see Chapter 6). A child may show different attachment emotions and behaviors toward different people, even people who do not seem dramatically different from each other.

Attachment also shows normal variations. A given child does not show exactly the same attachment behavior—like use of a secure base—every day, even though the situation and the people involved may be very similar.

Finally, and most importantly, attachment behavior does seem to follow the systems tenet that rules and functions can reorganize abruptly. Children's attachment behavior and emotions do not change instantaneously, but there is often a noticeably rapid transition from the fearless, convivial period of infancy to the characteristic behavior of a toddler who screams at the approach of a well-meaning stranger, or even a familiar family member. (For example, one child happened to be taken on a two-day trip by his mother at seven months; he was restless and unfriendly to other people. On reunion with the father at an unfamiliar campsite, he cried and turned away, a difficult response for the father.)

A useful concept related to systems theory is that of the transactional process.[14] This idea also provides an excellent framework for attachment. Transactional processes are repeated interactions, like many that occur between parents and infants. In each interaction, each person influences and changes the other a little, and this alteration changes the ways they are able to affect each other. At the end of many interactions, each person has changed, and their ways of interacting are different from what they were originally.

Attachment behaviors and emotions develop as part of a relationship, and as we saw in earlier chapters, both partners change. To see this as the result of a transactional process makes a great deal of sense. Take, for example, the development of secure base behavior. A parent might initially assume that a toddler who goes off exploring in a safe playground needs no special attention or interest; the adult might read the paper or talk to a friend, occasionally glancing at the child only for safety's sake. The child might then surprise and distress the parent by returning, climbing into a lap, demanding attention, and so on, before exploring again. After that occasion, the parent would probably become more attentive, watching the child, being available to return eye contact when the child looks back, and perhaps speaking to the child. Together, the two would work out how far away the child might go with comfort to both partners, and how much attention the parent needs to pay in order to support the child's exploration. After several more park visits, the transactional process would result in effective secure base behaviors, which involve seeking on the child's part and cooperating on the parent's. (If, on the other hand, the parent was insensitive to the child's signals, the result might be a degree of risk-taking behavior sufficient to grab the parent's attention.)

Both systems theory and the transactional process are useful ways to approach the complexity of attachment. Unfortunately, it is quite difficult to apply these ideas to the design of research on emotional development, or to interpret research that involves so many factors. In any case, these ways of thinking have helped us to get past some oversimplified perspectives on attachment.

Attachment and Theory of Mind. A fascinating and potentially fruitful new way of looking at attachment links the process with the development of *Theory of Mind.*[15] Theory of Mind (TOM) is also referred to as *mentalization* or *Reflective Function.* The term Theory of Mind describes the ability of all normal human adults to read minds—not literally, of course, but to make excellent guesses about what another person knows, wants, believes, hopes, and intends. We use TOM when we assume that all these human bodies around us, a lot like ours, have inside them the capacity to know and experience the world just as we do. In order to use TOM well, however, we must also understand that another person's knowledge, desires, intentions, and subjective experience are probably not identical to our own.

Communication with others depends on TOM. If we were to assume that speech was just mechanical, reflexive noise making, unconnected with a mind, we could not understand another person's intentions or make our own clear. When a guest refuses a second helping of mashed potatoes, our capacity to use TOM enables us to decide with some degree of accuracy whether to press the offer or let it drop, or even whether to take offense at the implication that our cooking might not be appetizing.

Of course, we as adults all know that we can do TOM tasks, even though we do not always do them very well. What does TOM have to do with attachment or any part of early emotional development? The connection comes in the course of early development and involves complicated steps. The description below is a highly simplified summary of a large body of research and theory, linking parents' abilities to mentalize their emotional

involvement with their children and with attachment and TOM development in the child.[16]

Events in development of TOM and attachment begin with *intersubjectiv-
ity*, the apparently innate tendency for the young baby and parent to respond
to each other in special, human ways. Although the baby may not really
know what a human being is, she acts as if she does, and from birth she looks,
listens, and interacts with a caregiver in quite different ways than she would
with inanimate objects. For example, the baby takes turns in interactions,
vocalizing and looking for a while, then waiting quietly while the caregiver
does the same. The baby also can and does imitate certain adult facial expressions. The caregiver responds by acting as if the baby intends to communicate, even though it seems impossible for us to know whether this is true.

In the course of these interactions with the young baby, the parent begins to mirror, or mimic, the baby's expression, with the imitation following a fraction of a second behind the baby. The baby, of course, does not
see herself in a mirror often. The adult's imitation provides a chance for the
baby to learn the connection between the subjective experience of emotion and the external movements that can reveal the internal emotional
state. "I feel like this," the baby may think, "and it looks like that." These
experiences build a foundation of emotion-linked knowledge that will later
help the baby read the mental processes of others.

Can this process go astray? A baby who is weak, sick, or distressed may
not respond well to a caregiver, who may in turn become depressed and
discouraged, and stop engaging with the child. A baby with facial problems
may not present an expression to which an adult can respond. A caregiver
who is depressed to begin with may not look at or listen to the baby, but
may simply go through caregiving routines mechanically. A caregiver who
is overstressed and preoccupied may mirror emotions inaccurately, or her
face may show only her own internal state, which may not be a good match
for the baby's emotions. And a caregiver with poorly developed TOM may
not pay attention to the baby's communications at all, instead behaving as
if the baby has no subjective experience whatever.

As the baby observes the world and begins to see patterns of behavior,
he or she develops a *teleological stance*—a set of expectations about what a
person will do next. This stance does not initially take into account the
person's intentions, knowledge or other parts of the mental state, but simply assumes that people do things that make physical sense (like taking the
shortest path to walk across a room). The baby is puzzled and interested
when behavior does not make sense, but has no way to understand the
internal state of mind that is guiding the action. (One 12-month-old,
newly walking, imitated his mother's attempts to swat a fly in every detail,
including swiveling his head as if following the insect's flight. But he paid

no attention at all to an actual fly nearby—showing that he did not understand the intention behind the movements.)

At about nine months of age, just as most are beginning to show concern about separation, infants begin to coordinate new behaviors with adults in the form of joint attention. The child uses the gaze to get the adult's attention and to point it to something interesting. For example, she looks at an adult until the adult looks back. Then, flicking her gaze toward the interesting puppy or new toy, she uses her eyes to point. Next, she looks back to check the direction of the adult's gaze, and if the adult is not looking in the right direction, she tries again. The sequence ends with a series of eye movements: the two look at the interesting sight, then back at each other with a smile, and then at the object again.

Joint attention may be the beginning of the intentional stance that makes TOM much more accurate, enabling the child to judge what another person plans and wants to do, not just what might reasonably happen. Paying attention to the direction someone looks, and to the person's facial expression, is a great help in understanding what is intended.

The new understanding of intention and desire is normally in place by about two years of age and alters communication and understanding a good deal. (When the little boy described above arrived at an intentional stance, he grabbed and waved the flyswatter, shouting, "Where dat fly!" in imitation of his mother's intention, not just her actions. He omitted the head swiveling that had been a feature of his earlier performance.) Although many two-year-olds have this much TOM and know what people want, they still do not understand that people may fail to do what they intend if they believe something that is not true. If a three-year-old sees someone put a cup in the dishwasher before leaving the room and someone else take the cup out and put it in the cupboard, the child will be mistaken about what will happen when the first person returns. Asked where the first adult will look for the cup, the three-year-old replies "in the cupboard," believing actions are always based on reality.

Not until age four or five do children realize that the adult's false belief will make her look in the wrong place. At that age, also, children begin to think about how they or other people know something—whether they saw it themselves, whether someone told them, whether they just figured it out. This step enables the child to understand the consequences of false belief, but also to have some insight into the chances that a belief is false, or that someone else may think it is.

How are these steps toward mature TOM related to attachment? First, TOM and attachment seem to develop as a result of similar social experiences. The sensitive, responsive caregiver, whom we have repeatedly mentioned as an important factor in attachment, is also the person who pays attention to the child, quickly and accurately mirroring the child's expression. The responsive caregiver quickly notices the child's gaze and joins in joint attention, looking as instructed and exchanging a smile and glance of pleasure with the child. The caregiver talks to the child and responds to and joins in pretend play, showing the affectionate, playful sociability that seems to be a foundation of attachment. At the same time, the caregiver is providing the language that helps to describe emotional states ("Is that a scary noise?"), and some practice in understanding intention and belief. The child may come to think about intention because the caregiver acts as if it is important. The caregiver's response to the child's intentions also provides quick comfort and a return to security. A familiar caregiver will understand the child's signals best and therefore be the best at comforting the child and providing a secure base.

Development of TOM is essential for negotiation, a significant step in the attachment process. To negotiate effectively, the child must recognize that the parent's intentions, desires, and beliefs may be different from the child's, and this means that to some degree, the child must be capable of reflecting on his or her own mental state. Negotiation involves attempts to move toward another's position without abandoning too much of one's own, and thus requires knowledge of both people's positions, which are based partly on TOM. Similarly, the development of the goal-corrected partnership involves progressive change in each partner's assessment of the other's knowledge and wishes. Parents can and do model this aspect of TOM by offering compromise, explaining their thinking, and admitting that they have had a false belief, if this is the case.

Finally, TOM seems to be necessary for development of an effective internal working model of social relations. Mature TOM involves ways of thinking both about the self and about other people. These capacities enable the individual to be aware of how his own intentions and beliefs are like those of other people and how they are different. It also enables the child to understand how others may read him, thus predicting safety, security, hostility, nurturing, or rejection by others. Such predictions can include how others will act and feel about themselves and how one will act and feel toward someone else. Importantly, mature TOM allows the understanding of individual differences and needs, a step that creates a different position in the internal working model for the vulnerable baby than for the adult enemy.

CONCLUSION: ATTACHMENT AND POLICY

So far in this chapter, we have seen answers to some important questions about attachment, but we have also seen that related practice and theory are very much in flux. Is it possible to use what we know about attachment to establish good policy and legal guidelines for the benefit of children and their families?

The step from research and theory to policy is one that requires great care. As Sir Michael Rutter, the eminent researcher who studied the adopted Romanian orphan group, has warned, it is possible for policy change to be based far more on evangelism than on systematic evidence.[17]

Jack Shonkoff, a noted leader in family policy, has given a similar warning. Shonkoff has pointed out that in establishing policy we have access to three categories of material: established knowledge based on strict rules of evidence; reasonable hypotheses that go beyond the limits of what we clearly know; and unwarranted assertions that can include "blatant distortion or misrepresentation ... of science."[18] Policy decisions can be based on established knowledge and, to some extent, can follow reasonable hypotheses, as long as these are used responsibly and with awareness that they may not be true. Unwarranted assertions, of course, should never form the basis of policy decisions.

This book has summarized a great deal of established knowledge and has presented some reasonable hypotheses about attachment. Some assertions were also reviewed and identified as unwarranted. Is it possible to use the information we have discussed to make recommendations about policy?

There are some areas in which we have enough established knowledge and reasonable hypotheses to support policymaking. These areas include day care, foster care, some aspects of adoption, and some aspects of divorce and custody decision-making. We have enough information on these topics to guide judges in certain types of decisions and to establish day care arrangements that support early emotional development. (We may not have the money available to do this, of course.)

Here are some important evidence-based conclusions that could be used to establish policy:

1. Newborn infants are little, if at all, affected by separation from the biological mother. The mother may be distressed by the loss, but there is no need to be concerned about a direct effect on the child.
2. Attachment develops as a result of consistent, sensitive, responsive care, especially in the first two years. For the best developmental outcomes, foster care and nonparental day care need to be planned with this foundation. Consistency may be the bugaboo of small minds, but is the essential factor in the social environment of small children.
3. From about six to eight months and on, abrupt long-term separations are disturbing to the child and interfere with sleeping, eating, playing, and learning. A child in this age group is old enough to be affected by

separation, but can also recover, especially if treated with sensitivity and responsiveness by new caregivers. Placement in foster care should be made with as few changes as possible, and foster or adoptive parents should receive guidance to encourage sensitivity, especially toward children who may not communicate well. Custody decisions following divorce should follow similar rules.

4. Adults' attitudes about relationships strongly influence children's attachment, and caregivers should be selected or guided in ways that help them show positive attitudes about attachment. The fact that they have reared their own children successfully is not necessarily evidence that foster or adoptive parents will be able to do a good job.

5. By the age of five or six years, children are much less influenced by separation than they were as toddlers, although they will still be sad about losses. Custody decisions for children of this age or older do not need to place stress on consistency of care, even though it was necessary earlier. School-age children and adolescents will not be emotionally traumatized by a custody change in and of itself, and other factors may be more important in such decisions.

Where More Work Is Needed

There are quite a few other areas where we presently do not have either evidence or sufficiently reasonable hypotheses about attachment to make policy decisions. Unanswered questions about emotional development are still being worked on.[19] For example, we do not know enough about what parents do in negotiating with preschool and older children, and how this style of negotiation contributes to the development of an internal working model of social relationships. The absence of this information makes it difficult for us to apply attachment theory to school policy or to our understanding of foster care and adoption of older children.

It is also unclear exactly what factors work together with attachment and loss to influence emotional development. In discussing conclusions drawn from the Romanian orphan studies, Rutter has made the following statement: "[It] is clear that parental loss or separation carries quite mild risks unless the loss leads to impaired parenting or other forms of family maladaptation." Poor family functioning would involve factors like persistent conflict, especially when it is negative attention aimed at a particular child; a lack of individualized caregiving; a lack of conversation and play; and experience with a social group that fosters undesirable behavior.[20] How these factors interact with loss is still so poorly understood, we cannot establish policy on this basis.

Not only are we without answers to important questions, but there is also little argument that attachment theory and research remain in a state of flux. Aspects of policy and law fluctuate too, while technology and social custom follow their own paths of change. A remarkable legal case in 2000 demonstrated clearly how little grasp we still have on the connections between modern life and family relations.[21] In this strange case, two families were in conflict after a mix-up in a fertility clinic. By error, a white woman who had come for fertility treatment was implanted not only with her own embryos but with those of a black couple. The white woman, Donna Fasano, gave birth to two boys of different skin shades; she named the black child Joseph and the white one Vincent. The black woman, Deborah Perry-Rogers, also received implanted embryos, but she did not have a successful pregnancy.

Mr. and Mrs. Rogers sought legal help and were given permanent custody of then five-month-old Joseph, renaming him Akiel. During the legal process, they had agreed to give the Fasanos visiting rights, but when they requested legal release from the agreement, they obtained it.

Part of the legal decision-making hinged on attachment issues, but not the sort this book has generally discussed. When the Rogers parents obtained custody of Akiel, "a judge ordered that Akiel and Vincent should visit each other regularly in the presence of psychologists, who would determine whether they had formed links as brothers during ... months *in the womb* [emphasis added] and in the Fasanos' home." However, a later ruling stated that the Fasanos had known of the mix-up soon after it occurred and had done nothing, making "any bonds that formed between the boys legally invalid."[22]

Here we have a startlingly incoherent legal application of the attachment concept, with nods to concepts like genetic factors in relationships and to prenatal development of emotional ties. We also seem to have the belief that psychologists can detect the existence of attachment, not only in children of less than six months, but between infants who are far too young to play the role of attachment figures for each other or give the cues that might initiate attachment behavior.

A Kabala scholar is supposed to have said, "Nonsense is always nonsense, but the history of nonsense is scholarship." Although scholarship still has much to do with the understanding of attachment, we have come far enough to be able to tell which ideas are nonsense. Application of systematic attachment evidence to law and policy is already possible. It is to be hoped that the helping and legal professions will join in carrying out this task.

Notes

CHAPTER 1

1. Jerrold M. Post, *Leaders and Their Followers in a Dangerous World* (Ithaca, NY: Cornell University Press, 2004); E. Bumiller, "Was a Tyrant Prefigured by Baby Saddam?" *New York Times*, May 15, 2004, B9.

2. Margaret Mahler, "Rapprochement Subphase of the Separation-Individuation Process," in *Rapprochement: The Critical Subphase of Separation-Individuation*, ed. R. Lax, S. Bach, and J. Burland (New York: Aronson, 1980).

3. Marshall H. Klaus, R. Jerauld, N. Kreger, W. McAlpine, M. Steffa, and J. H. Kennell, "Maternal Attachment: Importance of the First Post-Partum Days," *New England Journal of Medicine* 286 (1972): 460–463.

4. Daniel Yankelovitch Group for Zero to Three and Civitas, "What Grown-ups Understand about Child Development: A Benchmark Study" (Washington, DC: Zero to Three, 2000).

5. Jack P. Shonkoff, "Science, Policy, and Practice: Three Cultures in Search of a Shared Mission," *Child Development* 71 (2000): 181–187.

CHAPTER 2

1. Valerie Fildes, *Wet Nursing: A History from Antiquity to the Present* (New York: Blackwell, 1988).

2. Ibid., 115, 117.

3. R. de Saussure, "J. B. Felix Descuret," trans. R. de Saussure, *Psychoanalytic Study of the Child* 2 (1940): 420.

4. Philip Slater, "Child Rearing During the Early National Period" (PhD diss., University of California, Berkeley, 1970).

5. Ian Suttie, *The Origins of Love and Hate* (London: Penguin, 1935).

6. Irenaus Eibl-Eibesfeldt, *Ethology: The Biology of Behavior* (New York: Holt Rinehart Winston, 1970).

7. K. M. Wolf, "Evacuation of Children in Wartime," *Psychoanalytic Study of the Child* 1 (1945): 389.

8. Anna Freud and Dorothy T. Burlingham, *War and Children* (New York: Medical War Books, 1943).

9. Anna Freud and Dorothy T. Burlingham, *Infants Without Families: Reports on the Hampstead Nurseries, 1935–1945*, vol. 3, *Writings of Anna Freud* (New York: International Universities Press, 1973).

10. John Bowlby, *Attachment* (New York: Basic, 1982).

11. Bruno Bettelheim, *The Children of the Dream* (Cambridge, MA: Harvard University Press, 1969); S. Diamond, "Kibbutz and Shtetl: The History of an Idea," *Social Problems* 2 (1957): 71–99; and M. E. Spiro, *Children of the Kibbutz* (Cambridge, MA: Harvard University Press, 1958).

12. Bettelheim, *Children of the Dream*, 33.

13. Ibid., 108.

14. K. Johnson, H. Banghan, and W. Liyao, "Infant Abandonment and Adoption in China," *Population and Development Review* 24, no. 3 (1998): 469–510.

15. Michael Rutter, J. Kreppner, J. O'Connor, and English and Romanian Adoptees (ERA) Study Team, "Risk and Resilience Following Profound Early Global Deprivation," *British Journal of Psychiatry* 179 (2001): 97–103.

16. Michael Rutter, "Nature, Nurture, and Development: From Evangelism through Science Toward Policy and Practice," *Child Development* 73 (2002): 1–21.

CHAPTER 3

1. René Spitz, "Hospitalism: An Inquiry into the Genesis of Psychiatric Conditions in Early Childhood," *Psychoanalytic Study of the Child* 1 (1945): 53–74.

2. Jeremy Holmes, *John Bowlby and Attachment Theory* (London: Routledge, 1993); Inge Bretherton, "The Origins of Attachment Theory: John Bowlby and Mary Ainsworth," *Developmental Psychology* 28 (1992): 759–775.

3. Melanie Klein, *Contributions to Psychoanalysis, 1921–1945* (London: Hogarth, 1948).

4. Bretherton, "Origins of Attachment Theory."

5. John Bowlby, "Forty-Four Juvenile Thieves: Their Characters and Home Life," *International Journal of Psychoanalysis* 25 (1944): 19–52, 107–127.

6. James Robertson and Joyce Robertson, *Nine Days in a Residential Nursery* (Van Nuys, CA: Child Development Media, 1953) video.

7. Harry Harlow, "The Nature of Love," *American Psychologist* 13 (1959): 573–585.

8. John Bowlby, "The Nature of a Child's Tie to his Mother," *International Journal of Psychoanalysis* 39 (1958): 350–433; John Bowlby, "Separation Anxiety,"

International Journal of Psychoanalysis 41 (1960): 89–113; and John Bowlby, "Grief and Mourning in Infancy and Early Childhood," *Psychoanalytic Study of the Child* 15 (1960): 9–52.

9. Bretherton, "Origins of Attachment Theory."

10. Ibid.

11. Mary Ainsworth, M. Blehar, E. Waters, and S. Wall, *Patterns of Attachment* (Hillsdale, NJ: Erlbaum, 1978).

12. D. Teti and M. Nakagawa, "Assessing Attachment in Infancy: The Strange Situation and Alternative Systems," in *Interdisciplinary Assessment of Infants*, ed. E. Gibbs and D. Teti (Baltimore: P. H. Brookes, 1990), 91–214.

13. Mary Main and J. Solomon, "Discovery of an Insecure-Disorganized/Disoriented Attachment Pattern," in *Affective Development in Infancy*, ed. T. B. Brazelton and M. Yogman (Norwood, NJ: Ablex, 1986), 95–124.

14. Everett Waters and K. Deanne, "Defining and Assessing Individual Differences in Attachment Relations: Methodology and the Organization of Behavior in Infancy and Early Childhood," *Monographs of the Society for Research in Child Development* 50 (1985): 41–65.

15. C. George, N. Kaplan, and M. Main, "Adult Attachment Interview" (unpublished manuscript, University of California, Berkeley, 1995).

16. M. J. Bakermans-Kranenburg and M. van IJzendoorn, "A Psychometric Study of the Adult Attachment Interview," *Developmental Psychology* 29 (1993): 870–879.

17. Daniel Yankelovitch Group for Zero to Three and Civitas, "What Grownups Understand about Child Development: A Benchmark Study" (Washington, DC: Zero to Three, 2000).

18. Jean Mercer and Clyde McMurdy, "A Stereotyped Following Behavior in Young Children," *Journal of General Psychology* 112 (1985): 261–266.

19. J. L. Gewirtz, "Potency of a Social Reinforcer as a Function of Satiation and Recovery," *Developmental Psychology* 1 (1969): 2–13.

20. John Bowlby, *Darwin: A New Life* (New York: W. W. Norton, 1990).

CHAPTER 4

1. René Spitz, "Relevancy of Direct Infant Observation," *Psychoanalytic Study of the Child* 5 (1950): 66–73.

2. W. Ernest Freud, "Prenatal Attachment and Bonding," in *Course of Life*, vol. 1, *Infancy*, ed. S. I. Greenspan and G. H. Pollock (Madison, CT: International Universities Press, 1989), 467–484.

3. Donald Winnicott, "Transitional Objects and Transitional Phenomena," in *Collected Papers: Through Pediatrics to Psychoanalysis*, ed. D. Winnicott (Middlesex, England: Penguin, 1953), 1–25.

4. L. B. Adamson and C. L. Russell, "Emotion Regulation in the Emergence of Joint Attention," in *Early Social Cognition*, ed. P. Rochat (Mahwah, NJ: Erlbaum, 1999), 281–297.

5. René Spitz, "Hospitalism: An Inquiry into the Genesis of Psychiatric Conditions in Early Childhood," *Psychoanalytic Study of the Child* 1(1945): 53–74.

6. R. Weiss, "Loss and Recovery," in *Handbook of Bereavement*, ed. M. Stroebe, W. Stroebe, and R. Hansson (New York: Cambridge University Press, 1994), 271–284.

7. John H. Kennell and Marshal H. Klaus, "Caring for the Parents of a Still-born or an Infant Who Dies," in *Parent-Infant Bonding*, ed. M. H. Klaus and J. H. Kennell (St. Louis: Mosby, 1982), 151–266.

8. Marshal H. Klaus, R. Jerauld, N. Kreger, W. McAlpine, M. Steffa, and J. H. Kennell, "Maternal Attachment: Importance of the First Post-Partum Days," *New England Journal of Medicine* 286 (1972): 460–463.

9. Referred to by David M. Levy, "The Concept of Maternal Overprotection," in *Parenthood: Its Psychology and Psychopathology*, ed. E. T. Anthony and T. Benedek (Boston: Little, Brown, 1970), 387–409.

10. A. Sharma, M. McGue, and P. Benson, "The Psychological Adjustment of United States Adoptive Adolescents and Their Non-Adopted Siblings," *Child Development* 69 (1998): 791–802.

CHAPTER 5

1. Bowlby, "Forty-Four Juvenile Thieves," 19–52, 107–127.

2. Jerome Kagan, *Three Seductive Ideas* (Cambridge, MA: Harvard University Press, 2000).

3. M. A. Easterbrooks and W. A. Goldberg, "Security of Toddler-Parent Attachment," in *Attachment in the Preschool Years*, ed. M. Greenberg, D. Cicchetti, and M. Cummings (Chicago: University of Chicago Press, 1990), 221–244.

4. Mary Main and D. Weston, "The Independence of Infant-Mother and Infant-Father Relationships: Security of Attachment Characterizes Relationships, Not Infants," *Child Development* 52 (1981): 932–940.

5. Vivian B. Shapiro, Janet R. Shapiro, and Isabel Paret, *Complex Adoption and Assisted Reproductive Technology* (New York: Guilford, 2001).

6. Nancy Scheper-Hughes, *Death Without Weeping* (Berkeley, CA: University of California Press, 1992).

7. Ibid., 471.

8. Marinus van IJzendoorn, "Adult Attachment Representations, Parental Responsiveness, and Infant Attachment: A Meta-Analysis on the Predictive Validity of the Adult Attachment Interview," *Psychological Bulletin* 117 (1995): 387–403.

9. Mary Main and E. Hesse, "Parents' Unresolved Traumatic Experiences Are Related to Infants' Insecure–Disorganized/Disoriented Attachment Status: Is Frightened or Frightening Behavior the Linking Mechanism?" in *Attachment in the Preschool Years*, ed. M. Greenberg, D. Cicchetti, and M. Cummings (Chicago: University of Chicago Press, 1990), 161–184.

10. Robertson and Robertson, *Nine Days in a Residential Nursery*.

11. Jay Belsky and M. J. Rovine, "Nonmaternal Care in the First Year of Life and the Security of Infant-Parent Attachment," *Child Development* 59 (1988): 157–167; Jay Belsky and J. M. Braungart, "Are Insecure-Avoidant Infants with Extensive

Day-Care Experience More Independent in the Strange Situation?" *Child Development* 62 (1991): 567–571.

12. Inge Bretherton, B. Golby, and E. Cho, "Attachment and the Transmission of Values," in *Parenting and Children's Internalization of Values*, ed. T. Grusec and L. Kuczynski (New York: Wiley, 1997), 103–134.

13. R. Furman, "A Child's Capacity for Mourning," in *The Child in his Family*, vol. 2, ed. E. Anthony and C. Koupernik (New York: Wiley, 1973), 225–232.

14. Judith Wallerstein, "Children of Divorce: The Psychological Tasks of the Child," *American Journal of Orthopsychiatry* 53 (1983): 230–243.

15. R. Weiss, "Loss and Recovery," in *Handbook of Bereavement*, ed. M. Stroebe, W. Stroebe, and R. Hansson (New York: Cambridge University Press, 1994), 27–284.

16. S. Murphy, "Identifying Pattern and Meaning in Sibling-Infant Relationships: Using Multiple Forms of Family Data," in *Qualitative Methods in Family Research*, ed. J. Gilgun, K. Daly, and G. Handel (Newbury Park, CA: Sage, 1992), 146–171.

17. Murphy, "Identifying Pattern and Meaning."

18. P. Silverman and J. Worden, "Children's Reaction to the Death of a Parent," in *Handbook of Bereavement*, ed. M. Stroebe, W. Stroebe, and R. Hansson (New York: Cambridge University Press, 1993), 300–316.

19. E. M. Hetherington, M. Bridges, and G. Insabella, "What Matters? What Does Not? Five Perspectives on the Association Between Marital Transitions and Children's Adjustment," *American Psychologist* 53 (1998): 167–184.

20. Wallerstein, "Children of Divorce."

21. Ibid.; Hetherington, "What Matters? What Does Not?"

22. M. Cunliffe, C. Lee, A. Bashe, and M. Elliot, "'Thanks, Mom!' or 'Mom? No Thanks.' Emotion Regulation and Attachment in Adolescence," poster presented at Biennial Meeting of the Society for Research in Child Development (Albuquerque, NM, April, 1999).

23. David Elkind, *The Hurried Child* (Reading, MA: Addison-Wesley, 1981).

24. A. C. Huth-Bocks, A. A. Levendosky, C. A. Bogat, and A. von Eye, "The Impact of Maternal Characteristics and Contextual Variables on Infant-Mother Attachment," *Child Development* 75 (2004): 480–496.

CHAPTER 6

1. American Psychiatric Association, *Diagnostic and Statistical Manual of Mental Disorders*, 4th ed. (Washington, DC: American Psychiatric Association, 1994).

2. Rutter, "Nature, Nurture, and Development," 1–21.

3. Mary Main and J. Solomon, "Discovery of an Insecure-Disorganized/Disoriented Attachment Pattern," in *Affective Development in Infancy*, ed. T. B. Brazelton and M. Yogman (Norwood, NJ: Ablex, 1986), 136.

4. Ibid., 137.

5. Ibid., 138.

6. Ibid.

7. Ibid., 139.

8. Main and Hesse, "Parents' Unresolved Traumatic Experiences," 161–184.

9. Ibid., 175.

10. Ibid.

11. Ibid., 176.

12. Ibid.

13. John Bowlby, M. Ainsworth, M. Boston, and D. Rosenblith, "The Effects of Mother-Child Separation: A Follow-Up Study," *British Journal of Medical Psychology* 29 (1956): 211–247.

14. American Psychiatric Association, *Diagnostic and Statistical Manual.*

15. Rochelle F. Hanson and E. G. Spratt, "Reactive Attachment Disorder in Children: What We Know About the Disorder and Implications for Treatment," *Child Maltreatment* 5, no. 2 (2000): 137–145.

16. Frederick R. Volkmar, "Reactive Attachment Disorder," in *DSM-IV Sourcebook*, ed. T. A. Widiger, A. J. Frances, H. A. Pincus, R. Ross et al. (Washington, DC: American Psychiatric Association, 1997).

17. World Health Organization, *ICD-10* (Geneva, Switzerland: WHO, 1992).

18. Charles H. Zeanah, O. Mammen, and A. F. Lieberman, "Disorders of Attachment," in *Handbook of Infant Mental Health*, ed. C. H. Zeanah (New York: Guilford, 1993), 332–349.

19. Ibid., 343.

20. Ibid., 344.

21. Carl J. Sheperis, R. A. Dogget, N. E. Hoda, T. Blanchard, E. L. Renfro-Michael, S. H. Holdiness, and R. Schlagheck, "The Development of an Assessment Protocol for Reactive Attachment Disorder," *Journal of Mental Health Counseling* 25, no. 4 (2003): 291–310.

22. Constance G. Dalenberg, *Countertransference and the Treatment of Trauma* (Washington DC: American Psychological Association, 2000).

23. Mary Dozier, K. C. Stovall, K. Albus, and B. Bates, "Assessment for Infants in Foster Care: The Role of the Caregiver's State of Mind," *Child Development* 72 (2001): 1467–1477.

24. Alicia F. Lieberman, "The Treatment of Attachment Disorders in Infancy and Early Childhood: Reflections from Clinical Intervention in Later Adopted Foster Care Children," *Attachment and Human Development* 5, no. 3 (2003): 279–282.

25. Ibid., 281.

26. Ibid., 282.

27. Ibid.

28. Mary Dozier, "Attachment-Based Treatment for Vulnerable Children," *Attachment and Human Development* 5, no. 3 (2003): 253–257.

29. Ibid., 255.

30. Ibid., 256.

31. Stanley I. Greenspan, *Infancy and Early Childhood* (Madison, CT: International Universities Press, 1992).

32. Jean Mercer, L. Sarner, and L. Rosa, *Attachment Therapy On Trial* (Westport, CT: Praeger, 2003).

33. Ronald S. Federici, *Help for the Hopeless Child* (Alexandria, VA: Ronald S. Federici and Associates, 2003).

34. Vivian B. Shapiro, Janet R. Shapiro, and Isabel Paret, *Complex Adoption and Assisted Reproductive Technology* (New York: Guilford, 2001).

35. Daniel S. Schechter, "How Post-Traumatic Stress Affects Mothers' Perceptions of their Babies: Brief Video Feedback Intervention Makes a Difference," *Zero to Three* 24, no. 3 (2004): 43–49.

36. Ibid., 43.

37. Ibid.

38. Ibid., 47.

39. Ibid., 48.

CHAPTER 7

1. J. Sears, M. Sears, R. Sears, and W. Sears, *The Baby Book: Everything You Need to Know About Your Baby From Birth to Age Two* (New York: Little, Brown, 2003).

2. Gary Ezzo and R. Bucknam, *On Becoming Babywise: Parenting Your Pretoddler, Five to Fifteen Months* (Sisters, OR: Multnomah Books, 1995).

3. Robert W. Zaslow and M. Menta, *The Psychology of the Z-Process* (San Jose, CA: San Jose State University Press, 1975).

4. Mercer et al., *Attachment Therapy On Trial*.

5. Nancy Thomas, "Parenting Children with Attachment Disorders," in *Handbook of Attachment Interventions*, ed. T. M. Levy (San Diego, CA: Academic, 2000), 67–111.

6. The mental health practitioner who gave this description has given permission for its use, but has asked not to be named.

7. Elizabeth Randolph, *Manual for the Randolph Attachment Disorder Questionnaire* (Evergreen, CO: The Attachment Center Press, 2000).

8. Jirina Prekop, *Haettest du mich festgehalten* (Muenchen: Koesel, 1991).

9. J. Goldstein, A. Solnit, S. Goldstein, and A. Freud, *The Best Interest of the Child: The Least Detrimental Alternative* (New York: Free Press, 1996).

10. American Psychiatric Association, *Diagnostic and Statistical Manual*.

11. D. E. Arredondo and L. P. Edwards, "Attachment, Bonding, and Reciprocal Connectedness," *Journal of the Center for Families, Children, and the Courts* 146 (2000): 109–127.

CHAPTER 8

1. Everett Waters, K. Kondo-Ikemura, G. Posada, and J. Richters, "Learning to Love: Mechanisms and Milestones" in *Minnesota Symposia on Child Psychology*, vol. 23, *Self-Processes and Development*, ed. M. Gunnar and L. Sroufe (Hillsdale, NJ: Erlbaum, 1991), 217–255.

2. C. L. Bokhorst, M. J. Bakermans-Kranenburg, R. M. Pasco Fearon, M. van IJzendoorn, P. Fonagy, and C. Schuengel, "The Importance of Shared

Environment in Mother-Infant Attachment Security: A Behavioral-Genetic Study," *Child Development* 74 (2003): 1769–1782.

3. Daniel Bar-On, *Fear and Hope: Life-Stories of Five Israeli Families of Holocaust Survivors, Three Generations in a Family* (Cambridge, MA: Harvard University Press, 1995).

4. Glen Elder, "The Life-Course as Developmental Theory," *Child Development* 69 (1998): 1–2.

5. Vivian Shapiro, J. Shapiro, and I. Paret, *Complex Adoption and Assisted Reproductive Technology* (New York: Guilford, 2001).

6. Jay Belsky and M. J. Rovine, "Nonmaternal Care in the First Year of Life and the Security of Infant-Parent Attachment," *Child Development* 59 (1988): 157–167; Jay Belsky and K. M. Braungart, "Are Insecure-Avoidant Infants with Extensive Day-Care Experience More Independent in the Strange Situation?" *Child Development* 62 (1991): 567–571.

7. K. A. Clarke, "Infant Day Care: Maligned or Malignant," *American Psychologist* 44 (1989): 266–273.

8. G. R. Munoz, "A Relational and Sociocultural Approach in Services to a Mexican Family Across the Generations," *Zero to Three* 23, no. 3: 26–32.

9. F. Stott and R. Halpern, "Listening to the Voices of Families: Thoughts, Hopes, and Fears in a Latino Community," *Zero to Three* 23, no.3 (2003): 16–21.

10. R. Lurie-Hurvitz, "A Champion for Babies: An Interview with Joan Lombardi," *Zero to Three* 21, no. 6 (2001): 40–44.

11. Jeree Pawl, "Infants in Day Care: Reflection on Experiences, Expectations, and Relationships," *Zero to Three* 10, no. 3 (1990): 1–6.

12. R. Aslin, "Commentary: The Strange Attractiveness of Dynamic Systems to Development," in *A Dynamic Systems Approach: Applications*, ed. L. Smith and E. Thelen (Cambridge, MA: MIT Press, 1993), 385–399.

13. Jean Mercer and Clyde McMurdy, "A Stereotyped Following Behavior in Young Children," *Journal of General Psychology* 112 (1985): 261–266.

14. Arnold Sameroff, "Factors in Predicting Successful Parenting," in *Minimizing High Risk Parenting*, ed. V. Sasserath (Skillman, NJ: Johnson and Johnson), 16–24.

15. P. Fonagy, G. Gergely, E. L. Jurist, and M. Target, *Affect Regulation, Mentalization, and the Development of the Self* (New York: Other Press, 2002).

16. Ibid.

17. Rutter, "Nature, Nurture, and Development," 1–21.

18. Shonkoff, "Science, Policy, and Practice," 183.

19. Ross Thompson, "The Legacy of Early Attachments," *Child Development* 71 (2000): 145–152.

20. Rutter, "Nature, Nurture, and Development," 8.

21. A. Newman, "Visiting Rights Denied in Embryo Mix-Up Case," *New York Times*, Metro section, October 27, 2000.

22. Ibid., B3.

Bibliography

Adamson, L. B., and C. L. Russell. "Emotion Regulation and the Emergence of Joint Attention." In *Early Social Cognition*, edited by P. Rochat. Mahwah, NJ: Erlbaum, 1999.

Ainsworth, Mary, M. Blehar, E. Waters, and S. Wall. *Patterns of Attachment*. Hillsdale, NJ: Erlbaum, 1978.

American Psychiatric Association. *Diagnostic and Statistical Manual of Mental Disorders*. 4th ed. Washington, DC: American Psychiatric Association, 1994.

Arredondo, D. E., and L. P. Edwards. "Attachment, Bonding, and Reciprocal Connectedness." *Journal of the Center for Families, Children, and the Courts* 146 (2002): 109–127.

Aslin, R. "Commentary: The Strange Attractiveness of Dynamic Systems to Development." In *A Dynamic Systems Approach to Development: Applications*, edited by L. Smith and E. Thelen. Cambridge, MA: MIT Press, 1993.

Bakermans-Kranenburg, M. J., and M. van IJzendoorn. "A Psychometric Study of the Adult Attachment Interview: Reliability and Discriminant Validity." *Developmental Psychology* 29 (1993): 870–879.

Bar-On, Daniel. *Fear and Hope: Life-Stories of Five Israeli Families of Holocaust Survivors, Three Generations in a Family*. Cambridge, MA: Harvard University Press, 1995.

Barr, R. "Reduction of Infant Crying by Parent Carrying." In *Advances in Touch*, edited by N. Gunzenhauser. Skillman, NJ: Johnson and Johnson, 1996.

Beck, M. "Birthfather Registries." http://www.adoptivefamilies.com/article/PrinterFriendly.php?aid=233 (accessed May 4, 2004).

Belsky, Jay, and J. M. Braungart. "Are Insecure-Avoidant Infants with Extensive Day-Care Experience More Independent in the Strange Situation?" *Child Development* 62 (1991): 567–571.

Belsky, Jay, and M. J. Rovine. "Nonmaternal Care in the First Year of Life and the Security of Infant-Parent Attachment." *Child Development* 59 (1988): 157–167.

Bettelheim, Bruno. *The Children of the Dream.* New York: Macmillan, 1969.

Bokhorst, C. L., M. J. Bakermans-Kranenburg, R. M. Pasco Fearon, M. van IJzendoorn, P. Fonagy, and C. Schuengel. "The Importance of Shared Environment in Mother-Infant Attachment Security: A Behavioral-Genetic Study." *Child Development* 74 (2003): 1769–1782.

Bowlby, John. *Attachment.* New York: Basic, 1982.

Bowlby, John. *Darwin: A New Life.* New York: W.W. Norton, 1990.

Bowlby, John. "Forty-Four Juvenile Thieves: Their Characters and Home Life." *International Journal of Psychoanalysis* 25 (1944): 19–52, 107–127.

Bowlby, John. "Grief and Mourning in Infancy and Early Childhood." *Psychoanalytic Study of the Child* 15 (1960): 9–52.

Bowlby, John. "Separation Anxiety." *International Journal of Psychoanalysis* 41 (1960): 89–113.

Bowlby, John. "The Nature of a Child's Tie to his Mother." *International Journal of Psychoanalysis* 39 (1958): 350–433.

Bowlby, John, M. Ainsworth, M. Boston, and D. Rosenblith. "The Effects of Mother-Child Separation: A Follow-Up Study." *British Journal of Medical Psychology* 29 (1956): 211–247.

Bretherton, Inge. "The Origins of Attachment Theory: John Bowlby and Mary Ainsworth." *Developmental Psychology* 28 (1992): 759–775.

Bretherton, Inge, B. Golby, and E. Cho. "Attachment and the Transmission of Values." In *Parenting and Children's Internalization of Values,* edited by T. Grusec and L. Kuczinski. New York: Wiley, 1997.

Bumiller, E. "Was a Tyrant Prefigured by Baby Saddam?" *New York Times,* May 15, 2004, Metro section.

Clarke-Stewart, K. A. "Infant Day Care: Maligned or Malignant?" *American Psychologist* 44 (1989): 266–273.

Cunliffe, M., C. Lee, A. Bashe, and M. Elliot. April 1999. 'Thanks, Mom!' or 'Mom? No Thanks.' Emotion Regulation and Attachment in Adolescence. Poster presented at Biennial Meeting of the Society for Research in Child Development, Albuquerque, NM.

Dalenberg, Constance. *Countertransference and the Treatment of Trauma.* Washington, DC: American Psychological Association, 2000.

Daniel Yankelovitch Group for Zero to Three and Civitas. "What Grownups Understand About Child Development: A Benchmark Study." Washington, DC: Zero to Three, 2000.

De Saussure, R. "J. B. Felix Descuret." *Psychoanalytic Study of the Child* 2 (1946): 17–424.

Diamond, S. "Kibbutz and Shtetl: The History of an Idea." *Social Problems* 2 (1957): 71–99.

Dozier, Mary. "Attachment-Based Treatment for Vulnerable Children." *Attachment and Human Development* 5, no. 3 (2003): 253–257.

Dozier, Mary, K. C. Stovall, K. Albus, and B. Bates. "Attachment for Infants in Foster Care: The Role of Caregiver State of Mind." *Child Development* 72 (2001): 1467–1477.

Easterbrooks, M. A., and W. A. Goldberg. "Security of Toddler-Parent Attachment." In *Attachment in the Preschool Years*, edited by M. Greenberg, D. Cicchetti, and E. M. Cummings. Chicago: University of Chicago Press, 1990.

Eibl-Eibesfeldt, Irenaus. *Ethology: The Biology of Behavior.* New York: Holt, Rinehart, Winston, 1970.

Elder, Glen. "The Life-Course as Developmental Theory." *Child Development* 69 (1998): 1–2.

Elkind, David. *The Hurried Child.* Reading, MA: Addison-Wesley, 1981.

Emde, Robert N. "Social Referencing Research." In *Social Referencing and Social Construction of Reality in Infancy*, edited by S. Feinman. New York: Plenum, 1992.

Ezzo, Gary, and R. Bucknam. *On Becoming Babywise. Book Two: Parenting Your Pretoddler Five to Fifteen Months.* Sisters, OR: Multnomah Books, 1995.

Federici, Ronald S. *Help for the Hopeless Child.* Alexandria, VA: Dr. Ronald S. Federici and Associates, 2003.

Fildes, Valerie. *Wet Nursing.* New York: Blackwell, 1988.

Fonagy, P., G., Gergely, E. L. Jurist, and M. Target. *Affect Regulation, Mentalization, and the Development of the Self.* New York: Other Press, 2002.

Freud, Anna, and D. T. Burlingham. *Infants Without Families and Reports on the Hampstead Nurseries, 1935–1945.* New York: International Universities Press, 1973.

Freud, Anna, and D. T. Burlingham. *War and Children.* New York: Medical War Books, 1943.

Freud, W. Ernest. "Prenatal Attachment and Bonding." In *The Course of Life*, vol. 1, *Infancy*, edited by S. I. Greenspan and G. H. Pollock. Madison, CT: International Universities Press, 1973.

Furman, R. "A Child's Capacity for Mourning." In *The Child in his Family*, vol. 2, edited by E. Anthony and C. Koupernik. New York: Wiley, 1973.

Gardner, R. "Guidelines for Assessing Parental Preference in Child-Custody Disputes." *Journal of Divorce and Remarriage* 30, nos. 1–2 (1999): 1–9.

George, C., N. Kaplan, and M. Main. "Adult Attachment Interview." Unpublished manuscript, University of California, Berkeley, 1995.

George, J. "Long Thought Dead, A Child is Found Alive and Healthy." *New York Times*, March 3, 2004, sec. A.

Gewirtz, J. L. "Potency of a Social Reinforcer as a Function of Satiation and Recovery." *Developmental Psychology* 1 (1969): 2–13.

Gilbert, M., and R. Schulzinger. *Relinquishing Custody: The Tragic Result of Failing to Meet Children's Mental Health Needs.* Washington, DC: Bazelon Center for Mental Health Law, 2000.

Goldstein, J., A. Solnit, S. Goldstein, and A. Freud. *The Best Interest of the Child: The Least Detrimental Alternative.* New York: Free Press, 1996.

Greenspan, S. I. *Infancy and Early Childhood.* Madison, CT: International Universities Press, 1993.

Hanson, R. F., and E. G. Spratt. "Reactive Attachment Disorder in Children: What We Know About the Disorder and Implications for Treatment." *Child Maltreatment* 5 (2000), no. 2: 137–145.

Harlow, Harry. "The Nature of Love." *American Psychologist* 13 (1959): 573–685.

Hart, A. "Chinese Parents Not Tricked, Judge Says in Custody Case." *New York Times*, May 13, 2004, sec. A.

Hetherington, E. M., M. Bridges, and G. Insabella. "What Matters? What Does Not? Five Perspectives on the Association Between Marital Transitions and Children's Adjustment." *American Psychologist* 53 (1998): 167–184.

Holmes, Jeremy. *John Bowlby and Attachment Theory.* London: Routledge, 1993.

Huth-Bocks, A. C., A. A. Levendosky, G. A. Bogat, and A. von Eye. "The Impact of Maternal Characteristics and Contextual Variables on Infant-Mother Attachment." *Child Development* 75 (2004): 480–496.

Johnson, K., H. Banghan, and W. Liyao. "Infant Abandonment and Adoption in China." *Population and Development Review*, no. 3 (1998): 469–510.

Kagan, Jerome. *Three Seductive Ideas.* Cambridge, MA: Harvard University Press, 2000.

Kennell, J. H., and M. H. Klaus. "Caring for the Parents of a Stillborn or an Infant Who Dies." In *Parent-Infant Bonding*, edited by M. H. Klaus and J. H. Kennell. St. Louis: Mosby, 1982.

Klaus, M. H., R. Jerauld, N. Kreger, W. McAlpine, M. Steffa, and J. H. Kennell. "Maternal Attachment: Importance of the First Post-Partum Days." *New England Journal of Medicine* 286 (1972): 460–463.

Klein, Melanie. *Contributions to Psychoanalysis, 1921–1945.* London: Hogarth, 1948.

Leon, I. "Adoption Losses: Naturally Occurring or Socially Constructed?" *Child Development* 73 (2002): 652–663.

Levy, David M. "The Concept of Maternal Overprotection." In *Parenthood: Its Psychology and Psychopathology*, edited by E. J. Anthony and T. Benedek. Boston: Little, Brown, 1970.

Lieberman, Alicia F. "The Treatment of Attachment Disorders in Infancy and Early Childhood: Reflections from Clinical Intervention in Later Adopted Foster Care Children." *Attachment and Human Development* 5, no. 3 (2003): 279–282.

Lurie-Hurvitz, E. "A Champion for Babies: An Interview with Joan Lombardi." *Zero to Three* 21, no. 6 (2001): 40–44.

Mahler, Margaret. "Rapprochement Subphase of the Separation-Individuation Process." In *Rapprochement: The Critical Subphase of Separation-Individuation*, edited by R. Lax, S. Bach, and J. Burland. New York: Aronson, 1980.

Main, Mary, and D. Weston. "The Independence of Infant-Mother and Infant-Father Attachment Relationships: Security of Attachment Characterizes Relationships, Not Infants." *Child Development* 52 (1981): 932–940.

Main, Mary, and E. Hesse. "Parents' Unresolved Traumatic Experiences Are Related to Infants' Insecure-Disorganized/Disoriented Attachment Status: Is Frightened or Frightening Behavior the Linking Mechanism?" In *Attachment in the Preschool Years*, edited by M. Greenberg, D. Cicchetti, and M. Cummings. Chicago: University of Chicago Press, 1990.

Main, Mary, and J. Solomon. "Discovery of an Insecure-Disorganized/Disoriented Attachment Pattern." In *Affective Development in Infancy*, edited by T. B. Brazelton and M. Yogman. Norwood, NJ: Ablex, 1986.

Mercer, Jean, and C. McMurdy. "A Stereotyped Following Behavior in Young Children." *Journal of General Psychology* 112 (1985): 261–266.

Mercer, Jean, L. Sarner, and L. Rosa. *Attachment Therapy On Trial*. Westport, CT: Praeger, 2003.

Munoz, G. R. "A Relational and Sociocultural Approach in Services to a Mexican Family across Three Generations." *Zero to Three* 23, no. 3 (2003): 26–32.

Murphy, S. "Identifying Pattern and Meaning in Sibling-Infant Relationships: Using Multiple Forms of Family Data." In *Qualitative Methods in Family Research*, edited by J. Gilgun, K. Daly, and G. Handel. Newbury Park, CA: Sage, 1992.

Newman, A. "Visiting Rights Denied in Embryo Mix-Up Case." *New York Times*, October 27, 2000, Metro section.

Pawl, Jeree. "Infants in Day Care: Reflections on Experiences, Expectations, and Relationships." *Zero to Three* 10, no. 3 (1990): 1–6.

Post, J. M. *Leaders and their Followers in a Dangerous World*. Ithaca, NY: Cornell University Press, 2004.

Prekop, Jirina. *Haettest du mich festgehalten*. Muenchen: Koesel, 1991.

Randolph, Elizabeth. *Manual for the Randolph Attachment Disorder Questionnaire*. 3rd ed. Evergreen, CO: The Attachment Center Press, 2000.

Robertson, James, and J. Robertson. *Nine Days in a Residential Nursery*. VHS. Van Nuys, CA: Child Development Media, 1953.

Rutter, Michael. "Nature, Nurture, and Development: From Evangelism Through Science Toward Policy and Practice." *Child Development* 73 (2002): 1–21.

Rutter, Michael, J. Kreppner, T. O'Connor, and the English and Romanian Adoptees (ERA) Study Team of 2001. "Risk and Resilience Following Profound Early Global Deprivation." *British Journal of Psychiatry* 179 (2001): 97–103.

Sameroff, Arnold. "Factors in Predicting Successful Parenting." In *Minimizing High-Risk Parenting*, edited by V. Sasserath. Skillman, NJ: Johnson & Johnson, 1983.

Schechter, Daniel S. "How Post-Traumatic Stress Affects Mothers' Perceptions of their Babies: Brief Video Feedback Intervention Makes a Difference." *Zero to Three* 24, no. 3 (2004): 43–49.

Scheper-Hughes, Nancy. *Death Without Weeping.* Berkeley, CA: University of California Press, 1992.

Sears, J., M. Sears, R. Sears, and W. Sears. *The Baby Book: Everything You Need to Know About Your Baby from Birth to Age Two.* New York: Little, Brown, 2003.

Shapiro, Vivian B., J. R. Shapiro, and I. Paret. *Complex Adoption and Assisted Reproductive Technology.* New York: Guilford, 2001.

Sharma, A., M. McGue, and P. Benson. "The Psychological Adjustment of United States Adoptive Adolescents and their Non-Adopted Siblings." *Child Development* 69 (1998): 791–802.

Sheperis, Carl J., R. A. Dogget, N. E. Hoda, T. Blanchard, E. L. Renfro-Michael, S. H. Holdiness, and R. Schlagheck. "The Development of an Assessment Protocol for Reactive Attachment Disorder." *Journal of Mental Health Counseling* 25, no. 4 (2003): 291–310.

Shonkoff, Jack P. "Science, Policy, and Practice: Three Cultures in Search of a Shared Mission." *Child Development* 71 (2000): 181–187.

Silverman, P., and J. Worden. "Children's Reactions to the Death of a Parent." In *Handbook of Bereavement,* edited by M. Stroebe, W. Stroebe, and R. Hansson. New York: Cambridge University Press, 1993.

Slater, Philip. "Child Rearing During the Early National Period." Doctoral dissertation, University of California, Berkeley, CA, 1970.

Spiro, M. E. *Children of the Kibbutz.* Cambridge, MA: Harvard University Press, 1958.

Spitz, René. "Hospitalism: An Inquiry into the Genesis of Psychiatric Conditions in Early Childhood." *Psychoanalytic Study of the Child* 1 (1945): 53–74.

Spitz, René. "Relevancy of Direct Infant Observation." *Psychoanalytic Study of the Child* 5 (1950): 66–73.

Stott, F., and R. Halpern. "Listening to the Voices of Families: Thoughts, Hopes, and Fears in a Latino Community." *Zero to Three* 23, no. 3 (2003): 16–21.

Suttie, Ian. *The Origins of Love and Hate.* London: Penguin, 1935.

Teti, D., and M. Nakagawa. "Assessing Attachment in Infancy: The Strange Situation and Alternative Systems." In *Interdisciplinary Assessment of Infants,* edited by E. Gibbs and D. Teti. Baltimore: P. H. Brookes, 1990.

Thomas, Nancy. "Parenting children with Attachment Disorders." In *Handbook of Attachment Interventions,* edited by T. M. Levy. San Diego, CA: Academic Press, 2000.

Thompson, Ross A. "The Legacy of Early Attachments." *Child Development* 71 (2000): 145–152.

Tomasello, M. "Social Cognition Before the Revolution." In *Early Social Cognition,* edited by P. Rochat. Mahwah, NJ: Erlbaum, 1999.

Van IJzendoorn, Marinus. "Adult Attachment Representations, Parental Responsiveness, and Infant Attachment: A Meta-Analysis on the Predictive Validity of the Adult Attachment Interview." *Psychological Bulletin* 117 (1995): 387–403.

Van IJzendoorn, Marinus, and M. Bakermans-Kranenburg. "Attachment Disorders and Disorganized Attachment: Similar and Different." *Attachment and Human Development* 5, no. 3 (2003): 313–320.

Volkmar, Frederick R. "Reactive Attachment Disorder." In *DSM-IV Sourcebook*, vol. 3, edited by T. A. Widiger, A. J. Frances, H. A. Pincus, R. Ross, et al., Washington DC: American Psychiatric Association, 1997.

Wallerstein, Judith. "Children of Divorce: The Psychological Tasks of the Child." *American Journal of Orthopsychiatry* 53 (1983): 230–243.

Waters, Everett, and K. Deanne. "Defining and Assessing Individual Differences in Attachment Relations: Methodology and the Organization of Behavior in Infancy and Early Childhood." *Monographs of the Society for Research in Child Development* 50 (1985): 41–65.

Waters, Everett, K. Kondo-Ikemura, G. Posada, and J. Richters. "Learning to Love: Mechanisms and Milestones." In *Minnesota Symposia on Child Psychology*, vol. 23, *Self-Processes and Development*, edited by M. Gunnar and L. Sroufe. Hillsdale, NJ: Erlbaum, 1991.

Weiss, R. "Loss and Recovery." In *Handbook of Bereavement*, edited by M. Stroebe, W. Stroebe, and R, Hansson. New York: Cambridge University Press, 1994.

Whitehead, Mary Beth. *A Mother's Story*. New York: St. Martin's, 1980.

Winnicott, Donald. "Transitional Objects and Transitional Phenomena." In *Collected Papers: Through Pediatrics to Psychoanalysis*, edited by D. Winnicott. Middlesex, England: Penguin, 1953.

Wolf, K. M. "Evacuation of Children in Wartime." *Psychoanalytic Study of the Child* 1 (1945): 389–404.

World Health Organization. *ICD-10*. Geneva, Switzerland: WHO, 1992.

Zaslow, Robert W., and M. Menta. *The Psychology of the Z-Process*. San Jose, CA: San Jose State University Press, 1975.

Zeanah, Charles H., O. Mammen, and A. F. Lieberman. "Disorders of Attachment." In *Handbook of Infant Mental Health*, edited by C. H. Zeanah. New York: Guilford, 1993.

Index

threat, 43, 51, 60, 66, 76, 94
time-out, 93
Tinbergen, Nikolaas, 33
toddlers, 51
traditional societies, 157
transactional process, 59, 163
transference, 117, 118
transitional object, 4, 162
trauma, 118, 125, 145

Uganda study, 41, 42

video feedback, 125

visiting relationship, 89–92
voice patterns, 108

wariness, 59
wet nursing, 14–15, 16
Winnicott, Donald, 57, 128
World Association for Infant Mental
    Health, 160
World War II, 20–23, 26, 33, 76

Zaslow, Robert W., 135
Zeanah, Charles, 46, 111–116
Zero to Three, 7, 160–161

About the Author

JEAN MERCER is a professor of Psychology in the Division of Social and Behavioral Sciences at Richard Stockton College and President of the New Jersey Association for Infant Mental Health. She is also coauthor of *Attachment Therapy On Trial* (Praeger, 2003).